Other books in the series

IRS Managing Absence and Leave – 0754519538
IRS Managing Employee Representatives – 0754519546

Related titles from Tolley:

Tolley's Managing Dismissals: Practical guidance on the art of dismissing fairly –
075451255X
Tolley's Managing E-mail and Internet Use: A practical guide to employers' obligations and employees' rights – 0754513947
Tolley's Employment Tribunals Handbook: Practice, procedure and strategies for success – 075451488
Tolley's Managing Fixed-term and Part-time Workers: A practical guide to employing temporary and part-time staff – 0754 516 628
Tolley's Managing Business Transfers: TUPE and takeovers, mergers and outsourcing – 075451661X

Visit our websites:
www.irsonline.co.uk
www.XpertHR.com

For further information on IRS books, please contact the Marketing Department on
020 7354 6747. For further information on Tolley books, please contact Customer
Services on 020 8662 2000 (or by fax on 020 8662 2012).

FOREWORD

Managing diversity is a term which is now commonly used, not just in HR departments but in relation to an organisation's strategic development. The benefits of managing diversity are becoming widely recognised, but what is it?

Many organisations have had equal opportunities policies in place for some time. So why should they be considering a strategy for managing diversity? Is it not the same thing under a different guise?

Managing diversity involves much more than drawing up a policy which states very laudable aims of an organisation in relation to traditionally disadvantaged groups. With equal opportunities, it has been easy for organisations to have an 'add on' policy which supplements other employment practices. Far too often, agreeing the policy is more or less where it ends. Recent employment tribunal decisions have demonstrated that it is not enough to have an equal opportunities policy in place; employers must be able to demonstrate that it is actively implemented.

So how does a diversity strategy differ from the traditional equal opportunities policy? Firstly, equal opportunities has concentrated on creating equality of opportunity, regardless of difference. In other words, everyone has the same right of access to, say, promotion opportunities. But the barriers facing some groups of employees, such as lack of childcare provision for women, are not addressed.

Managing diversity involves recognising difference and, more importantly, valuing that difference. A diversity strategy recognises that different groups of people have different skills and capabilities to offer but, in order to give them the opportunity to exercise those talents, an organisation has to ensure that their different needs are also recognised.

Secondly, far too often an equal opportunities policy has simply been an additional HR policy and, once in place, has been largely ignored. A diversity approach cannot be ignored if properly pursued. A key aim in implementing a diversity strategy is to ensure the 'mainstreaming' of the diversity vision. This means that the commitment to diversity permeates the whole organisation, affecting not just employment policies but also marketing, advertising, training, customer care, service delivery, financial planning; in fact, every facet of the organisation's activities. This, of course, implies major change within an organisation; a change of culture whereby everyone shares the aims and values of a diversity approach.

This book provides comprehensive guidance for HR specialists and other managers whose task it is to lead the development of a diversity strategy within an organisation.

Chapter One, What is Diversity? – The history and definitions of managing diversity are explained in this chapter, with a detailed discussion of the differences between diversity and equal opportunities. It sets the scene for the following chapters.

Chapter Two, Understanding the Organisational Case for Diversity – This chapter deals with the 'preparation' required before an organisation's strategy on diversity can be agreed. It sets out the 'organisational' case for diversity, pointing out that it is not just the business benefits which come into the equation, but also the legal and moral imperatives.

Chapter Three, Developing the Strategic Plan and Business Objectives for Diversity – This is a crucial chapter for those embarking upon a diversity approach. It explains how to present the arguments for a diversity strategy and how to fight for its inclusion into the organisation's business strategy and business plan. It stresses the importance of diversity being part of the overall strategy of the organisation, illustrating ways in which it can be used to help the organisation achieve its stated aims and objectives.

Chapter Four, Measuring the Success of a Diversity Strategy – An important part of any strategy is measuring outcomes, and this is dealt with in this chapter. Measuring the success of a diversity strategy is crucial to its continuing support from senior management, and this chapter explains how its success can be demonstrated.

Chapter Five, Implementing and Managing Diversity – This chapter sets out and explains various aspects of managing a diverse workforce. For many organisations with equal opportunities policies in place, these areas will be familiar. But the chapter takes the issues a step further, and demonstrates how equal opportunities policies support diversity policies.

Chapter Six, Diversity and the Law – One of the main drivers for the implementation of a diversity policy is the law. There has been an increase in the amount of legislation in the area of discrimination, and there is more to come, covering a wider range of issues such as age, sexual orientation and religion or belief. The increased awareness of the legislation and the need to comply with these minimum requirements have led to more and more organisations thinking about how they can ensure compliance with the law. This chapter sets out the legal framework. However, adopting a diversity strategy means going beyond the minimum protection provided by statute.

Chapter Seven, Case Studies on Diversity – Throughout the book, examples and short case studies are used to illustrate the points made. This is taken a step further in this chapter and there are detailed case studies of a number of organisations which have been at the forefront of developing diversity policies.

Chapter Eight, Model Policies – This chapter provides model policies, again from organisations at the forefront of developments. These policies provide useful benchmarks for any organisations developing their own strategy.

Introducing a diversity strategy can bring huge benefits to an organisation and, of course, to the communities affected by it. But it will only succeed if the issues are understood, and clear strategies are put in place. It also requires commitment, not just from senior management but throughout the organisation. This book will help the manager who has responsibility for pushing forward the diversity agenda to gain that commitment and understanding, and to successfully implement a strategy which will reap benefits for the organisation.

Sue Johnstone
Executive Editor

ACKNOWLEDGEMENTS

The publishers wish to express their thanks to:

Angela Ishmael
B&Q
Bonnie Mitchell
Bradford and Bingley plc
British Telecommunications plc
Chris Logan
Claire Traylen
Gary Bowker
Harrogate Borough Council
Jenine Wong
Jennie Dunn
John Twitchin
JPMorgan Chase
London Borough of Camden
Nationwide Building Society
Sue Johnstone
Yorkshire Electricity

ABOUT THE AUTHORS

Executive Editor

Sue Johnstone
Contributor to Chapter Six.
Sue Johnstone is the Editor of the IRS specialist journal, *Equal Opportunities Review* (EOR) and its website (www.EORdirect.com). Prior to that, Sue was a Principal Lecturer in Law, lecturing and researching in employment law. Sue has specialised in discrimination law for the last 15 years, and has previously written on the law and managing diversity. Sue also sits as a member of the employment tribunal. sue.johnstone@butterworths.com

Contributors

Gill Kirton BA(Hons), MA, LicIPD
Contributor to Chapter One.
Gill Kirton is a Senior Lecturer in HRM and Employment Relations at the London Metropolitan University, where her teaching specialism includes diversity management. Gill is co-author (with Anne-Marie Greene) of *The Dynamics of Managing Diversity*, Butterworth-Heinemann (2000). Gill is engaged in research on gender, race, equality and diversity and is the author of several published articles and book chapters in this area. g.kirton@unl.ac.uk

Kay Allen, Diversity Services Director, Grass Roots Group
Contributor to Chapters Two, Three, Four and Five.
Kay Allen has worked for 16 years in HR and Diversity Management, most recently for B&Q. Kay was appointed as a Commissioner for the Disability Rights Commission in 2000, and regularly speaks on all aspects of diversity management. Kay is currently working as a consultant on diversity and is actively involved in the UK debate on the single equalities initiative. kayallen801@hotmail.com

Colin Hann, Head of MDA (Managing Diversity Associates)
Contributor to Chapter Five.
Until recently Colin Hahn worked with top law firm DLA, with whom his consultancy group retains an association. Colin was also Director of Communications and Strategy at the Commission for Racial Equality, where he was responsible for various award-winning advertising and other campaigns, as well as leading a number of policy and legal initiatives, including formal investigations. Colin has recently been reviewing organisations on diversity issues and advising on effective diversity strategies, including internal communications. Colin has also published widely on areas and issues relating to diversity. colinhann@managingdiversityassociates.com

Linda Johnson, LLB, LLM, MPhil, Cert Ed, Dip Ashe
Contributor to Chapter Six.
Linda Johnson is Subject Field Director of Business Law and Programme Leader for

MA European and International Business Law at the University of North London Business School. Linda has been teaching employment law at undergraduate and postgraduate level for 20 years and specialises in comparative discrimination law. Research includes race discrimination laws and the impact of EU Equality Directives on Member States. Linda also carries out consultancy work for a number of large retailers. l.johnson@unl.ac.uk

Carol Foster BA(Hons), MA
Contributor to Chapter Seven.
Carol Foster has worked on equal opportunities and diversity issues in employment for over 19 years. For the past four years, she has worked on *Equal Opportunities Review* (EOR), undertaking independent case study-based research into various aspects of employers' equal opportunities and diversity policies and practices in both the public and private sectors. Prior to joining EOR, Carol worked for the Equal Opportunities Commission (EOC) for 15 years, where she acquired an in-depth knowledge of gender equality and related multi-discrimination issues. Her work at the EOC included legal strategy and policy development. carol.foster@butterworths.com

Sarah Podro, Research Officer on Equal Opportunities Review
Contributor to Chapter Seven.
Sarah Podro has worked for *Equal Opportunities Review* (EOR) since 1996, researching and writing on a wide range of equal opportunities and diversity issues. Prior to joining EOR, Sarah worked as a freelance researcher producing reports on gender-related issues for the European Commission, the European Foundation for the Improvement of Living and Working Conditions, the International Labour Organisation, the Institute of Employment Studies and the Department for Education and Employment). Sarah has also carried out community-based research for a number of migrant and refugee groups. sarah.podro@butterworths.com

Editorial Board Members

Gary Bowker, Senior Consultant, Mercer Human Resource Consulting
Gary Bowker is an employment law consultant, specialising in diversity and discrimination law with Mercer Human Resource Consulting. He is a former Editor of *Equal Opportunities Review* (EOR) and *Discrimination Case Law Digest*.
Gary has researched and written on discrimination law and equal opportunities for the past 20 years. A law graduate and an industrial relations postgraduate, Gary is a member of the Chartered Institute of Personnel and Development (CIPD) Steering Group on equal pay, and a member of the EOR advisory panel. Gary is also a trustee of the national equality charity, the Wainwright Trust. gary.bowker@mercer.com

Angela Ishmael, Head of Dignity at Work Community, The Work Foundation
Angela Ishmael is responsible for leading the Dignity at Work Community's consultancy campaign for The Work Foundation (formerly the Industrial Society), whose purpose is to improve working life (www.theworkfoundation.com/solutions/

consultancy/dignity/index.jsp). Angela is accountable for the research, development and design of client interventions in areas such as diversity and discrimination, organisational culture and climate, harassment and bullying, and working relationships. Angela has extensive experience in advising at board and strategic levels across all sectors.

Angela is also author of *Harassment, Bullying and Violence at Work*, The Industrial Society (1999) and *No Fear: Challenging Harassment and Bullying*, Spiro Press (due to be published January 2003). aishmael@theworkfoundation.com

John Twitchin, FCIPD, Director of Diversity Works

John Twitchin was in charge of BBC TV Management Training output for 20 years, producing 90 documentary training videos, four books and 18 manuals on managerial competencies for valuing diversity at work. He has also written articles for *Training Journal and Public Service Review*.

He is the Department for Education and Skills Recommended Provider on Equalities, and has been consultant/trainer to the employment tribunals, The Employment Service, the Race Relations Employment Advisory Service (part of the former Department for Education and Employment) and NHS Executive.

Among Diversity Works' specialisms are anti-discrimination law and cross-cultural communication. This includes tutoring the UK's only post-graduate course in Intercultural Communication in Business and Public Services (www.diversityworks.co.uk). johntwitchin@diversityworks.co.uk

CONTENTS

Chapter One

What is Diversity?

OVERVIEW

This chapter covers the following issues.

- How diversity can be defined and how it differs from traditional equal opportunities (see p **5**).

- The areas covered by diversity (see p **8**).

- Why organisations should adopt a diversity strategy (see p **9**).

- Different approaches to diversity strategy (see p **10**).

- How diversity issues in the external environment impact on organisational policy and practice (see p **11**).

- The role of diversity policy in the workplace (see p **17**).

- Some of the problems in the implementation of a diversity strategy (see p **19**).

INTRODUCTION

'Managing diversity' has become a popular catch phrase in UK management literature. In order to understand the concept and how it can be translated into policy and practice, it is important to consider its origins.

The term was imported from the USA in the early 1990s, where it had been used to signify a departure from traditional equal opportunities policies and their association with the unpopular 'affirmative action' approach underpinned by US legislation. As well as the increasing backlash against affirmative action, the USA was also facing major demographic changes, which, as heralded by the influential *Workforce 2000* report,[1] were about to transform the ethnic and gender composition of the workforce.

With its emphasis on celebrating all types of difference, managing diversity promised a means of overcoming the resentment and hostility provoked by the US policy of affirmative action, which had focused on women and ethnic minorities. Managing diversity also promised a strategy for enabling organisations to recruit and retain employees from diverse demographic backgrounds. In this way, the concept of managing diversity was aligned with organisational objectives, rather than with the social and moral concerns of equal opportunities; namely, discrimination and disadvantage.

Whilst the USA and the UK share some social and economic features (such as the increasing employment rates of women within the context of a growing service industry), there are also many significant differences in the labour market context (such as a smaller UK ethnic minority population). The legal context is also very different, with positive discrimination (seen as equivalent to the US affirmative action) outlawed by UK legislation. The different contexts produce different problems, challenges and opportunities, which need to be confronted by diversity policy-makers. From this point of view, it is not only desirable but essential that the UK diversity concept takes a different shape to that of the USA. This is the premise of this chapter as it seeks to explain what diversity is and how the issues confronting UK organisations can be understood. Many of the issues dealt with in this chapter are covered in more depth in subsequent chapters.

DIVERSITY AND EQUAL OPPORTUNITIES

Equal opportunities policies (EOPs) now have a long history in the UK, having been part of employment policy and standard business practice since the early 1980s. Recent evidence shows that around two thirds of British workplaces are covered by formal written EOPs.[2] Within the ambit of EOPs, organisations developed a range of procedures and practices to eliminate discriminatory behaviour by managers and other employees. These were strongly influenced by the necessity to comply with legislation (in particular the *Sex Discrimination Act 1975* (*SDA 1975*) and the *Race Relations Act 1976* (*RRA 1976*)), and policies tended to concentrate on eliminating sex and race discrimination. Disability has received more policy attention since the advent of the *Disability Discrimination Act 1995* (*DDA 1995*), whilst other dimensions, such as age, sexuality and religion, were often tagged on to the list of areas covered by the policy, but with little evidence of meaningful policy initiatives. The focus was generally on recruitment and selection procedures, and on harassment policies. It was thought that greater formalisation of recruitment and selection processes would eliminate discrimination at the point of entry to the organisation, and that the existence of a harassment policy would deter potential harassers and provide appropriate avenues of complaint where harassment occurred.

Some organisations went further than the requirements of the legislation (ie not to discriminate) by developing initiatives designed to achieve greater representation of social diversity; for example, training programmes targeted at women and ethnic minorities. Clearly, equality legislation combined with EOPs, provide important safeguards against discrimination in employment. However, the equal opportunities approach has met with considerable criticism in recent years.

Criticism of Equal Opportunities Policies

One of the main criticisms of 'equal opportunity' has been that it is negative; failure to comply with the law carries penalties and any individual found contravening the policy is likely to be disciplined.

There is little emphasis on how an organisation and its members might *gain* from equality, and more on how it could *suffer* if discrimination were discovered. For example, employment tribunal cases can result in large compensation awards, not to mention the possibility of negative media coverage which could tarnish the reputation of the business. Whilst this might seem reason enough to take some action to avoid complaints of discrimination, it does not compel organisations to actually promote equality in a positive manner. In contrast, diversity policy stresses the benefits of *valuing difference*, rather than seeing it as a problem needing a solution. Advocates of diversity also argue that if members of an organisation can be convinced of the benefits of diversity, it will be easier to get them on board in proactively seeking and valuing diversity.

The emphasis on treating people the same is another of the major criticisms of EOPs. The main arguments are as follows.

- Individuals are not all the same, so it is not always appropriate to treat them the same.
  For example, adjustments to buildings or work processes might be needed to enable some disabled people to work. In other words, disabled people might need to be treated differently from non-disabled people. Women who are mothers might need to work flexible hours or take time off during school holidays, and they might need to be treated differently from people without similar responsibilities. On the other hand, not all disabled people need adjustments to be made for them and not all women are mothers, or want to be treated as though they will become mothers. EOPs have seldom accommodated the complexities of difference.

- Treating everyone the same has not achieved *equality of outcome.*
  This is partly because of the type of issues raised above, but also because treating everyone the same assumes a level playing field and does not take into account past discrimination and under-representation of certain groups (for example, women and ethnic minorities in management). Most EOPs have concentrated on rules and procedures to eliminate unfair discrimination, rather than being concerned with employment outcomes; eg who gets recruited, who gets promoted and who gets the highest performance-related pay awards?

- Treating everyone the same requires conformity and assimilation.
  Many social groups are now asserting their own identities in a positive manner, making it clear that they do not want to assimilate into the dominant group.

For example, some ethnic minority groups are adopting 'traditional' dress and hairstyles. The emphasis of EOPs on 'sameness' presents difficulties for the positive recognition of cultural and social diversity.

Key point: If treating everyone the same has not been entirely successful in achieving the representation of diverse groups in all organisations and at all levels, will recognising difference be any more effective?

IS A DIVERSITY STRATEGY THE ANSWER?

One of the main weaknesses is tying diversity strategy to business strategy. Will difference only be valued if it contributes to specific organisational objectives?

If the answer were yes, this is dangerous from the point of view of equality for all because, in any given organisation, it seems unlikely that all dimensions of diversity would, or could, contribute equally or tangibly to organisational goals.

Will highlighting difference simply enable organisations to see more clearly which type of difference would contribute most to their business objectives, encouraging them to undervalue other types of difference?

Some organisations, for example, might provide a better service to customers if they employ older people. This is something that DIY (do–it–yourself) stores in particular have tapped into because of the older profile of their customers. There is a clear business case here for actively recruiting and valuing older employees. However, would other types of business benefit equally from employing older people? Does age always matter? Does age have any significance for the achievement of business objectives? If the organisation cannot see how it would actually benefit from employing older people, should it worry about age diversity? What this example illustrates is the contingent nature of the business case. Whether or not there is a clear and indisputable business case for diversity depends on the context and objectives of the organisation. This is discussed in more detail in the section headed '*Why adopt a diversity strategy?*' (see p **9**).

Another main potential disadvantage with a diversity approach is that, in emphasising difference, stereotypes may be reinforced.

Stereotyping has been recognised as a major barrier to equal treatment and equal opportunity in employment; it is usually negative and can perpetuate prejudice and discrimination. The question for diversity policy is, will organisations use stereotypes to understand and think about difference? For example, will the organisation assume that all older people share the same interests and characteristics?

Related to this is the problem of over-playing difference at the expense of sameness or similarity.

People can be different from one another in some ways and similar in others. For example, the overwhelming majority of women become mothers, taking on the main family carer role. In this way women are similar to one another, and most will benefit from a range of 'family friendly' policy initiatives. However, although the role women play in the family influences their patterns and experiences of employment in countless ways, the picture is not entirely uniform. Whilst white women are most likely to work part-time when their children are dependent, black women have far higher rates of full-time work. In this way women are different to each other.

There is little comprehensive information available about the extent to which UK organisations have developed or implemented diversity policies. At present in the UK, when organisations talk about diversity policy it appears that they are usually referring to a set of procedures and practices which they would once have labelled 'equal opportunities'. The difference is that these procedures and practices are *now* seen as essential to the achievement of organisational goals and, therefore, all members of the organisation, especially managers, have an interest in ensuring that they are implemented. In this sense, equality and diversity are inter-related policy orientations (see **CHAPTER EIGHT – MODEL POLICIES**).

Definitions of Diversity

The management of diversity complements established approaches to equal opportunities.

For example, the approach to diversity favoured by the Chartered Institute of Personnel and Development (CIPD) is as follows.

> 'Managing diversity requires equality to be dealt with in a strategic, co-ordinated way. It broadens the concept of equal opportunities beyond the issues covered by law. It welcomes difference and seeks to avoid bias on the basis of issues which unfairly block personal development. It recognises that people have different abilities to contribute to organisation goals and performance, and that action might be needed to give everyone a chance to contribute and compete on equal terms. It acknowledges that organisational cultures may need to become more flexible and adaptable in order to realise the full potential of a diverse workforce. Changing the way in which things have always been done is a fundamental requirement.'[3]

There is evidence that the organisations with established equality policies are the ones which have started to develop a diversity policy, which fits in with the CIPD concept.

Therefore, the adoption of a diversity strategy does not usually signal an abandonment of equal opportunities (especially as there is still a need to comply with the various legislation in this area), but it does often signal new priorities or a new underpinning philosophy.

Diversity or equal opportunities?

Table 1 below lists some of the terminology used in diversity and provides definitions. Although the definitions vary to some degree, whichever term is chosen, at the heart of the diversity concept is the idea that difference will be valued to enable everyone to contribute effectively to the organisation. The emphasis on difference does mark a departure from traditional equal opportunities, which stresses the importance of treating everyone the same in the interests of fairness.

Table 1: Diversity terminology

Term	Definition
Managing diversity	'Managing diversity accepts that the workforce consists of a diverse population of people. The diversity consists of visible and non-visible differences, which will include factors such as sex, age, background, race, disability and work style. It is founded on the premise that harnessing these differences will create a productive environment in which everybody feels valued, where their talents are being fully utilised and in which organisational goals are met.'[4]
Diversity model of equal opportunity	'A commitment by the employer to create a workplace which facilitates the inclusion of all social categories and enables everyone to contribute to the business.'[5]
Diversity management	'Diversity management refers to a strategic organisational approach to workforce diversity development, organisational culture change and empowerment of the workforce. Ideally it is a pragmatic approach, in which participants anticipate and plan for change, do not fear human differences or perceive them as a threat, and view the workplace as a forum for individual's growth and change in skills and performance with direct cost benefits to the organisation.'[6]

Table 2 below includes examples of organisational statements on diversity and indicates how organisations are themselves defining diversity, and whether emerging and evolving diversity approaches are influencing organisational policies.

Table 2: Examples of organisational statements on diversity

Organisation	Statement on diversity
British Telecom (BT) www.groupbt.com/Betterworld/ Employees/Employees.htm	'BT has, for some time, been particularly active in establishing the business case for equality. Compliance with legislation is critical but, if we want to take a lead position in world markets, we need to be increasingly flexible, innovative, creative and able to accommodate a range of backgrounds and perspectives.'
JPMorgan Chase www.jpmorganchase.com	'Diversity is an integral component of strengthening our ability to compete in a highly global and competitive marketplace. We are building a culture that respects the value of differences among us and encourages individuals to contribute their very best.'
British Airways www.britishairwaysjobs.com	'To be the best managed company, British Airways wants to attract and develop the most talented people. Ensuring equality of opportunity and valuing diversity will help British Airways to understand the needs of, and provide the best possible service to, its customers.'
HSBC Bank www.hsbc.co.uk/diversity	'We seek to employ a workforce which reflects the diverse community at large, because we value the individual contribution of people, irrespective of sex, age, marital status, disability, sexuality, race, colour, religion, ethnic or national origin. Diversity brings positive benefits, which will improve and strengthen our business.'
Shell www.shell.com/home/Framework	'We believe that by attracting and developing the best people of all backgrounds and experience, we uphold our value of "respect for people" and improve our ability to form relationships and compete in diverse cultures and markets.'

The main points above reflected in the diversity statements of the large organisations can be summarised as follows:

- discrimination and disadvantage are not central diversity concerns;

- fairness and equality are not the major concerns; and

- there is no indication that everyone will be treated the same.

The main areas emphasised in these organisational definitions reflect a diversity approach as defined in *Table 1*, in that they:

- link diversity to business goals;

- stress the benefits of diversity; and

- use positive language to talk about diversity.

This is not to suggest that organisations adopting a diversity approach are not practising equal opportunities, or that they are not interested in eliminating discrimination and disadvantage or achieving fairness of treatment. What it does suggest is a *shift in emphasis*, and a new way of thinking about future policy developments.

This section of the chapter has highlighted some of the similarities and differences between equal opportunities and diversity approaches in order to define diversity. The case for grafting diversity policy onto existing equal opportunities policy is two-fold.

- Equal opportunities policy provides important safeguards against unfair discrimination, requiring a high degree of consistency in the treatment of individual employees (or sameness of treatment); whilst diversity allows for the positive recognition of difference.

- Equal opportunities policy involves a commitment to eliminating discrimination, unfair treatment and disadvantage for its own sake; in other words, a moral commitment to equality. In contrast, diversity makes a business case for valuing difference as well as arguing the moral and legal case. Both approaches are important for organisations wishing to be proactive and 'employers of choice'.

Key points

In understanding and defining diversity, and examining how diversity differs from equal opportunities, the following characteristics of diversity emerge.

- Diversity builds on and complements existing equal opportunities approaches.

- Diversity emphasises social and cultural difference, but should also recognise sameness.

- A diversity approach constructs a business case for action and intervention, as well as recognising the moral and legal case.

What Does Diversity Cover?

Some authors[7] argue that diversity should cover all individual and social differences. However, there is a risk that, if the areas covered by a diversity policy become too broad, in trying to do everything nothing will be achieved. After all, everyone is different in countless ways. In UK policy and practice, an assumption of group identity still underlies diversity definitions and initiatives, just as it did with equal opportunities initiatives. The difference is that diverse group identities are valued and seen as having a positive contribution to make.

It is important for organisations to define issues of priority for policy initiatives. The next consideration is how to decide which dimensions of diversity to prioritise. No organisation functions in a vacuum; organisations are situated within local communities and a wider society. It is clear from the section below, looking at how diversity issues in the external environment impact on organisational policy and practice (see p **11**), that social, group-based employment inequalities still exist. This suggests that society is not yet ready to value diversity; simply saying it will not make it happen. Organisations need to acknowledge the inequality, disadvantage, discrimination and prejudice preventing the valuing of diversity; they need to develop policies for tackling the problems as well as policies for taking advantage of the opportunities of diversity.[8] This means continuing to think about diversity in terms of group-based social and cultural difference, whilst allowing room for consideration of the individual.

Key point: The concept of diversity advocated in this book is one which moves beyond the narrow definition associated with traditional equal opportunities and includes broader and overlapping dimensions of diversity.

Why Adopt a Diversity Strategy?

The cornerstone of the business case for diversity is that diversity will deliver benefits to the organisation. The proponents of diversity approaches usually emphasise four main advantages to business.[9]

1. Taking advantage of diversity in the labour market: The principal concern is the changing make-up of the British labour market, outlined below (see p **11**). The main demographic changes are the decline in young people entering full-time, permanent employment and the increase of women seeking employment. However, the truly diverse organisation will want to cast its net more widely to take in the breadth of diversity indicated in subsequent chapters of this book.

2. Maximising employee potential: Here organisations are urged to harness the skills and experience possessed by diverse groups in order to improve organisational performance. This should also avoid low morale and poor performance caused by prejudice and discrimination, and, in this sense, it is possible to make links with the concerns of traditional equal opportunities.

3. Managing across borders and cultures: This is particularly important for the global organisation, which needs to recruit and retain diverse employees in order to thrive.

4. Creating business opportunities and enhancing creativity: The assumption here is that organisations could gain access to new customer markets by tapping the culturally-specific experiences and insights of a diverse workforce.

Critics of the business case for diversity[10] believe that if the organisational benefits to be gained from diversity are too narrow or short-term, the result might be a partial rather than a comprehensive policy, ie one addressing the most obvious and immediate concerns only. Also, a narrow approach might lead organisations to value certain types of diversity over others, depending on the business and labour market contexts. The alternative is to create a broader vision and to consider a fifth advantage to business.

5. Conducting ethical business/providing service equality: This includes social, ethical and environmental issues, so that, even where short-term gains are not apparent, organisations would attach importance to workforce diversity. The central idea is that organisations need social legitimacy if they are to survive and flourish in the longer term. This area is emphasised in **CHAPTER TWO –UNDERSTANDING THE ORGANISATIONAL CASE FOR DIVERSITY**, where the wider remit of diversity is discussed in detail.

The distinction between reactive and proactive diversity policy

Table 3 below demonstrates how proactive diversity policy builds on the successes and safeguards of the organisation's EOPs to develop a broad diversity agenda underpinned by an ethical approach to business.

Table 3: Types of diversity approach[11]

	Reactive diversity policy	*Proactive diversity policy*
Ideology	Utilitarian instrumentalism Business case Diversity viewed as a cost	Ethical rationality Social justice Diversity viewed as an asset
Triggers	Labour and skills shortages Declining profits Shareholders' needs	Corporate reputation Attracting investors Multiple stakeholders' needs
Characteristics	Abandons EOPs Legal compliance Focus on recruitment Add-on initiatives Managerial autonomy Mission statement Dependent on statements of intent Management-led Narrow agenda Short-term	Builds on EOPs Goes beyond the law Focus also on promotion blocks Mainstreaming Managerial accountability Ongoing publicity Dependent on monitoring and auditing Consultation with stakeholders Broad agenda Long-term

HOW DO DIVERSITY ISSUES IN THE EXTERNAL ENVIRONMENT IMPACT ON ORGANISATIONAL POLICY AND PRACTICE?

Gender, race and ethnicity, age and disability are all factors which influence *patterns of employment*, as well as people's *actual experiences* of organisations. Other dimensions of diversity also impact on employment experiences, including religion and sexuality. The labour market patterns of different groups of employees should be considered because they shape the context in which diversity policy is developed. It is also important to consider the ways in which the experiences of the various groups of employees can help inform diversity initiatives and interventions. This section looks at the external environment of organisations (the wider labour market) and briefly considers the diversity policy issues for organisations. The concepts of the 'glass ceiling' and 'sticky floor' (see p **15**) are also explained.

Women

Female employment in the UK is now at the highest rate ever, with women comprising 45% of the workforce and just below 70% of women being in employment. The largest employment rate increase in the last decade has been among women with children aged below five, although most of these work part-time. The vast majority of women (88%) work in the service industries and the main occupations for women are clerical (24%), professional/technical (22%), personal/ protective (16%), managerial (12%) and sales (12%).[12] These factors point to greater gender diversity in the labour market than previous generations have witnessed and indicate that organisations might need to adjust their employment strategies in order to recruit and retain this increasingly important labour source.

Policy issues

- Initiatives need to be developed to ensure that women are encouraged to apply for positions and stay with the organisation, otherwise a valuable resource is lost. Such initiatives might include flexible working patterns, enhanced (ie above statutory requirement) maternity leave, maternity pay, carer's leave, childcare and career breaks.

- Women must be treated equitably in payment systems, performance appraisal systems, promotion decisions and in the allocation of training and development. This will involve monitoring and auditing of systems.

- It is also important to recognise the diversity of women. For example, although it is presently the case that the majority of women leave employment for a period after childbirth, not all women will take this path if there are viable and affordable alternatives.

Race and Ethnicity

Non-white ethnic minority people comprise about 6% of the British workforce. Recent analysis of Labour Force Survey data shows that ethnic minorities are disproportionately found in lower-skilled and lower-grade jobs. In particular, they are under-represented in senior management grades in large organisations,[13] despite progress having been made by most ethnic minority groups in qualification levels. It is notable that in terms of occupational and educational attainment, there are considerable differences *between* different ethnic minority groups.[14] This underscores the diversity within ethnic minorities. The Trades Union Congress (TUC) also highlights the pay inequalities experienced by ethnic minorities; the difference between the average weekly earnings of white and black men is £97.[15]

Policy issues

- Organisations might need to develop initiatives to attract ethnic minority employees in order to achieve ethnic diversity. Such initiatives could include advertising jobs in the ethnic minority press, targeting graduate recruitment at universities with a higher-than-average ethnic minority student population, producing new recruitment materials with ethnic diversity at the forefront and avoiding word-of-mouth recruitment, which tends to have the effect of reproducing the existing ethnic composition of the workforce.

- Targeted training programmes, coaching and mentoring schemes/networks could help to increase ethnic diversity at the more senior levels of the organisation.

- Monitoring and auditing would identify any wage inequalities.

Religion

Inequality and discrimination on religious grounds are often bound up with issues of race and ethnicity, although this is not always the case. Some of the most economically disadvantaged ethnic minority groups (Pakistani and Bangladeshi people) are Muslim. Minority religious groups often have greater difficulty in taking time off work for religious observance and festivals, although various forms of flexible working can help with this. The significance of religion in a multi-cultural society has been heightened in the aftermath of the events of 11 September 2001 and the widespread vilification of Muslims. Various bodies, including the Government and the Commission for Racial Equality, have called for religious tolerance.

Policy issues

- Arrangements could be made allowing religious observance, including time off for religious festivals and for prayer.

- The dietary needs of different religious groups should be taken into account in any catering facility.

- The organisation's social and business networks should not exclude some religious groups. For example, activities centred on alcohol should be avoided as these could have the effect of excluding some religious minorities.

- Consideration needs to be given to uniforms and informal dress codes to ensure that religious observance can occur.

Disability

Disabled people make up 13% of the working-age population. They are over-represented in low-skilled, low-status jobs and are three times more likely than non-disabled people to be unemployed. The likelihood of an organisation employing disabled people is linked to size (larger organisations are *more likely* to employ) and sector (manufacturing organisations are *most likely* to employ).[16] In one survey[17], 13% of employers admitted that they would only employ disabled people for certain types of jobs and 6% admitted that they would not employ disabled people under any circumstances. Although this is a small minority of employers, it is still worrying that this proportion of employers are prepared to admit to excluding disabled people from employment.

Policy issues

- Adjustments to buildings, premises and equipment might be necessary to accommodate certain types of disability. The advice of relevant agencies and disability organisations should be sought.

- Work processes and organisation might need to be flexible to accommodate some types of disability; this could include work hours, work roles and tasks.

- Because disability is so enormously varied in terms of duration, severity, impairment and treatment required, employment policies in this area need to flexible enough to consider the needs of the individual.

Older People

Ageism is sometimes described as the fourth main form of discrimination in employment. Age intersects with other diversity issues; especially with gender, race and disability. Women, ethnic minorities and disabled people all experience age disadvantage to the greatest extent. People over the age of 50 are disproportionately represented among the long-term unemployed, and older employees are less likely to receive training from their employers.[18]

Policy issues

- It is important to ensure that job adverts do not send coded messages signalling (intentionally or otherwise) that older people are not welcome. The Code of Practice for Age Diversity (1998) contains advice on this area.

- Monitoring and auditing, especially of training and development programmes, is important to uncover any discriminatory practice which goes against the valuing of age diversity.

Sexuality

In the work context, many lesbians and gay men choose to conceal their sexuality in order to avoid discrimination and harassment. This can have the effect of excluding lesbians and gay men from some social and business networks. Surveys confirm that many lesbians and gay men believe that they have been refused a job or denied promotion because of their sexuality.[19] Some organisations extend various employee benefits to opposite-sex partners or spouses only, producing discrimination in remuneration packages.

Policy issues

- A harassment policy helps to deter would-be harassers so that lesbians and gay men can be open about their sexuality if they choose.

- Employee benefits, including pension provisions, travel concessions, discounts, etc, should be available to all long-term partners.

- Provisions for special leave on death of a partner or adoption of a child should also extend to lesbians and gay men.

Transexuals

The rights of people undergoing gender reassignment are now specifically protected by the *SDA 1975* (following the introduction of the *Sex Discrimination (Gender Reassignment) Regulations 1999 (SI 1999 No 1102)*) and it is, therefore, unlawful to discriminate against someone on the grounds of their transexual identity. Undergoing gender reassignment is a process that involves crossing a gender boundary, which, given the relatively fixed nature of gender roles in society, raises issues about how the transition will be managed and how others will view it. Consideration might need to be given as to when, and whether, colleagues and clients are informed. There is also likely to be an ambiguous gender status at some point in the process, which can create problems of a practical nature in the employment context.

Policy issues

- When gender reassignment is in progress, individuals will need time off for various treatments.

- Return to work following the various stages of the reassignment process needs to be handled sensitively, with consideration given to any practical issues involved; for example, dress codes, uniforms, use of single-sex facilities.

- The organisation needs to recognise that various forms of indirect discrimination could take place, including exclusion by peer groups from social and business networks.

The 'Glass Ceiling' and the 'Sticky Floor'

Most people are now aware of the concept of the 'glass ceiling' and it is widely recognised to exist in organisations for women and ethnic minorities. There are many initiatives at organisational level designed to increase the representation of these groups at higher levels. There are also a number of national initiatives, such as *Opportunity Now* (originally *Opportunity 2000*), a campaign to increase the numbers of women in senior positions, and *Race for Opportunity*, to increase employment and career development opportunities for ethnic minority employees. Less policy attention is paid to the 'sticky floor'. But what do these terms mean?

- The 'glass ceiling' refers to the intangible, invisible barriers in an organisation which prevent some groups from rising to positions above a certain level.

- The 'sticky floor' refers to the way that some groups cannot even climb up from the bottom rung of the organisational ladder and remain stuck in low-paid and undervalued jobs.

For example, highly-qualified women often encounter the 'glass ceiling' midway through their careers. In other words, they might reach junior or middle management levels but be unable to progress any further. Diversity policy could tackle this problem through a number of initiatives, such as including women in senior management training programmes, creating mentoring and coaching schemes, setting up women managers' networks and career break schemes for mothers. For women on the 'sticky floor', the problems and solutions are often less obvious. Initiatives may be needed to improve basic skill levels, to tackle pay disadvantage and to assist with childcare costs and family responsibilities.

Key points

- The labour market tends to produce inequalities of pay and opportunities among diverse social groups, rather than value their diversity. In other words, in the world of employment many people experience discrimination and inequality. This is the external social and economic context in which organisations develop diversity policy.

- This context seems to lead to the conclusion that although the aims of diversity are laudable, they are not easily achieved because of the continued existence of inequality, discrimination and disadvantage. However, organisations can take action; practical initiatives and interventions need to be developed. These need to be capable of both valuing diversity at all levels of the organisation and providing for fair and consistent treatment of groups and individuals.

Table 4 below provides examples of organisational diversity initiatives. The initiatives are varied in nature, but share an intention to improve the experiences and opportunities of diverse groups of employees. Importantly, there is also a commitment to plans, targets and monitoring, without which no diversity policy can claim success.

Table 4: Examples of organisational initiatives on diversity

Organisation	Initiative
JPMorgan Chase (see **CHAPTER EIGHT**)	*Opportunity 2000* programmes to develop and advance women. Range of 'work–life balance' initiatives. Diversity plans for senior executives. Gay and lesbian employees' support group. Recruitment fair for gay and lesbian graduates.
HSBC Bank	Graduate recruitment fairs aimed at ethnic minority students. Work skills retraining for over 50s. Employee benefits for same-sex partners. Disabled employees network – Disability Equality Action Group. Career break scheme. Family leave. Working parents' network. Women's development training. *Women's networks.*
British Telecom (see **CHAPTER EIGHT**)	Positive measures to encourage recruitment of any under-represented group. Monitoring of policy initiatives. *Harassment and bullying policy.*
Shell	Global diversity and inclusiveness standard, involving annual reports on diversity. Diversity action plans tailored to the context of each country. *Targets for the representation of women at senior levels.*
Littlewoods	Ethnic monitoring and local targets for the recruitment of ethnic minorities. 'Dignity at work' policy. Company climate survey to get staff feedback on diversity initiatives. Asian-style uniforms. *Mentoring, especially aiming at ethnic minority young people.*

THE ROLE OF A DIVERSITY POLICY IN THE WORKPLACE

No matter how well intentioned the diversity policy or how strong the top-level commitment, it is important that policy levers are developed to embed the policy into everyday organisational practice. This section briefly outlines four major policy areas. These are discussed in more detail in **CHAPTER FIVE – IMPLEMENTING AND MANAGING DIVERSITY IN THE WORKPLACE**. The role of HR (human resources) practitioners and line managers in diversity policy are also considered. Finally, the section outlines some problems with policy implementation.

Policy Areas

Following are brief outlines of the four main areas which should be covered in a diversity policy: recruitment and selection; training and development; terms and conditions of employment; and monitoring and auditing.

Recruitment and selection

From a traditional 'equal opportunity' perspective, good practice in recruitment and selection is usually taken to mean formalised and standardised procedures, with the aim of eliminating bias and potential discrimination. These procedures should be followed by anyone involved in the selection process and usually include full job descriptions and person specifications, the use of an application form in preference to CVs and a set of pre-agreed questions to be put to all candidates during interview. Diversity policy should not abandon 'good practice', but should extend the recruitment and selection activity to encourage applications from previously under-represented groups.

Training and development

There are three ways in which training and development can act as a diversity tool.

1. Diversity policy training can be used to communicate the aims and objectives of the policy. The idea is to get all members of the organisation on board and committed to making the policy real. Managers and other employees would receive information on their roles and responsibilities within the policy; for example, performance indicators would need to be covered especially for managers.

2. Diversity awareness training seeks to create positive attitudes towards work-force diversity and break down negative stereotypes of certain groups.

3. Diversity training can be targeted towards helping groups break through the 'glass ceiling' or break free from the 'sticky floor'. For example, some

organisations have developed training courses to assist women and ethnic minority employees to progress their careers.

Terms and conditions of employment

The focus in this area should be on ensuring that terms and conditions are fairly and equitably applied to all employees and that indirect discrimination does not occur. For example, job share arrangements, parental leave and career break schemes should be available to all men and women in the organisation and not just to women or senior staff. An equal pay review would ensure equality in pay across all groups. All employee benefits should be available to lesbians and gay men. In practice, this involves 'diversity proofing' the contract of employment.

Monitoring and auditing

This is essential for evaluating the successes and failures of diversity policy initiatives. It also makes good business sense for organisations to know what resources they have and where they stand so that diversity policy can be linked to business objectives. The audit will establish whether the organisation is under–utilising the skills and abilities of diverse employees, and in this way addresses business case concerns.

Key point: 'In an increasingly competitive environment, where according to a plethora of human resource management (HRM) literature, people are deemed to be an organisation's "most valued asset", can companies afford not to be making high quality decisions with regard to their personnel? Arguably, a thorough monitoring policy, covering gender, ethnic grouping, disability and age, may become a competitive advantage in the future.' [20]

The Equal Opportunities Commission (EOC), the Commission for Racial Equality (CRE) and the Chartered Institute of Personnel and Development (CIPD) all recommend monitoring, and it can also be tied in with broader ethical business case arguments. The findings of an audit will provide information on the extent of workforce diversity and should indicate the extent to which diversity is valued. In other words, if some groups appear to be facing disproportionate difficulty in obtaining promotion, or seem to be achieving lower performance ratings, the audit will identify this and action can then be taken to address the problem so that the claim to value diversity holds good. The role of monitoring and its pitfalls are discussed in detail in CHAPTER FOUR – MEASURING THE SUCCESS OF A DIVERSITY STRATEGY (see p **78**).

The Role of HR Practitioners

Traditionally, personnel practitioners were not only the guardians of equal opportunities policies, they also had responsibility for the implementation of equal opportunity initiatives. More recently there has been a general trend towards devolving some HR responsibilities to line managers (for example, performance appraisal, and grievance and discipline), whilst HR practitioners take on a more advisory, or sometimes strategic, role. This means that it is likely to fall to HR practitioners to develop the case for diversity, and to advise on and design the initiatives that will translate the policy into practice. The HR specialist's role is likely to involve coaching, training, facilitating, supporting and monitoring managers and other employees, to ensure that the policy becomes embedded in everyday management and organisation practice. The positioning of diversity within the organisation is discussed in detail in **CHAPTER TWO** (see p **47**) in the context of the wider remit of diversity.

The Role of Managers

The enhanced role played by managers in diversity has certain benefits because of the managers' day-to-day involvement with employees and their important role in delivering business objectives. In other words, the involvement of managers in the implementation of diversity policy provides an opportunity to 'mainstream' diversity; to filter diversity considerations through to all areas of business activity. In fact, it is likely that diversity policy cannot succeed without the co-operation of managers.

However, there are also possible disadvantages. In the decentralised context it becomes particularly important for line managers to 'buy into' the diversity ideal, otherwise they could have the capacity to act in a manner which prevents policy from being translated into practice. Strong business case arguments are most likely to win over managers responsible for the 'bottom line', and diversity awareness training can help in making the connections between diversity and business goals. It is also important that managers are not under so many pressures that diversity objectives are placed at the bottom of their list of priorities. This is, of course, easier said than done. One safeguard is to build diversity objectives into managers' performance indicators. This will ensure that diversity is always an issue to be addressed. The diversity audit will also reveal any areas of concern. The representation of diverse groups at all levels of management should strengthen commitment to the diversity ideal and its implementation.

Problems with Implementation

One of the criticisms of the diversity literature in the USA has been its 'upbeat naivety';[21] the way it de-emphasises the conflicts, problems and dilemmas involved in attempting to develop meaningful diversity interventions. Conflicts, problems and dilemmas arise for a number of reasons.

- Increasing diversity in organisations leads to loss of privilege for some groups, as previously under-represented groups start to compete for promotions or training and development.

For example, white men dominate management levels in most organisations. They will find themselves competing with larger numbers of people if diversity initiatives to increase the representation of women and ethnic minorities are successful.

- There may be resource constraint issues which mean that responding to the needs of one group might involve neglecting the needs of others, who may be equally disadvantaged or under-represented.

  For example, because of changing demographic patterns and the decrease in the number of young people available for permanent employment, organisations often put the greatest effort into attracting women, which might mean neglecting other diverse groups.

- Special measures to assist under-represented groups, such as some of the organisational initiatives shown in *Table 4* above (see p **15**), might be perceived as preferential treatment by people not benefiting from them, inducing feelings of resentment and hostility.

  It is likely that this will run against a culture of valuing diversity. For example, some studies, particularly in the US context, report a backlash from white men against initiatives such as management training programmes for women and ethnic minorities.

- Diversity might not increase creativity; instead it might create divisions and disagreements in work teams and arouse conflict among members of the organisation, which prevent them from working together effectively.

  If people are not used to working with diversity, performance might suffer, at least in the short term, as they learn to adapt to the new environment.

- If the organisation's rhetoric on diversity is not matched by employees' actual experiences and perceptions, and by meaningful initiatives, the policy risks doing more harm than good.

  This is especially important in relation to auditing and monitoring, which might uncover problems requiring action; otherwise employee relations problems could occur.

- The organisation needs to have a diverse workforce to begin with; it is impossible for an organisation to value something it does not have.

- Special initiatives for under-represented or disadvantaged groups might stigmatise the individuals involved and worsen their position rather than improve it.

  This is a dilemma because without special initiatives change might not occur or might be very slow to occur.

- The wider societal context of the organisation makes it difficult to address some diversity issues.

For example, an employer in the engineering sector seeking to increase the proportion of women engineers will not find it easy to do so because of women's under-representation on engineering courses.

Following is a cautionary tale involving one of the world's most well-known brand names; Coca–Cola. Despite being ethnically diverse and having a 'core philosophy' of diversity, the company has still run into trouble for its employment practices in relation to black employees. The new procedures and practices implemented as part of the settlement deal involve new standards, which should force the company to live up to its diversity ideal.

CASE STUDY: The diversity bubble bursts for Coca-Cola in the US

Coca-Cola is one of the world's most ethnically diverse companies and yet over the last couple of years it has faced charges of race discrimination. Coca-Cola is a company whose 'core philosophy is diversity, whose ties to Atlanta's black colleges, foundations and not-for-profit organisations have made it a model for other corporations'. In a law suit a group of black employees claimed that they were paid less than their white counterparts, or were passed over for promotion. The law suit documents how black employees were directed into departments such as human resources or community affairs, whereas white employees went to divisions such as corporate finance, which offered more responsibility and better career prospects.

A deal in settlement of the complaints has been reached. It requires Coca-Cola to:

- pay substantial compensation to all African-Americans who worked for the company between April 1995 and June 2000;

- create a fund to reward black people promoted to posts where there had been under-representation and bring black workers' pay up to the level of others doing the same jobs;

- set up an independent task force to ensure 'fair, equitable and effective' implementation of the agreement;

- commit its board to 'review and remain informed' about the company's progress and establish a schedule for receiving reports from the board's diversity council, the task force and the HR department;

- establish a 'public issues and diversity review committee' to oversee its equal opportunities performance;

- together with the claimants, appoint two industrial psychologists to review HR policies and practices and report to the task force;

- appoint an ombudsman, reporting to the chief executive officer, to address allegations of 'discrimination and retaliation' and monitor HR's handling of complaints; and

- tie managers' bonuses in with the company's equality performance.[22]

Key point: The aim of this handbook is to help HR managers or diversity champions to avoid those pitfalls outlined above, and to introduce a diversity strategy into their organisation in the most effective way, taking account of the business, legal and moral case for such a strategy (see **CHAPTER TWO**).

Key points

- In practice, not all organisations have achieved workforce diversity, so it is important to ensure that the policy is tailored to tackle the issues facing the individual organisation, and to recognise where it is starting from in developing diversity policy. For some organisations this might mean beginning with recruitment and identifying ways of attracting more diverse candidates. For other organisations, diversity might exist at lower levels of the hierarchy, but not at higher ones. In this case, the organisation will need to identify ways of achieving diversity higher up. Performance appraisal and training programmes might be the appropriate HR tools.

- Whatever the starting point, if organisations are to develop successful and meaningful diversity policies, the problems with implementation have to be identified and confronted, rather than glossed over. The example above indicates that diversity can be a contentious area, therefore, support from all organisational stakeholders is necessary. Diversity policy will sit uncomfortably, however, with a drive for lower costs because resources will be necessary to make the policy successful and meaningful.

- HR practitioners and line managers both play a key role in ensuring the successful implementation of diversity policy. This means that although HR practitioners are most likely to develop and champion the policy, line managers will need to be convinced of the gains to be had from implementation.

CONCLUSION

Diversity policy needs to build on the strengths and successes of traditional equal opportunity, whilst developing new arguments and initiatives for tackling some of the weaknesses and failings. The policy must articulate a strong case for diversity on broad ethical business grounds, and show how, in practical terms, the goal of valuing diversity is to be achieved by making clear links to specific policy initiatives. However, the policy should not lose sight of discrimination and disadvantage. The barriers to valuing diversity should not be underestimated. Policy-makers should recognise that there is no once-and-for-all set of practices to meet diversity objectives because the internal and external environments of organisations are in a dynamic state of flux. Organisations must also be prepared to confront the problems and dilemmas involved in implementing diversity policy.

References

1. Johnston W and Packer A, Workforce 2000: Work and Workers for the Twenty First Century, Hudson Institute (1987).
2. Cully M, Woodland S, O'Reilly A, Dix G, *Britain at Work*, Routledge (1999).
3. Chartered Institute of Personnel and Development, *Managing Diversity: An IPD Position Paper* (1996).
4. Kandola R and Fullerton J, *Managing the Mosaic*, Cromwell Press (1994).
5. Webb J, *The Politics of Equal Opportunity, Gender, Work and Organisation*, 4(3) 159–167, Blackwell (1997)
6. Arredondo P, Successful Diversity Management Initiatives, Sage (1996).
7. See for example, Kandola R and Fullerton J, *Managing the Mosaic*, Cromwell Press (1994).
8. Kirton G, Developing Strategic Approaches to Diversity Policy, in Davidson M J and Fielden S L (eds), Individual Diversity in Organisations, Wiley (2002).
9. Cornelius N, Gooch L, Todd S, Managing Difference Fairly: An Integrated 'Partnership' Approach, in Noon M and Ogbonna E (eds), Equality, Diversity and Disadvantage in Employment, Palgrave (2001).
10. See for example, Dickens L, The Business Case for Women's Equality. Is the Carrot Better than the Stick?, Employee Relations, 16(8) 5–18, MCB UP (1994); Kirton G and Greene A M, The Dynamics of Managing Diversity, Butterworth-Heinemann (2000).
11. Kirton G, Developing Strategic Approaches to Diversity Policy, in Davidson M J and Fielden S L (eds), Individual Diversity in Organisations, Wiley (2002).
12. Trends in Female Employment, Equal Opportunities Review, No 96, IRS (March/April 2001).
13. Hoque K and Noon M, Racial Discrimination in Speculative Applications: New Optimism Six Years on?, Human Resource Management Journal, 9(2) 71–82, IRS/CIPD (1999).
14. See Kirton G and Greene A M, *The Dynamics of Managing Diversity*, Butterworth-Heinemann (2000).
15. Trades Union Congress, Black and Underpaid. How Black Workers Lose Out on Pay (April 2002).
16. Honey S, Meager N and Williams M, *Employers' Attitudes Towards People with Disabilities*, Institute of Manpower Studies (1993).
17. Morrell J, *The Employment of People with Disabilities, Research into the Policies and Practices of Employers,* Department of Employment, Employment Services (1990)
18. Department for Education and Employment, *Labour Market and Skill Trends 1997/98* (1997).
19. See for example, Palmer A, *Less Equal than Others*, Stonewall (1993); Snape D, Thomson K and Chetwynd M, *Discrimination against Gay Men and Lesbians*, Social and Community Planning Research (1995).
20. Noon M, Racial Discrimination in Speculative Applications: Evidence from the UK's Top 100 Firms, Human Resource Management Journal, 3(4) 35–47, IRS/CIPD (1993).
21. Prasad P, Mills A, Elmes M, Prasad A, *Managing the Organisational Melting Pot*, Sage (1997).
22. Liu B, Coca-Cola Faces the Race Test, the Financial Times (30/05/00); Cooper C, Coca-Cola Pledges to be the Real Thing on Racial Equality, People Management (14/06/02).

Chapter Two

Understanding the Organisational Case for Diversity

OVERVIEW

This chapter covers the following issues.

- The reasons for gaining an understanding of the case for diversity – the legal, moral and bottom line benefits (see p **24**).

- The legal case for a diversity policy (see p **25**).

- The moral and civil rights issues (see p **30**).

- The potential business benefits (see p **31**).

- A step-by-step approach to launching a diversity initiative (see p **40**).

- How to gather 'diversity intelligence' (see p **44**).

- Where to position diversity within an organisation and determine who should drive the diversity agenda (see p **47**).

INTRODUCTION

The remit of diversity is extending far beyond the reach of the employment relationship. Organisations cannot ignore the impact that knowledge of diversity can have on employees, brand reputation, customer loyalty and supplier relationships. The impetus for this change is being driven by market forces and demanded by new discrimination legislation. In addition, people's expectations of fair treatment are a growing force. These factors all contribute to the widening remit of diversity management.

Changing legislation is raising people's expectation of the equalities agenda in service delivery as well as employment. People are becoming more aware that they have the right to expect the same or similar service as any other customer, as well as expecting equal employment rights irrespective of their individual needs. If an organisation is keen to secure customer and employee loyalty, it must understand how the individuality and differing needs of people impact upon the business. New legislation on race and disability requires organisations and service providers to think much more widely about diversity in relation to customers. Gathering this 'diversity intelligence' and understanding how diversity could impact on the organisation is becoming a fundamental management tool which needs to find a niche in the boardroom.

An organisation which is diversity-aware, and has developed diversity as a business management tool, will be quick to make the logical link between employee and customer expectations and take a more holistic approach to increasing its corporate knowledge on diversity. Ad hoc initiatives which separate employment issues from customer service will not benefit from the synergy that can be gained from having a single diversity programme with the objective of achieving a change in culture, leading to an understanding of how diversity can impact on every aspect of the organisation.

The overall aim of this chapter is to explore the expanding remit of diversity beyond pure employment and to delve into the potential organisational benefits that diversity management can bring in areas of customer service and brand reputation. This chapter discusses how gathering intelligence on diversity can contribute to the success of the organisation and considers how to start the process of developing a diversity strategy as an essential business planning and management tool.

THE WIDER REMIT OF DIVERSITY MANAGEMENT

This section explores the widening remit of the legal, moral and business cases for having a diversity strategy and provides an understanding of the rationale of these three areas. This provides the foundations for the diversity research exercise that is needed in order to explain where an organisation is in relation to diversity. By having a clear picture of where an organisation stands in relation to legal compliance, respect for people and the business opportunities, the organisation will be in a stronger position to decide what action to take.

The Legal Case

Equal opportunities legislation has been around for over 25 years and, during that time, there has been a whole range of new legislation which defines discrimination. It is interesting how this evolving legislation has seen the remit of equal opportunities venture outside the employment relationship.

The *Disability Discrimination Act 1995* (*DDA 1995*) saw the introduction of the 'anticipatory duty' under *Part III* of the Act (which applies to discrimination in relation to goods, facilities and services). Service providers have to start to make reasonable adjustments to physical features in anticipation of the legal duty which takes effect in 2004. The Disability Rights Commission (DRC) has issued a Code of Practice (Rights of Access: Goods, Facilities and Services 2002) to provide guidance for employers and service providers.

Legislation demands that organisations be able to demonstrate that they are learning, and will continue to learn, about disability and that they understand that discrimination against disabled people is as big a problem in the area of goods and services as it is in employment. The law is encouraging organisations to develop processes which address the broader economic inequalities that are evident in society. The anticipatory duty is important because it means that organisations can no longer be 'reactive'. A weakness of past discrimination legislation (and indeed existing legislation in other areas) is that it allowed organisations to be passive and do virtually nothing until there was a complaint or problem. At the point of complaint a reactive solution was allowed. Now, however, breach of the legislation occurs much earlier.

Key point: Organisations must be able to produce evidence that they are taking a much more 'proactive' approach, and they should be able to show how they are continuing to learn and monitor the situation.

Example 1

A large sports complex amended its 'no dogs policy' to allow entry to guide dogs. It offered guide dog users a tour of the building to acquaint them with the routes. However, an alteration took place due to building works which made it difficult for guide dog users to negotiate their way. The sports complex decided to offer appropriate additional assistance during the alteration to help overcome the problem.

Similarly, the *Race Relations (Amendment) Act 2000 (RR(A)A 2000)*, as it applies to public authorities, was a response to the finding in the Stephen Lawrence Enquiry of 'institutional racism' and the barriers which can exist in the provision of services, employment practices and other functions of an organisation. The law now recognises that discrimination can be the result of long-standing ways of doing things. This fundamental shift in perspective brings with it a whole new set of principles for equalities managers. Organisations must be able to extend their knowledge and understanding of diversity from the narrow issue of employment to a much wider approach which covers, customers, suppliers, community partnerships and other stakeholders.

Key point: It is clear that institutional racism needs institutional change.

The cost of failing to comply with the law

There is a great deal of evidence, both in the public and private sector, which demonstrates the consequences of failing to understand and comply with discrimination legislation. Such failure can have huge cost implications.

Employment tribunal awards for race, sex and disability discrimination are on the increase. However, it is not only the financial costs of tribunal awards or settlements which should be considered, but also the costs in management time, damage to reputation and affect on staff morale and attitudes.

There is no limit to the level of compensation that can be awarded by employment tribunals in discrimination claims. In *Table 1* below are the highest awards made in 2001. *Table 2* shows the number of claims made to employment tribunals in 2000.

Table 1: Awards made by employment tribunals in 2001[1]

Category	Compensation award	Injury to feelings (including aggravated damages)
Disability discrimination	£278,801 (see *Newsome v The Council of the City of Sunderland (27 November 2001) Case No 6403592/99)*	£24,000 (see *Parsons v Deltron Components Ltd (29 May 2001) Case No 187314/99)*
Race discrimination	£63,069 (see *Jarrett v Dataphone (UK) Ltd (19 December 2001) Case No 1900569/2001)*	£17,500 (see *Jarrett v Dataphone (UK) Ltd (19 December 2001) Case No 1900569/2001)*
Sex discrimination	£190,663 (see *Shepherd v Bentwood Bros (Manchester) Ltd (9 February 2001) Case No 2100872/00)*	£40,000 (see *Cotterill and Westmoreland v (1) Millenium Air Products Ltd, (2) Majestic Enterprises UK Ltd, (3) Kevin Robinson, (4) Malcolm Billing, (5) Craig Russell, (6) Lindsey Broderick (22 May 2001) Case No 2603242/00, 2603246/00)*

Table 2: Employment tribunal applications in 2000[2]

	Total Claims	Settled	Withdrawn	Employment tribunal judgement	Other
Sex discrimination	9,082	3,047	1,926	1,128	2,981
Race discrimination	4,153	1,322	1,303	1,041	487
Disability discrimination	4,422	1,647	1,102	679	994

Table 3 below shows the average and median total awards for discrimination claims in 2001 (with figures for 2000 shown in brackets).

Table 3: *Average and median awards in 2001 for discrimination claims*[3]

	Average	*Median*
Disability discrimination	£24,202 (£13,046)	£7,218 (£5,175)
Race discrimination	£9,743 (£13,817)	£5,000 (£6,833)
Sex discrimination	£9,035 (£9,450)	£5,125 (£4,847)
All discrimination awards	£11,800 (£11,165)	£5,346 (£5,231)

In 2001 compensation totalling £3.88 million was paid out for unlawful discrimination, an increase of 10% on the previous year. In these cases there was not just a financial cost but a considerable cost of time and effort to all concerned and to the reputation of the organisations involved.

Example 2

Following a claim in the employment tribunal, Isabelle Terrillon was paid £70,000 by Nomura, the Japanese bank, in a settlement over alleged sex discrimination. Whatever the facts of the case the reality was that it made headline news in most of the tabloids. The real cost in this case is the damage to brand reputation of the city finance house who may now struggle to recruit highly-qualified female employees. In addition, Nomura may find its own clients asking questions about appropriate and acceptable behaviour. Organisations, such as Barclays Bank plc, which are working hard on their own diversity strategies are asking suppliers to produce evidence of equal opportunities policies as a requirement of their own procurement processes.

Key point: Failure to comply with the law can have a much wider impact and be much more costly than just a failed employment tribunal case.

The new demands of the law

In the past, one criticism of equal opportunities legislation has been that it is an externally-imposed standard, which results in organisations being interested in achieving only minimum compliance.

However, the new legislation, and that yet to come on age, sexual orientation and religion, is actually very demanding, especially on the public sector. The *RR(A)A 2000* and the requirement to produce a race equality scheme (RES) are placing legal compliance beyond the role of an equalities officer. Public bodies covered by the *RR(A)A 2000* can no longer hide behind policies and ad hoc initiatives. The new legislation demands that organisations take a proactive approach to equal opportunities from policy and strategy to employment.

The mere existence of an equal opportunities policy does not eradicate discrimination. As stated above (see p **25**), this was the key learning from the Stephen Lawrence Enquiry, which highlighted that 'long-standing ways of doing things build in hidden barriers which result in unfair treatment'. *Institutional racism* was the phrase used to describe this collective failure of an organisation. It was a recognition that the existence of an equal opportunities policy did little to encourage the organisation to learn about race relations. This leads on to the concept of mainstreaming as the future direction for diversity. It is no longer appropriate to abdicate responsibility for diversity management to a specialist function. Ownership and understanding of diversity and its constituent parts must be driven throughout the organisation.

The equal opportunities policy is being made redundant and replaced by action plans and evidence-based reports. The idea of 'evidence-based equality' is likely to become embedded in new legislation with the implementation of the revised Equal Treatment Directive (Directive 76/207/EEC) by 2005. It raises the issue of 'equality action plans' and envisages all employers producing such a plan in relation to sex discrimination.

This 'joined-up' approach to diversity will be reinforced by a new single equality body which is likely to be established in the future. In addition, the public sector has seen equality standards on race replaced by a generic equalities standard.

Key point: The new legal direction should be taken into account when considering where to place responsibility for diversity management and when implementing the diversity strategy. A best practice approach would be a management process which ensured accountability for the equalities agenda was driven throughout the organisation from the senior team to the staff dealing with customers.

Summary of the legal remit for diversity

- The legal case for understanding diversity is a compelling argument within itself. Minimum compliance is not so easy to achieve and the cost of failure is becoming increasingly high.

- The challenge for an organisation embarking on a diversity journey is to ensure that this knowledge of the legal responsibilities is owned and understood by everyone in the organisation, and not left to the few specialist employees in the HR (human resources) and equalities department.

- Before embarking on any diversity action plan it is important to understand fully how the law affects the organisation, and to identify areas of potential risk in failing to comply with the law.

- The days of the stand-alone equal opportunities policy are numbered. Organisations need to move towards integrated diversity action plans.

The Moral Case

It has become widely accepted that employers have a responsibility to help create a fair and equal society.

For example, the DRC has adopted a vision statement highlighting its desire for 'a society where all disabled people can participate fully as equal citizens', which clearly advocates the civil rights position. However, some writers have argued that the moral case for diversity is too 'soft' a management phrase and the civil rights issues have disappeared from the equalities agenda in favour of a 'harder' business case approach.

In an attempt to gain credibility for a subject which can be hard to explain, and even harder to manage, much is being made of the business benefits of diversity, which are important, though this should not be at the expense of understanding core values about respect and fairness.

There is a strong ethical argument for diversity management which should not be diluted. Treating people with respect should be a fundamental value of any progressive diversity strategy. This argument is especially true when exploring diversity within supply chain relationships and community partnerships where there is no specific legal imperative for doing something and where certain actions may result in a cost to the business, but are clearly the right things to do.

For many years this notion of 'doing the right thing' has been confined to the charity model that has its roots in the paternalistic approach of 'giving something back to the community'. However, the management of Corporate Social Responsibility (CSR) is also experiencing a maturity and many of the business benefits of CSR are rooted firmly in the ethical management case. Grayson, in his book, *Everybody's Business*,[4] demonstrates how ignorance of these issues can add to operating costs and hurt a company's reputation. Diversity managers need to be students of CSR as well as diversity and understand how the two issues are inextricably linked.

The equal opportunities agenda was defined by the legal case and it was responsible for introducing the concept that equality meant treating everyone the same. This argument has been challenged and most definitions of diversity now promote the idea of *difference being valuable*. The ethical arguments for diversity management show how the 'equity' argument supports the new diversity definition. Equity does not mean treating everyone exactly the same in order to ensure fairness. Instead, it means giving everyone equal access to, and the right to participate in, society. It also means not denying people the opportunity to contribute because of individual needs. A diversity policy means valuing the differences.

The cost of ignoring the moral case

In looking at the widening remit of diversity, it should not be forgotten that most organisations operate out of a local community. Even global chains such as HSBC, Barclays Bank plc and B&Q have a local focus on the high street, and public bodies clearly have a community which they serve. The value of respecting one's neighbourhood should be found at the heart of most diversity strategies. B&Q, for example, has a 'good neighbour policy', which has a strong diversity focus from local schemes and helps disabled people recognise religious festivals.

The new FTSE4GOOD Index is starting to have an impact, and membership of this ethical rating index is becoming a strategic objective for many management boards. Organisations such as the Co-operative Bank see this moral case as a basic principle.

Key point: Setting a diversity objective because it is the right thing to do should not be seen as a negative cost but as a positive benefit, especially when positioning the organisation as an employer of first choice.

Summary of the moral case

- When developing a diversity strategy and identifying the overall vision and action plan, the core value of simply treating people with respect and understanding should not be underestimated.

- The positive effect of having a good moral core to a diversity strategy will be hard to calculate; this should be accepted. It may be simpler to just take the moral case for ensuring equity for all as the given starting point for all diversity strategies.

- This should not weaken the organisational case for diversity, nor should it be perceived as a 'soft' issue. It should be a powerful demonstration that an organisation respects the quality of life of all the people it touches.

- Being recognised as socially responsible is essential if an organisation wants to become an employer of first choice.

The Business Benefits

The expanding remit of diversity has widened the scope for potential 'bottom line' or business benefits to be realised. The potential impact can be extended to cover employment, customer service, stakeholder involvement and brand reputation.

Key point: The widening remit of diversity has enabled a much more strategic approach to be taken in identifying measurable outcomes for diversity management and has helped to place diversity on the agenda of the boardroom.

Understanding the diverse needs of all the people who are involved with the organisation will enable that organisation to develop more targeted action plans for all areas, including, advertising strategies, product development, customer service, employment strategies and brand reputation.

The various potential business benefits are discussed below. Many generalisations are made when discussing the business benefits, however, is up to each individual organisation to investigate the areas upon which diversity can have a measurable impact, and to identify the specific benefits.

The benefits to customer service

The private sector has long sought 'intelligence' on customer behaviour. Whole industries have been built on delivering information from, for example, customer focus groups and mystery shoppers, to enable organisations to deliver excellence in customer service. This information is vital if an organisation is going to make informed strategic decisions on new products and marketing strategies designed to ensure a strong customer base. It is, therefore, a logical step to start to analyse customers within a diversity framework.

Example 3

London Transport employed disabled people to carry out a research project which analysed its customer service, in order to identify the actions needed to take to comply with the *DDA 1995*.

Example 4

An organisation in Leicester ran focus groups with Asian families to find out how it was perceived as a service provider. The feedback from this type of exercise can start to generate much clearer objectives for a diversity action plan aimed at improving customer service. The project in Leicester resulted in a greater understanding of the customer service needs of, potentially, the majority customer base for a supermarket. This resulted in the provision of language translation, different foods being offered for sale and holy days and religious festivals being respected.

Organisations need to gather information which will help them realise the benefits to customer service.

Following are the areas which should be investigated.

Understanding customer needs

Key point: Understanding the needs of customers is a crucial step in delivering excellence in customer service.

> ### Example 5
>
> An NHS out patients department in Leeds experienced a high number of cancellations. On further investigation, a correlation was shown to exist between certain religious festival dates and the pattern of cancellations. A multi-faith calendar was introduced and appointments were avoided on Fridays involving the Muslim holy day and main festivals. There was an immediate decrease in cancellations.

Customer service

Key point: Understanding diversity can help deliver niche markets.

There is a logical link between customers and employees which can be a powerful force in attracting a customer base and maintaining customer loyalty.

> ### Example 6
>
> With B&Q there is measurable evidence of the benefits of employing older workers to deliver DIY advice to customers (see CHAPTER SEVEN – CASE STUDIES ON DIVERSITY). Being able to respond with alternative media for disabled customers is another example.

If customers receive excellent customer service an organisation will start to build loyalty. This loyalty can be cultivated. For example, an organisation may want to be one which welcomes and respects gay and lesbian customers, and targets, therefore, some £40 billion of available spending power. Its diversity strategy could include, working with Stonewall as a diversity champion, sponsoring *Gay Pride week*, advertising in the *Pink News* and introducing progressive employment policies.

Marketing strategies

Key point: Marketing managers need to become more diversity aware as niche markets develop and because mistakes can be costly.

Advertisers need to be sensitive to the diversity of their audience. For example, Van der Berg foods ran a TV advert featuring the 'Chicken Tonight' sauce which attracted complaints from the Hindu community because of its portrayal of a woman meditating to a chicken. The combination of the Hindu-style chant and the fact that the advert encouraged meat eating offended followers of the Hindu faith who are largely vegetarian. This showed a poor understanding of the viewing audience. The company bowed to pressure and withdrew the advert.

Use of TV adverts can also position brand image. If only white married couples appear in adverts, this is going to relay a message not only to customers but also to potential employees.

Example 7

B&Q featured an employee with a disability in a mainstream advert. There was nothing special or different about the advert but it was able to send a clear message to the viewing audience that B&Q employs disabled people; even though the advert was about buying a drill. This was seen as such a positive step that the advert was shown on the evening news, giving B&Q even greater brand value.

Example 8

Bass Breweries were forced to drop an advert which showed bikini-clad women performing the Haka. This was offensive to New Zealanders because it portrayed women performing a male war dance.

Key point: Diversity awareness training rarely makes it to the marketing team as most organisations concentrate on training service staff who deal with customers. However, there needs to be a much wider delivery of diversity awareness.

Supplier relationships

Key point: It is becoming increasingly common for commitment to diversity to be demanded in supplier contracts.

It is common place to see standards demanded as part of a supplier–purchaser contract whether it is health and safety, quality assurance standards such as BS5750 or a guarantee on delivery. Increasingly environmental issues have become part of this relationship.

For example, Barclays Bank plc is now asking for evidence of a commitment to equal opportunities in supplier contracts. It will become increasingly common in the public sector as public bodies try to ensure that they are complying with the requirements of the *RR(A)A 2000*, where a private organisation supplies a public service.

Community partnerships

Key point: Reaching out into the local community can increase local knowledge, enhance local reputation and build up strong community relations.

Local authorities whose ethnic minority populations may not be so evident, such as Essex County Council, will have to work hard to secure community partnerships compared with local authorities, such as Tower Hamlets, where there is a strong voice from the Bangladeshi community. However, both such authorities will benefit from building their reputation in the community.

Example 9

The West Bromwich Building Society in Handsworth has a potential customer base, 30% of which is of Asian background. A global money transfer system was offered in conjunction with Global Money Transfer Limited. By paying attention to Asian customer needs the West Bromwich Building Society has developed a significant competitive advantage over other providers in the area.

The employment benefits

There are some generally accepted areas of employee benefits that can result from managing diversity.

Attracting candidates

Key point: Creativity in employment strategies can often yield associated benefits. Attracting candidates in the first place is a crucial step in helping to change an organisation's employee profile. Organisations which adopt more innovative recruitment strategies attract a wider pool of candidates.

In the UK, 16% of the white population have degrees, compared to 21% of the black and Asian community. 33% of refugees have a degree or professional qualification. Only 18% of the UK population speak two languages, whereas 65% of refugees speak two languages in addition to their mother tongue. Yet Asian graduates are twice as likely to be unemployed, whilst refugees are three times as likely to be unable to find permanent work. The cost of supporting refugees in Britain in 2001 was £751 million, and yet over half of the people seeking work reported being discriminated against.[5]

Attracting candidates takes up a great deal of HR management's time. A recent survey of graduates[6] found that decisions about choosing employment were more likely to be affected by work–life balance and working for an organisation which respected people and the environment, rather than a high salary.

Example 10

GAP, in partnership with Sabre Employment, helped secure long-term employment for nine disabled people in the flagship store on Oxford Street. The added benefits to the store included employee involvement and commitment to learn British Sign Language (BSL), which in turn saw an increase in deaf customers using the store.

Example 11

The Dome experienced similar benefits when 15 disabled people, who had never worked before, were employed to work there. They experienced a 100% retention rate for the full year's contract and were able to redeploy all 15 people.

Candidates are attracted not only as a direct result of job adverts. An organisation's brand, *where* it advertises and the recruitment agencies it uses can all have an impact. For example, organisations which use agencies to help them head-hunt and manage the recruitment process are in danger of continuing to recruit the same type of person.

Example 12

Bartlett Scott Edgar have realised that if they are going to remain competitive in the recruitment agency market they must be able to help organisations solve their employee profile issues. In 2002 they commissioned a piece of research, *Diversity. Big Difference or Indifference*,[7] which examined changing recruitment strategies. From this they have been able to influence the recruitment campaigns of their clients in attracting a more diverse range of candidates.

Retention rates

Key point: Diversity management can have a significant impact by helping organisations to understand how they can be more responsive to employee needs and, thus, improve retention rates. A recent survey by Accenture cited retention and people issues as the main advantages of introducing flexible working arrangements.[8]

Employers want the best person for the job and understanding how diversity can impact upon recruitment is a good first step. But many organisations then proceed to lose the best people for the job because they are inflexible in their approach to employment or suffer from absenteeism and de-motivated employees. Few organisations take the time to conduct effective confidential exit interviews to discover why people are leaving their jobs, or to really investigate absenteeism.

Turnover rates are a huge drain on an organisation's resources. Diversity management can help retain employees for a lot longer and thus reduce the high cost of staff turnover.

Example 13

In the employment tribunal case of *Chief Constable of Avon and Somerset Constabulary v Chew [2001] ALL ER (D) 101 (Sep)* a police officer returning from maternity leave was told that she could not work regular shift patterns, as requested, for a period of time in order to help with childcare arrangements and that, instead, she

> would be subject to the shift rota. Irrespective of the subsequent cost of the discrimination case, such an organisation can no longer simply ignore the needs of its employees. If the police force recognises the need to recruit more women then it must also become more intelligent about how it employs women in today's society. Simply put, if not enough attention is given to the way people work, staff will go elsewhere.

A report on *New Ways to Work*[9] highlighted the fact that Boots, who had had problems attracting women back to work, witnessed a rise from 4% to 49% of women returning to work over a four-year period after a range of work–life balance schemes were introduced.

Investment in training

Key point: Retaining staff by recognising diversity will result in a reduction in an organisation's training budget.

A natural extension of the argument on staff recruitment and retention is the return on investment made in staff. Organisations invest in staff through standard induction, further job training and through collective experience. This enables employees to become better at their jobs and feed the succession planning. If investment is consistently made in staff training but not in subsequent retention of staff, this is bound to have an effect on the training budget.

Example 14

BT reported a success rate of 96% of women returning to work after maternity leave as a result of the new employment philosophy on flexible working.

Example 15

Sainsbury's has a high investment rate in training all its staff, especially in customer care and induction. It now enjoys an 80% return-to-work rate after maternity leave as a result of flexible work options.

Employees as a resource

Key point: Employees are a great source of creativity and ideas; the more diverse the workforce, the greater the variety of new ideas.

Once the effects of a diversity strategy are starting to produce changes in the employment profile, the associated benefits will start to materialise. For example, older, experienced employees can act as mentors to younger employees.

Example 16

Nationwide Building Society experienced a huge loss of corporate memory when a large number of over-50s left the organisation following a merger. This loss was one of the driving forces behind its subsequent adoption of an age diversity policy (see CHAPTER EIGHT — MODEL POLICIES).

Example 17

Asda recruited many older workers in order to address the need for more part-time staff who could be flexible.

Summary of the business benefits

- Diversity management can be shown to help reduce the cost faced by organisations of recruitment and retention.

- A good diversity strategy can see an increase in return on investment from training and career breaks.

- The employment profile of an organisation can be managed to reflect the customer profile and can help deliver more effective customer services strategies.

By having a more holistic overview of diversity, it becomes really clear how synergies can be made across the organisation. The main benefits to the business start to have a more dramatic impact when this wider view of diversity is understood.

USING THE ORGANISATIONAL CASE FOR DIVERSITY

Three aspects of diversity which could contribute to the overall success of an organisation have been presented. The potential impact of the legal case, the moral case and the business benefits are capable of affecting all aspects of an organisation, and together make up the *organisational case* for the implementation of a diversity policy.

Having understood the organisational case, the next steps are to research the organisation, to apply this knowledge on diversity and to identify a business case which will justify committing time and resources in developing a diversity action plan. The challenge for an organisation is to establish the business benefits.

Research will enable the organisation to recognise:

- issues on recruitment within the organisation;

- the employee profile against customer profile;

- who is leaving, why and at what cost; and

- the impact diversity could have on employee retention, customer loyalty and brand reputation.

Knowledge of diversity management needs to be translated into a practical understanding of how these three areas could actually have a real impact upon the organisation. The case for diversity needs to be argued to the senior managers of the organisation in order to get them to understand why and how a diversity strategy can add value to the organisation.

Key point: It is crucial to be able to show where an organisation stands in relation to all three aspects of the organisational case in order to develop the right action plan to deliver the right results for that organisation.

The task is to make the organisational case for diversity based on compelling arguments which help senior managers understand:

- the legal case for compliance and the cost of failure;

- the moral case for treating people with respect and the benefits this can bring; and

- the business benefits available to help achieve the overall strategic objectives.

How can this knowledge of the potential impact of diversity be translated into identifiable and measurable action plans which will have an impact on the organisation?

RELATING DIVERSITY TO THE STRATEGIC PLANS OF AN ORGANISATION

Key point: The success of a diversity strategy lies in being able to relate the benefits to the overall strategic objectives of the organisation.

Organisations have strategic objectives, employ staff, communicate with customers and deliver some form of service or output. Within this overall concept there are specific legal requirements which apply in various ways to different types of organisations, and there will be differences between demographics and employee needs.

Being able to identify and communicate the organisational case is a vital first step in developing a diversity strategy. It is necessary to construct a robust argument when trying to secure top-line commitment and financial approval for an action plan. For a diversity strategy to carry credibility it must be based on strong, measurable evidence and not unsubstantiated claims.

A PROCESS FOR MANAGING DIVERSITY

Organisations have a reason for existing and a means by which they achieve their desired aims and objectives. The reason for existing is identified in a *strategic plan* that encapsulates the discussions around the principles and vision of the organisation. The strategic plan is 'owned' by the senior team and is used to maintain direction and communicate the goals which the organisation is working towards.

Once the strategic plan is agreed discussions need to take place and decisions must be made setting out what the organisation is going to do towards achieving its desired aims. This is the *business plan*. It should identify the actions required and set the pace for change. Both the strategic plan and the business plan require information on the present state of the organisation to enable informed decisions to be made on a future desired position.

A failure of many diversity initiatives is that they are launched in isolation from the main strategic plan. The diversity initiatives are not managed as part of a process. **CHAPTER THREE – DEVELOPING THE STRATEGIC PLAN AND BUSINESS OBJECTIVES FOR DIVERSITY**, explains how to develop a strategic plan and a business plan for diversity.

DIVERSITY STEPS

Diversity consultants, the Grass Roots Group (GRG), have identified four stages, called *diversity steps*, which need to be worked through before a diversity initiative is launched.

Figure 1: GRG diversity steps diagram

Further explanation of the four steps identified by GRG follows below.

- *Step 1: Understanding diversity – Diversity research.*
  An organisation must understand how diversity could impact upon every aspect of its work and all its stakeholders. It must also understand where it *currently stands* in relation to the legal case, the moral case and the business case.

- *Step 2: Identifying where the organisation wants to be – Strategic plan.*
  An organisation needs to work with senior managers to identify the vision, aims and objectives. An organisation needs to be clear what aims it is working towards.

- *Step 3: Agreeing on an action plan – Business plan.*
  Once an organisation is clear on what it wants to achieve it can set about devising an action plan that can be clearly communicated and implemented.

- *Step 4: Measuring and reporting on success – Annual report.*
  A sustainable diversity strategy must be capable of being measured for impact upon the organisation. Clear benchmarks, measurement targets and honest reporting are crucial to the ultimate success of a diversity strategy.

The rest of this chapter concentrates on Step 1 of the process, but also gives an overview on how to devise a strategy (this is discussed in more detail in **CHAPTER THREE**).

Step 1

The importance of Step 1 cannot be over-emphasised. All too often this step is not completed effectively or is missed out all together. Only by understanding diversity and the relationship between diversity and the organisation can that organisation begin to explore where it wants to be; and only then can a coherent, long-term strategy be agreed upon and implemented.

Jumping to Step 3 will only result in a random series of short-term quick fixes which invariably rely on the enthusiasm of an individual and rarely become embedded in the culture of an organisation.

Key point: When trying to bring about behaviour change, ad hoc initiatives will produce selective results that will fail to change the collective behaviour of an organisation.

Understanding what diversity means for the organisation

Many organisations make the mistake of trying to tackle managing diversity by simply providing for a series of initiatives aimed at solving a particular issue. A common mistake is for an organisation to move straight to an action plan without first taking the time to understand what diversity means for all its stakeholders and why certain situations arise. This can result in a diversity initiative being too reactive to a particular business need.

Finding the right solution

A monitoring exercise reveals that an organisation does not have enough representation of women at middle and senior management grades. It decides on a diversity solution that involves introducing a *Women into Management Network Group* and mentoring scheme. However, if the organisation does not understand why it had so few women managers in the first place, the 'solution' may not address the problem.

Different organisations have different problems.

- A police force lost a high profile sex discrimination case which received much media attention. It had a reputation for being a difficult environment for women to work in and for failing to respect the need for flexibility. As a result women were reluctant to apply for promotion because of the shift patterns and unsociable hours.

- A breakdown service is perceived as operating long shifts which are inflexible. Also, the main recruitment pool is qualified mechanics, but there are problems attracting women to these courses. Consequently, there are fewer women qualified to do the job.

- A city bank has a reputation for pay inequality. The number of graduates qualified to work at the bank include equal numbers of men and women, but few women want to apply to the bank because of its reputation.

If the reason behind the poor statistical profile of women in senior roles in the police force was a 'long hours culture' and a reputation for harassment of women, it would need a different diversity solution to that needed by the city bank or the breakdown service.

Key point: Diversity initiatives can be viewed as 'lip service' and 'tokenism' and may even provoke a backlash from other staff; it is important, therefore, that the right solutions are put in place.

Example 18

The Avon police force actively pursued its employment targets for employing more Asian police officers. It then found itself accused of 'priority' promotion. Also, an Asian officer took sick leave on grounds of stress (he felt he had been promoted too quickly), whilst the remaining white officers felt they had been overlooked for promotion.

Monitoring is an important way of measuring the effectiveness of policies and highlighting problem areas. However, monitoring is much more than just collecting data. It is vital that the information is analysed and the evidence understood. The statistical profile will highlight a problem area, but much more 'diversity intelligence' needs to be gathered if an organisation is going to be able to deliver the appropriate solution to the problem and produce results. For example, turnover statistics may show that a high number of women over the age of 35 are leaving the organisation; only by carrying out exit interviews is it possible to analyse the reasons for this.

It is crucial that the success of a diversity strategy should be measured and appraised on improvement and not be driven by target achievement. However, the result of having too many initiatives is that an organisation ends up having several unconnected action plans which try to address several diversity issues. It becomes increasingly difficult to communicate what all these actions are trying to do and how they fit into the organisation's strategic objectives. This damages the credibility of diversity management and weakens the business argument. A further consequence of this approach is that middle managers fail to see how diversity can impact upon the organisation and, as a result, commitment can be patchy and understanding can be limited.

The benefits of diversity are often widely quoted as being able to solve most problems from recruitment and retention to employee satisfaction, and increase competitive advantage. However, for an organisation to take full advantage of the benefits of diversity it must take time to understand what diversity means to it, to its employees, customers, community and other stakeholders, and to develop the right strategy and action plans for that organisation.

The need to gather diversity intelligence

If diversity management is to become an integral part of an organisation's corporate knowledge, the organisation must have a clear vision of what it intends to achieve and why. Clarity around this vision will enable the diversity strategy to be communicated to all the stakeholders. Many authors suggest that the starting point for developing a diversity strategy is to agree a strong vision and gain clear commitment from senior management. However, it is difficult for senior managers to give their commitment if they don't have all the information.

Example 19

When B&Q developed its diversity strategy, the directors all agreed that treating individuals with respect was the right thing to do and no one had any doubts that the organisation should have a diversity strategy. The moral case was clearly understood. The legal case added weight to the argument; minimum compliance in itself was an onerous task and the risk of failure can carry a heavy penalty. However, the board wanted to know much more about the business benefits of diversity, including employee attitudes and needs, customer service, business development and the impact on brand reputation. More questions than answers were raised by the board when the diversity initiative was considered, and the initial outcome was not a diversity vision statement but a task to go away and find out much more information on how diversity could impact upon B&Q.

Key point: The B&Q example demonstrates the importance of recognising the inter-dependence of the three strands of the business case for diversity.

The experience at B&Q showed that, in principle, all the directors had a willingness to express support for diversity but they wanted more 'market intelligence' on what diversity could mean for the company. As retailers, if the directors were considering introducing a new product they would want a whole host of data such as pricing, competition, packaging, customer feedback, potential advertising campaigns, a risk assessment, supply chain implications and training for staff. They treated diversity with the same level of interrogation and they demanded information on employees, customers, stakeholders, the community and the law.

Ross and Schneider[10] discuss a five-stage strategic approach where the first step is called diagnosis (defining the starting point). They discuss three areas for diagnosis: the statistics, the personnel policy and the prevailing culture. At B&Q this was a useful starting point but the directors needed to go much further and gather information from customers, stakeholders and community representatives. They wanted to know what people thought about B&Q. Did they need to change people's perceptions? Was B&Q ahead of competitors in this field?

They needed to establish where the organisation stood, both internally and externally, before they could assess where they wanted to be and how ambitious the vision statement could be.

The message from the board of directors was clear:

- they did not want to set themselves up for failure;

- they wanted clear targets that could be ambitious but achievable;

- they wanted clear benchmarks and clear objectives with quantifiable outcomes and identifiable measures for success; and

- the budget would be awarded in relation to the potential impact upon brand reputation and the bottom line.

Gathering diversity intelligence

The first step in producing a diversity strategy is to spend time researching a whole range of factors which should include the following.

(*a*) Internal issues.

    (i)   Employee monitoring statistics.

    (ii)   Employee attitude survey.

    (iii) Employee focus groups.

    (iv) Research of maternity leave and women returning to work.

    (v)   Assessment of how well the equal opportunities policy was understood.

    (vi) Exit interviews.

(*b*) External issues.

    (i)   Customer complaints.

    (ii)   Customer focus groups or other market research, eg mystery shoppers.

    (iii) Benchmarking and research on competitors.

    (iv) Research on which organisations are seen as adopting good practice.

(*c*) Community/political issues.

    (i)   How is the organisation perceived within the local communities?

    (ii)   How much political influence does the organisation have?

(*d*) Legal implications.

    (i)   Risk assessment against legislation.

(ii)   Analysis of the cost of discrimination issues and the cost of claims taken to the tribunal, including settlement costs and management time.

(iii) Potential impact of future legislation using a ten-year forecast.

Key point: The reason why B&Q has enjoyed so much success with its diversity strategy is that the organisation always takes the time to understand why it is doing something and what it wants to achieve.

Most organisations are to keen to do something without going through this first step. As Ross and Schneider state:

> 'There has been much solution orientated thinking and not enough diagnostics.'[11]

Statistical evidence, which is presented in isolation from any analysis, can result in decisions being made that are based on incomplete information. It is important that some qualitative information is gathered from, for example:

- focus groups;
- mystery shopping exercises;
- customer feedback;
- employee feedback; and
- demographic analysis (to help explain the picture that the statistics are presenting).

The results of Step 1

The result of Step 1 should be a position paper of where the organisation currently stands in relation to the legal, moral and business case for diversity.

This paper should:

- identify the risks and the potential benefits of a diversity strategy; and
- enable the board to make strategic decisions and assess how much resource to allocate to the diversity strategy.

Producing such a paper enables discussion with key directors and for questions to be answered before they meet to discuss the proposals.

It will be easier for a board to agree on a vision and core values if the directors know where they currently stand.

POSITIONING DIVERSITY WITHIN THE ORGANISATIONAL STRUCTURE

Having constructed the argument for a diversity strategy, and completed Step 1 in the diversity process, there is a need to identify where the role of diversity fits within the organisation.

Traditionally, HR management has held the equality agenda because of the clear links to the employment relationship. However, the remit of diversity is wider and it must be decided, therefore, where responsibility for managing the diversity agenda should be placed within the organisational structure. There are various options to consider.

Sustainability, CSR and Diversity

Consider the following facts.

- 77% of the public would like their pension funds to adopt an ethical policy provided it did not harm financial returns.[12]

- 25% of the world's financial wealth is made up from intangibles of brand value.[13]

- 86% of consumers express a clear preference for a company which treats people with respect.[14]

- Brand value and corporate reputation are becoming so important that reputation indexes like the FTSE4GOOD Index are emerging.

- The Dow Jones Sustainability Group Index representing ethically-managed stocks outperformed the Dow Jones by 36% over the past five years.

- The value of portfolio screening for Socially Responsible Investment (SRI) funds in the UK is worth £25 billion.

In short, this is a commercial response to people's changing values and how they view the image of business. Charles Fombrun calls this economic value of a company's reputation its *'reputational capital whose currency is credibility'*.[15]

If values are part of the intangible assets of a company, how do companies go about building their reputation and earning trust? And what part does diversity play in the currency of credibility?

Sustainable development, Corporate Social Responsibility (CSR) and diversity all share a similar foundation; they are about values of respect. All seek to enhance reputation, contribute to performance and increase stakeholder loyalty.

Therefore, it may make sense to position diversity within a new definition of this reputational capital in an organisation's structure. If an organisation is really going to embed its values, it needs to change its way of thinking and talk about sustainable development, CSR and diversity, almost as synonymous assets which are central to the business and can work more closely together. These internal partnerships are important and the relationship should be clear when developing a diversity strategy. For example, B&Q has already brought these issues together and has a Sustainability and Diversity Department.

Brand Reputation

As the organisational case for diversity is made, it is an ideal opportunity to re-position the diversity role and to seek a senior position that reports to the board. The position of the diversity manager is crucial in relaying how much importance the organisation is attributing to diversity.

Some organisations may wish to form a 'Reputation Board' as the mechanism for delivery on CSR, sustainability and diversity. The objective of this team would be to inspire everyone who is involved with the organisation to recognise the same values. This team could be the 'custodians' of brand reputation and seek to influence the corporate behaviour of the organisation. This will ensure that ad hoc fragmented initiatives are turned around into clear strategies, raising the stakes for diversity and giving it the same status as CSR.

The Diversity Manager

An alternative is to split the diversity role into employee issues and customer facing issues and have two lead roles; but these roles must have a linked strategy. It is important that the role is clearly defined and the job title will influence how diversity is seen within the organisation.

Example 20

Centrica has a diversity manager who is responsible for customer facing issues and a HR manager who is responsible for staff issues. However, they have recognised that the two diversity programmes should be synchronised.

Diversity practitioners are key players in this development. The positioning of diversity within an organisation can in itself deliver a powerful signal about the organisation and the level of commitment to change.

Key point: Most of the organisations currently delivering an effective diversity strategy all have senior diversity managers. It is clear that diversity cannot be managed as part of another role; it must have a clear role within the organisational structure.

A Stakeholder Approach to Diversity

Wherever the ultimate responsibility for implementation of diversity lies, diversity solutions need to be positioned within a wider framework of management accountability. This means having 'joined-up' strategies across all areas of management, such as customers, employees and community relations.

For example, a typical diversity issue is that monitoring statistics reveals low representation of ethnic minorities amongst employees. Where is the starting point for presenting a strategy for improvement and the budget justification needed to implement real initiatives? Perhaps the standard reaction is to put employment as the starting point, looking at recruitment. But what if the organisation's ability to recruit more black and Asian employees is seriously affected by its reputation in the community or by customer perception. The impact of any positive recruitment campaign will be weakened by the actions taken in other areas. What is needed here is a holistic approach to managing a diversity issue.

The diversity issue, whether it is age, disability, gender, race etc, needs to be placed at the centre of the stakeholder and business issues which have been identified. For example, if achieving a more age-balanced workforce is the issue to be improved upon, there needs to be an understanding of how age diversity could impact on all the stakeholders, and what influence they could have on the employment profile.

In planning the diversity strategy, an organisation needs to be aware of all the work going on with various stakeholder groups.

- Understanding customers means not only starting to meet their expectations in products and services but also building the organisation's reputation.

- Partnership in the community reinforces the message to customers, which adds to the currency of credibility.

- The organisation's supply chain must be known.

- How the organisation acts as a neighbour will have an impact.

- As credibility is built up, customers and neighbours will want to become employees.

- Loyalty and credibility are transferable between stakeholder groups.

- Robust employment practices are vital to avoid discrimination, but reputation is key in attracting candidates in the first place.

It is not uncommon to hear statements from HR teams that companies want to employ more disabled people, older people or people from different community backgrounds, but that they simply do not receive the applications!

For example, a high street retailer has only 4% ethnic minority employees in junior positions and the performance of its stores is below target in areas of high black and Asian communities. By understanding how policies impact on all the stakeholders, it results in a change to the starting point for introducing solutions.

It may start with the celebration of religious festivals in stores, the selling of holy day cards, understanding language in customer services needs, respecting what is happening in shared cultures in the supply chain and establishing a community partnership programme. These actions will transfer credibility to the employment solution as a natural progression.

The net result is a holistic strategy which can be clearly communicated. The organisation can then respond to the new demands of stakeholders, putting diversity in a position of strength both in terms of performance and profitability.

CONCLUSION

Diversity is a complex issue to define and manage. It is a subject that cannot be confined to employment as easily as the equal opportunities agenda. It naturally wants to exert an influence on customers as well as employees and, often, the results of an action in one area will be felt in another. Diversity wants to play a part in building brand reputation and in determining the agenda for CSR.

Diversity management is driven by the three strands: the legal case, the moral case and the bottom line or business benefits. These can be hard to define and measure but are capable of delivering undeniable benefits. Those organisations which are beginning to get to grips with this subject are doing so because they have put in place a clear strategic vision and a business plan designed to deliver the right solutions to particular diversity problems. The main weakness of diversity management lies in poorly-defined objectives, incomplete research and ill-defined measurement.

Key ingredients that provide the foundations for success include:

- diversity research;
- understanding the impact of diversity;
- positioning diversity within the organisational structure; and
- adopting a holistic approach.

CHECKLIST

✔ Do senior managers within your organisation understand the wider remit of diversity and the potential impact of the diversity argument in the three areas: the legal case, the moral case and the business benefits?

✔ Has your organisation identified the potential benefits and risks associated with diversity management?

✔ Have you completed a diversity mapping exercise of your own organisation, which would identify how potential benefits could impact on all areas of the business?

✔ Have you identified all the stakeholders involved?

✔ Have you constructed an argument for a holistic approach to diversity?

✔ Has it been decided where diversity management should be positioned within your organisational structure and where management accountability should lie?

References

1. *Equal Opportunities Review*, No 108, IRS (August 2002).
2. Advisory, Conciliation and Arbitration Service, *Annual Report 2000/01*.
3. *Equal Opportunities Review*, No 106, IRS (August 2002).
4. Grayson D and Hodges A, *Everybody's Business*, DK (2001).
5. London Research Centre, *New Earnings Survey* (1998).
6. Coopers and Lybrand, International Student Survey Report (1997).
7. Bartlett Scott Edgar, *Diversity. Big Difference or Indifference*, Bartlett Scott Edgar internal paper (2002).
8. Accenture, *The High Performance Workforce*, London Accenture (2001).
9. www.new–ways.co.uk.
10. Ross R and Schneider R, *From Equality to Diversity*, Pitman Publishing (1992).
11. Ross R and Schneider R, *From Equality to Diversity*, Pitman Publishing (1992).
12. NOP poll reported in the *Financial Times*, May 2000.
13. Business in the Community. *Winning with Integrity* (2000).
14. Adkins S, *Cause Related Marketing. Who Cares Wins*, Butterworth-Heinemann (1999).
15. Fombrun C, *Reputation: Realising Value from Corporate Image*, Harvard Business School Press (1996).

Chapter Three

Developing the Strategic Plan and Business Objectives for Diversity

INTRODUCTION

The problem with diversity management is that the benefits are not always understood and it is one of those areas that some managers feel is 'nice to have', but only when there are not more pressing business objectives to achieve. If diversity management is to have a real influence in the organisation and gain commitment, all managers need to see the sense behind it and understand how they and the business will benefit from any proposed actions. To aid this progression, senior decision-makers need to be convinced that diversity management is a pressing business objective for all aspects of the business. This is discussed in detail in CHAPTER TWO – UNDERSTANDING THE ORGANISATIONAL CASE FOR DIVERSITY.

Key point: Key decision-makers need to be sufficiently convinced by an argument in order for them to devote time to developing a strategic plan and a business action plan for diversity. Diversity management needs to secure a credibility which places it alongside marketing, product development, finance and operations if the potential benefits are going to be fully realised.

The *strategic plan* encapsulates the discussions around the principles and the vision for the organisation. The *business plan* sets out what the organisation is going to do to create the momentum to move the organisation forward towards meeting its desired aims. The diversity manager should work within a similar framework. This chapter examines how to develop a strategic plan and a business plan for diversity, and how to present a persuasive argument which will win credibility and influence key decision-makers and managers. The roles played by champions and employees are considered, together with the impact they have on the success of the diversity business plan and how communication of the strategy is a critical factor in sustaining change.

THE ROLE OF THE DIVERSITY MANAGER

It is clear that diversity cannot be managed as part of another role. Most organisations currently delivering an effective diversity strategy have a senior diversity manager. For example, Barclays Bank plc, HSBC, Ealing County Council and Royal Bank of Scotland have all appointed diversity directors. Diversity can be dealt with in different ways within an organisation, but in this chapter it is assumed that a 'diversity manager' has been appointed and reference to that role is made throughout. This title, however, simply refers to the person whose job it is to take this complex subject forward within the organisation, whatever his or her actual job title. The term 'managers' refers to anyone who has managerial responsibility within the organisation; senior people are referred to as 'key decision-makers'.

The role of the diversity manager is crucial in the initial stages of developing a diversity strategy. (Later in the chapter the concept of mainstreaming diversity and encouraging ownership throughout the organisation is discussed (see p **55**)). However, as with any initiative, diversity management needs clear direction and someone to ensure that the business plan sustains its momentum. By developing the role of the diversity manager, an organisation will be in a stronger position to influence key decision-makers and, ultimately, mainstream diversity into the organisation.

Managing Expectations

If an organisation is still in the early stages of understanding diversity, there are a number of basic principles to help in the task of developing the role of the diversity manager. These will help to prepare the groundwork for a strategic plan and manage any scepticism or 'lip service', and overcome managers' passive reluctance to accept diversity as a business benefit. By applying the following basic principles, people's expectations of what diversity management can do can be influenced and managed.

- *Basic principle:* Use the same rationale, language and format as the strategic plan to underpin the diversity strategy.

Achieving the overall strategic plan will always be the number one priority for key decision-makers. After all, it enshrines why the organisation exists in the first place and is often linked to bonus payments and performance appraisals. In order to convince people of the benefits of diversity, the existing strategic plan should be used as the foundation for the diversity strategy. Why key decision-makers set a particular business strategy, and the rationale behind the language and aspirations used, should be understood.

- *Basic principle:* Link the diversity action plan to issues which are important to managers. Demonstrate how diversity management can help achieve the overall business aims.

  One weakness of diversity action plans is that they are often written in isolation from the main business plans. This hinders the process of gaining management commitment and creates a feeling that diversity is yet another initiative or short-term interest. A diversity business plan which supports the overall business plan can be positioned as a helpful management tool and one that is integral to the success of the business. Managers would not then see it as yet another action plan which must be achieved but rather as a supporting document that will enable them to be more successful.

- *Basic principle:* Demonstrate robust, intelligent diversity measurement, which is capable of reporting success.

  A cry often heard from equalities managers is that diversity is still a 'bolt-on' subject, and one which has to compete for management time and resources. If diversity is an integral part of the overall strategic plan it makes this battle easier to win. An organisation should examine what it already measures and consider how success is determined. Diversity measurement could then be built into existing procedures. CHAPTER FOUR – MEASURING THE SUCCESS OF A DIVERSITY STRATEGY, deals with measurement in much more detail (see p **83** and p **92**).

- *Basic principle:* Ensure that that there is a common understanding of diversity and equality of opportunity amongst managers in order to secure ownership and commitment.

  CHAPTER ONE – WHAT IS DIVERSITY? (see p **5**) discusses the definition of diversity and equality. Whatever definition is used, it is important that common language is used consistently to explain what diversity means for an organisation. This definition should also explain that diversity is the responsibility of everyone and help position diversity within the overall values of the organisation.

Ownership of Diversity

Key point: The role of the diversity manager is not one of custodian of the equality policy. Instead he or she should drive people's expectations and push forward mainstream approaches to change.

It is important to involve people in the ownership process right from the beginning. Diversity management is something that sweeps across the organisation and embraces a wide remit. If managers are involved in the early stages of the research process, through, for example, focus groups and customer surveys, they will have been given the opportunity to express their views and understand what the diversity strategy is trying to achieve.

The concept of mainstreaming is becoming enshrined in law; for example, the *Race Relations (Amendment) Act 2000 (RR(A)A 2000)* encourages its use. Mainstreaming diversity has many advantages; principally it prevents people from abdicating responsibility for diversity and hiding behind a written policy which fails to deliver change. However, there is a weakness in the mainstreaming argument; that it underestimates the role of the diversity manager as a champion who maintains the momentum for change. It should be remembered that the best racehorse in the world will always need a committed owner who believes in its potential, an experienced trainer and a good jockey to maintain the right direction and speed if a win is be achieved. Mainstreaming diversity does not mean that the diversity manager will be letting go of the reins; it does, however, mean that a role is carved out which influences the process of involving and engaging all employees in the ownership of the business plan.

Key point: Mainstreaming diversity, or any initiative, does not happen by itself; it must be managed. The process of mainstreaming diversity starts with a cascade of knowledge and understanding which must be driven by the senior management team throughout the organisation. The diversity manager's first task must be to engage senior managers to act as a catalyst for this process.

Engaging Senior Managers

There are some key strategies which can be employed to engage the attention and commitment of senior managers.

- Time should be set aside by key decision-makers in order to hold a debate on diversity and develop a vision for diversity. The objective is to involve key decision-makers in understanding diversity, acknowledging where the organisation currently stands and agreeing where the organisation should be in relation to diversity. This vision setting needs to be formalised within a strategic plan for diversity.

- A diversity 'away day' is the best solution for preparing the strategic plan, as it enables key strategic staff, who might not have a place in the boardroom or main decision-making body, to contribute to the debate; for example, communications and the public relations (PR) team. It also allows for staff representation. An away day enables 'critical friends' to be invited who will be able to stimulate and challenge the debate.

  Involving a wider group of people is especially useful in the public sector where public accountability and local strategic partnerships are an essential element of best value reviews and best practice.

- As new equalities legislation further promotes accountability, organisations in the private sector may have to embrace the idea of consultation much more. They may be asked to explain how they developed their action plans and to demonstrate how they are putting them into practice. Demonstrating legal compliance may require robust evidence that consultation played a part in the development of equality action plans.

Key point: Key decision-makers need to be aware of the potential change in legal thinking, as equality action plans are likely to make the old-style equal opportunities policies obsolete.

- Securing an away day is important both for developing a strategic plan and for establishing an understanding of the wider remit of diversity. This kind of development day has a crucial part to play as it will result in a vision being set which communicates commitment and direction, and sets the tone for the communication plan and language to be used for diversity. Language is an important part of delivering success for the diversity action plan. It should be agreed from the beginning and then built into a communication plan. Once the strategic vision has been agreed, the business plan and budget debates can take place as regular discrete agenda items within the usual framework of the board meetings.

- Securing a whole day with all the key decision-makers can be a difficult task but it is possible to prepare, gather support and diffuse any opposition before the strategy planning stage is reached.

- The task of the diversity manager is to present a persuasive argument showing how diversity management can contribute to performance and profits and why senior managers should devote real time to vision setting.

- Once the diversity away day, or other forum in which to present the case for diversity, has been secured, the key decision-makers will, in effect, be representing the views of those reporting directly to them as well as determining the overall position for the organisation. It would be wise to have engaged these people in the debate before the actual away day. Preparation is crucial for a successful outcome. People need to understand the potential implications of what they may be committing to and they need to be able to back up the strategy with actions.

- Preparation for the away day should involve a *diversity positioning paper* that will inform the board debate and present all the evidence to the key decision-makers well in advance of any board meeting.

Presenting a Persuasive Argument for Diversity

People cannot be expected to make decisions without fully understanding all the facts. A persuasive practical paper is needed which demonstrates an understanding of the business and utilises all the facts and figures investigated during the research phase. (See p **59** below and CHAPTER TWO, p **46**)

In preparing key decision-makers for this debate, diversity managers need to follow a logical process, which includes:

- engaging key decision-makers in the debate;

- raising the knowledge of managers on the wider remit of diversity issues;

- involving teams in looking at the issues;

- informing managers of the views of stakeholders;

- answering concerns of managers; and

- encouraging 'champions'.

Bringing diversity issues to the attention of managers is important for gaining long-term commitment. This could be done by:

- holding traditional workshops;

- using external consultants;

- having internal or external conferences and seminars on diversity for senior managers; and

- holding focus groups with staff to debate the problems and concerns that the Step 1 diversity research highlighted (see p **42** in CHAPTER TWO). (This is probably the most cost-effective way of engaging managers.)

During the research phase all the relevant people should have had the opportunity to air their views and discuss the issues with their own teams. This team interaction is an important point to think about early on in the research process and as part of any feedback to staff. The use of staff focus groups starts the process of engaging people in the formulation of plans and actions. It helps to generate ideas about language and starts to manage people's expectations of diversity. This feedback will help add a dimension of reality to the arguments presented to key decision-makers.

Language which will capture the attention of managers must be used. Following are two statements; consider which would have the most impact upon the managers.

CASE STUDY: Diversity statements

Diversity Statement 1

The business environment is changing as a result of demographic changes. We need to be able to attract the best mix of employees. Women form a significant proportion of the available talent pool and currently comprise just less than 50% of the workforce in the UK. We know that we do not have enough women in senior management roles to reflect our customer base and the UK demographics. We are, therefore, recommending a board away day to look at what action we can take to recruit more women.

Diversity Statement 2

The problem: Upon analysis of our staff turnover figures, it was discovered that in the last two years over 35% of people leaving the organisation were female aged between 28 and 35. In turn, this is reflected in a poor representation of women in management roles because they are not staying long enough to be promoted. The cost to the business of this staff loss was calculated at £120,000 in lost production, additional recruitment costs and overtime payments. Having fewer women in management is having an adverse effect on our brand image of being an employer of choice. This is damaging our ability to attract highly-qualified women to new posts. Of the 1,000 applications received last year for 100 vacancies in management, only 15% were from women, which does not reflect UK demographics. This in turn is limiting our ability to reflect the needs of female customers and understand their buying behaviour in our retail stores.

The cause: By using focus groups and a series of exit interviews, and by listening to women who have stayed in the organisation, we have established that childcare in the area is limited and costly. We have started to understand the needs of women in management and consider the impact on the organisation of failing to help women into management roles.

Potential solutions: We would like to explore the potential benefits of a *cost-neutral payroll salary sacrifice scheme* for childcare payments and flexible start times for work. In addition, we would like to investigate the cost of securing childcare for parents at work.

Key point: When presenting the argument for diversity to managers, the evidence should be presented in a way which identifies the problem for the organisation, the cause of the problem and a potential solution.

It is much more powerful to present the kind of evidence-based argument shown in Diversity Statement 2 above than it is to use vague expressions that diversity management is the panacea for all employee problems. The diversity manager must learn to position arguments within a framework of robust evidence relevant to managers. The evidence from Step 1 (see **CHAPTER TWO**, p **30**) must be presented in this format within the diversity positioning paper.

Writing a Diversity Positioning Paper

The aim of a diversity positioning paper should be to inspire key decision–makers so that they will be keen to attend an away day. This preparation will enable people to hold an informed debate and give them the opportunity to become committed to an evolving process, as opposed to feeling caught up in a diversity revolution.

The diversity positioning paper should set out the current state of play for the organisation; identifying the opportunities and the risks for all the stakeholders. It should reach the inevitable conclusion that diversity management warrants a debate at board level. The paper should include the following.

(*a*) An explanation of the wider remit of diversity management. (See **CHAPTER TWO**, p **25** for more detail.)

(*b*) An impact assessment. Having gathered all the information on where an organisation stands in relation to diversity at Step 1, a risk assessment and cost benefit analysis on diversity can now be given. This will refer to all the stakeholder groups and give feedback, for example, from focus groups, mystery shoppers, statistical analysis and a legal overview. In the public sector this could provide evidence of where the organisation stands in relation to the generic equality standards.

(*c*) Information presented under the following headings.

    (i)   The problem.

    (ii)   The cause.

    (iii) Potential solutions

(*d*) Reference to the overall strategic plan for the organisation and how the organisation can make a contribution.

(*e*) Support for the business plan. Having assessed the business action plans, the potential role and benefits of diversity management should be identified against the core objectives for the business, illustrating how diversity can support the overall business plan.

Example 1

If one of the key business objectives for Comet, the electrical retailer, is to achieve 10% year-on-year growth in customer sales, the position paper needs to demonstrate how

> understanding diversity can influence the spending power of different parts of the UK community. Comet could, for example, market directly to the gay and lesbian community through advertising and sponsorship; thus securing customer loyalty from a large number of people not previously reached by Comet.

(f) An explanation of why diversity needs a vision statement and a business plan, and the role of managers in setting this agenda. It should also include feedback from stakeholders.

The diversity position paper should aim to secure commitment from key decision-makers, and it can be used later as part of the communication strategy to a wider management audience. If possible, the paper should be presented at team meetings and feedback should be welcomed from staff and managers at all levels. The paper should allow the opportunity for discussion at meetings in order to develop ideas. This process also helps to identify those people who would be willing to champion the issues and identifies opposition and potential blocks to the progress of a diversity business plan. The position paper will become a valuable reference document during the later stages of agreeing the business plan and the communication and training programme.

Diversity Champions

In some organisations it is clear that certain key decision-makers carry more credibility than others. It is a useful 'early win' if the champion on the board is the director most likely to attract respect from within the organisation. This is not always the most obvious person, however. For example, if research has highlighted TV advertising as an area which could impact upon diversity, the director who holds this portfolio should be encouraged to become the champion.

It is also useful to start some preliminary discussions with the finance director at this early stage. A diversity business plan cannot be implemented without resources, so it is wise to start managing these expectations right at the start of the process. Other budgets which might be available and funds which could potentially be secured need to be considered.

Key point: Funding is bound to be a question raised by senior managers. A good diversity manager will have anticipated this and be able to construct a robust response.

Preparing Managers for a Change in Approach

As the diversity management process begins to cascade down through an organisation, managers will feel better prepared for change if they can see the natural evolution of processes rather than a revolution driven by radicals. Introducing the idea of a new diversity vision and business plan does not mean throwing out all previous good work and starting again. Preparing managers for a change in approach will mean educating them that diversity includes customers, PR, community involvement, suppliers, brand reputation and employees. They need to understand the holistic remit of diversity and move beyond thinking of equality of opportunity and employment issues as separate from diversity.

If Step 1 (see CHAPTER TWO, p **30**) of the process has been conducted thoroughly, managers and employees will have been involved along the way. The profile of diversity will already have been raised (for example, using customer focus groups to identify specific service issues for disabled people) and the process of raising people's expectations will have begun. Managers are always keen to hear what people think about their organisation, especially customers and service users. If the Step 1 fact-finding involved mystery shopping and customer feedback, this will easily attract the attention of the board. In the public sector, feedback from residents' surveys and citizen panels provide similar information.

By presenting this information, managers will start to identify areas of synergy for diversity.

Example 2

The B&Q Macclesfield store's experiment on age diversity (see CHAPTER SEVEN – CASE STUDIES ON DIVERSITY) delivered greater customer satisfaction, loyalty from older customers, access to a new recruitment pool, reduced turnover and increased staff morale. In addition, it provided a focus for PR, charitable partnerships with Age Concern, government influence in the pension debate and a platform for building external credibility. The issue of age needed co-operation from all departments and, instead of defining age as Corporate Social Responsibility (CSR), PR or employment, it became a diversity issue which cut right across the business. The Employers' Forum on Age wrote, 'B&Q in one bold step caught the attention of the public, media and the Government.'

Example 3

Company X is a large UK-wide high street retail organisation which has a significant customer base and employs over 30,000 people. It has a well-established equality programme for employees and has been managing race diversity in employment for two years. This has resulted in some excellent ad hoc work being completed for selected employees. For example, Asian graduates were targeted and there was an increase in the number of applications from this target group.

However, the TV advertising campaign did not reflect this commitment to race diversity and failed to portray a diverse employment and customer base. In addition, the company received some adverse publicity in a newspaper regarding its treatment of an Asian member of staff. The employment initiatives were selective and owned by the HR (human resources) department and had not been communicated across the company. The affects of this adverse publicity and the failure of the marketing department began to have an unfavourable impact on the positive recruitment campaign for graduates which had been launched the previous year. The HR team did not see the expected increase in the number of graduates from black and Asian backgrounds, despite a national increase in the number of Asian students graduating with a degree.

By embracing a more holistic stakeholder approach the company could have investigated what people from different community backgrounds thought about it both as an employer and as a retailer. It could then have tailored the recruitment campaign accordingly.

Example 4

A northern police force launched an expensive advertising campaign in a bid to attract more women into the force. On the same day, an employment tribunal announced its verdict that the same force had discriminated against a female officer. This story appeared in most tabloids. This must surely have had a damaging effect on the potential results of the advertising campaign.

Key point: The skill of the diversity manager will revolve around being able to build internal partnerships, enabling senior managers to understand the wider remit of diversity and see how the risks and benefits of diversity management would impact upon all aspects the business. This will drive the process of mainstreaming.

Ensuring Commitment to Diversity

It is widely acknowledged by several authors on diversity (McEnrue,[1] Thiederman[2] and Ross and Schneider[3]) that top-level commitment is vital to success. McEnrue, in her model, presented three reasons for gaining top-level commitment.

- It communicates a vision that motivates employees.

- Only top managers can ensure that an initiative is carried out.

- A commitment of time and resources will be need to be sanctioned by managers.

Another important point is that if the key decision-makers own the strategic plan for diversity, gaining the commitment of middle managers, as the business plan is cascaded, will be far easier to achieve. Senior-level commitment needs to very visible and ongoing. When producing a communication strategy to launch diversity, having a credible and respected person heading up the campaign will be a key ingredient for success.

Key point: Diversity management is essentially a change management process which requires people at all levels in the organisation to embrace change.

The key to ensuring commitment is to make sure that everyone understands what is involved in the research phase and that people are given the opportunity to input their ideas into the development of action plans.

Summary

- The role of a diversity manager is to drive forward the equality and diversity agenda. This should happen via a systematic process which involves fact finding, presenting a robust argument of the benefits of diversity management and gathering momentum for change.

- The process should also have identified a key decision-maker as a sponsor who will present the argument for an away day to his or her colleagues.

- The preparation should have an effect and the organisation should be ready for developing the strategic plan for diversity.

DEVELOPING THE STRATEGIC PLAN

The strategic plan enables a vision to be communicated to everyone, which they in turn can own and support. This is important because of the potential to interpret the meaning of diversity and equality in different ways. In the past, equality statements were often written in a negative way using language which told an organisation what it would not do, or they were empty statements where commitment was hard to see. Many organisations have now developed strap lines for their adverts which have a more inclusive feel. For example, the appointments pages in *People Management* saw an array of statements, such as the following.

- 'Committed to equal opportunities' – Stage Coach UK Bus.

- 'Actively working towards equality of opportunity' – West Herts College.

- 'We value our diverse workforce. All sections of the community are welcome to apply' – Dudley Metropolitan Borough Council.

- 'Creating opportunity for all' – Barnet London Borough.

It is important that these strap lines are grounded within a vision statement which is much more than just a simple sentence. The strategic plan should commit to language which is appropriate for the organisation and should lay down guiding principles that will help address the problems identified in the research. The objective of the strategic plan should be a recognition of where the organisation currently stands in terms of diversity (which should be an honest reflection of the diversity research) and a commitment to moving towards where key decision-makers believe the organisation should be.

At this stage, the key decision–makers are asked not to agree any particular action, but to set direction, agree language and develop an internal branding for diversity. Raising awareness on diversity at the beginning of a meeting might help to provide a focus.

Example 5

The original diversity planning day at B&Q included a 20-minute presentation from a diversity consultant who is a wheelchair user. He placed his Visa Gold Card on the table, explained that he drove a Mercedes and had four children. He continued, if his four children each required a new pair of trainers and he had a choice of going to two shops, one was accessible and the other was not, which shop would he choose? That simple exercise exploded a few myths on disability from institutional care to financial independence. Having a facilitator who is experienced in engaging key decision-makers is crucial to the success of the day. The diversity manager would be well advised to find a suitable partner to help him or her deliver key messages quickly and succinctly in a way which relates to the problems and causes identified in the position paper.

Vision Setting

A strategic plan for diversity should:

- link the diversity vision to the core business objectives (for example, West Bromwich Building Society linked business growth objectives to the ethnic minority communities' need for flexible banking);

- focus on delivering results;

- use language which is inclusive;

- identify clear aims and a timescale; and

- identify where responsibility and ownership lies.

The strategic plan should also identify:

- why senior managers believe diversity management is important, based on the evidence of the initial research;

- what success will look like; and

- how progress will be measured and reported.

Items for discussion at the strategic planning meeting should include:

- the organisation's current position;

- what the competition are doing;

- potential unique selling points;

- vision setting (brainstorming on where the organisation wants to be);

- the language to be used (agreeing common terminology);

- the timescale (what is to be achieved by when); and

- potential priority areas.

The strategic planning meeting should result in:

- a vision statement;

- a commitment to progress;

- agreement on priority areas;

- commitment to discuss a business plan; and

- a statement of how the process will be managed and by whom.

Linking Diversity to Brand Identity

Developing an instantly recognisable brand for diversity is an easy and practicable first step. At Essex County Council there is talk of the 'Essex Total Approach', and in the London Borough of Tower Hamlets there is a diversity brand of 'Celebrating Diversity'. Developing this kind of brand identity starts to identify the language of diversity which it is right for an organisation.

Example 6

Essex County Council needed to develop a race equality scheme (RES) in order to comply with the *RR(A)A 2000*. In researching the RES requirements it was clear that the Council would benefit from a more holistic diversity strategy. The pressing timescale for the RES enforced this as a priority action. However, Essex County Council decided to position all the equal opportunities initiatives, including the RES, within a more comprehensive diversity strategy. The Council took time to develop a brand that could be linked to the corporate plan. There was already a brand called 'The Essex Approach' and it was decided that the diversity strategy would be called 'The Essex Approach to equality and diversity', and that specific action plans would be positioned within this. This would enable all the past work on equality to be pulled together and re-positioned within a more 'joined-up' strategy.

Essex County Council will need a specific action plan on race in order to meet legal requirements. However, by developing a common framework and a brand, the Council will find it much easier to start to communicate to 30,000 employees why certain actions are being implemented and how these actions fit into the overall community plan. This will also enable the Council to launch plans in the future for disability and age, as part of an ongoing commitment to diversity.

Key point: Developing a strategic plan does not mean throwing away past good work and starting afresh. On the contrary, it means taking the time to understand what has been achieved so far and how well initiatives have worked in the past. It enables a revitalisation of current practices and it facilitates the communication process.

Managing Diversity within the Organisational Structure

A crucial part of the strategic planning process is to agree how diversity will be managed within the organisation. It is important to agree clear lines of communication and identify clear accountability. Accountability should be driven throughout the entire organisation; however, the reality is that the process will need to be managed and co-ordinated. Someone needs to provide the expertise and sustain change. The key people must be identified and the reporting structure must be communicated to all employees, otherwise there is confusion and no one to take responsibility.

Example 7

One organisation had an Equalities Steering Group, a Stephen Lawrence Action Plan and an Equalities Team; three separate groups all busy producing action plans in isolation of each other. The message to employees was one of confusion.

Example 8

An NHS Trust, which had been recently re-organised, realised on 3 May that it had to complete its RES by 31 May. It had to quickly assign responsibility of this onerous task to one person, who, of course, had another full-time job in the Trust. Ultimately, a decision had to be taken to delay the launch of the RES in favour of adopting a more strategic approach.

Example 9

The position of the diversity manager within the organisation sends out a clear signal of how important the issue is considered to be. In B&Q this was a key part of the strategic plan. The chief executive officer (CEO) took direct responsibility and a regular interest in diversity. The diversity manager reported directly to the CEO each month through regular meetings, as did all other direct reports. This gave the diversity manager easy access to the other directors and helped to build confidence with middle managers. The diversity team was small with two key members of staff who were able to form the centre of excellence and drive forward the diversity agenda.

The process and structure by which the organisation expects diversity to be managed must be clear and communicated throughout the organisation. Once the strategic plan and the management process have been agreed, they need to be communicated and the language of diversity introduced throughout the organisation.

Summary

- The purpose of the strategic planning meeting is to agree the values which reflect what the organisation wants in relation to respect for people. There must be an understanding of what the issues are within the organisation and what the current situation is. From this, a vision statement needs to be set which will encourage the organisation to move towards achieving commitment to diversity management.

- By the end of this stage in the process, key decision-makers should have a good understanding of the issues and problems in the organisation, an agreement on the language that will be used to convey this understanding and a vision that will move the organisation forward. There should also be a clear understanding of how the diversity agenda will be managed.

DEVELOPING THE BUSINESS PLAN

The strategic plan will communicate the long-term goal and secure commitment from senior management. However, employees need to understand how this will be translated into action. Decisions need to be made about what the organisation is going to do to achieve its desired aims. These actions need to be set down in a business plan for diversity.

The organisation cannot attempt to do everything at once. Therefore, some form of priority setting must also take place. Action plans can develop over time and they should not, therefore, be seen as rigid documents but as evolving commitments that can be responsive to changing business needs. However, they should have a reporting function built into them with agreed timescales for showing progress. Indicators for measuring success and impact must also be identified within the action plan. The role of such action plans will become more evident as equalities legislation strengthens the desire to see evidence-based change. For example, changes have been agreed to the Equal Treatment Directive (Directive 76/207/EEC) which will mean a proactive approach to managing equality (see **CHAPTER SIX – DIVERSITY AND THE LAW**).

Developing a business plan is a common-sense approach to managing diversity that will undoubtedly become a robust legal defence in the future as equality laws become increasingly complex.

In developing the business plan for diversity, the evidence put together in the position paper will need to be used. During the research the legal, moral and business case for diversity will have been identified, and the position of the organisation will have been mapped against the legal requirements and the business needs. Evidence of issues under the headings of problem, cause and possible solutions will also have been identified by the research.

Clearly, any potential risk of non-compliance with the law will form the basis of an action plan and help with the setting of priorities. The cost to the business of past and potential failures should have been calculated. The position paper should also have identified the problems faced by the organisation from a stakeholder perspective. The action plan will start to identify priority areas based on this evidence. It will also start to build the argument for a budget and the resources which will be needed.

In setting priorities, the organisation's weak points should be identified. The action plan should be designed to encourage sustainable change which is both practical and affordable, and which can show measured progress.

Some progress can always be made in an area of diversity at a very low cost, such as partnership building and awareness raising with the people who will be producing literature and advertisements for the organisation. If money is a real constraint, actions that have a low-cost impact should be a priority.

The Business Plan

The business plan should be written using the same style and language as the overall business plan where it is appropriate to do so. An alternative is to develop a model specifically for diversity but which links to the objectives in the business plan. Fundamentally, the diversity manager needs to identify the problem, the cause and the solution and phrase these in such a way that they link to the overall objectives.

Headings for the diversity business plan could include the following.

- What the organisation needs to be better at (link to business objectives).
- How the organisation is going to get better.
- The level of resource which will be needed to implement change.
- How the impact will be measured.

Following are examples of business plans for high street retailers.

Example 10

What we need to be better at	*How we will get better*	*What this will cost*	*How we will measure success and report on results*
The research indicated that over a two-year period, 35% of women who took maternity leave did not return to work. This cost the organisation £120,000.	1. Understand why women fail to return to work by conducting a series of exit interviews and focus groups. 2. Benchmark against competitors/comparators. 3. Identify appropriate solutions.	£5,000	1. Produce a report on the feedback by *[specified date]* and recommend solutions. 2. We aim to see a return rate of 80% of women within two years with cost savings of £80,000.
We have identified that within store management roles, women represent fewer than 23% of decision-makers. We need to improve the promotion, retention and recruitment of women in senior roles.	1. Interview women managers and understand their concerns. 2. Evidence and track career progression of women. 3. Identify the recruitment pool for manager vacancies. 4. Identify what support is required to enable women to progress into management.	£10,000	1. Produce a report by *[specified date]* on the issues and concerns of women managers. 2. We aim to identify solutions that will see an increase of 20% in the number of women available from the internal recruitment pool for manager vacancies.

Example 11

What we need to be better at	*How we will get better*	*What this will cost*	*How we will measure success and report on results*
The feedback from the mystery shopping revealed that black and Asian women were twice as likely to be dissatisfied with the customer service than white women.	1. Understand why black and Asian women feel more dissatisfied by holding a series of focus groups. 2. Benchmark against competitors/comparators. 3. Identify appropriate solutions, such as language translation, respecting religious requirements, understanding customer needs and the potential spending power of black and Asian women.	£10,000	1. Produce a report on the feedback by *[specified date]* and recommend solutions. 2. We aim to see an increase of 21% in customer satisfaction rates against a comparative mystery shopping exercise within one year.

We have identified that within store management roles, black and Asian women represent less than 0.5% of decision-makers. We need to understand the impact that this has on our brand reputation with the black and Asian community.	1. Understand what the ethnic minority community thinks about the organisation. 2. Understand the profit impact upon stores whose customer base has an ethnic minority of over 12% of the total people. 3. Understand the relationship between customer satisfaction and the recruitment profile. 4. Understand what we can do to improve recruitment of ethnic minority people.	£20,000	1. Produce a report by *[specified date]* on the issues and concerns of ethnic minority employees. 2. We aim to identify solutions that will see a year-on-year increase in the number of ethnic minority employees.

The organisations in Examples 10 and 11 above will be able to show progression as the action plan matures so that, upon completion of the first report, the action can be strengthened for the following year. Some organisations make the mistake of setting unrealistic targets too soon in the process; for example, a 30% increase in the number of women managers within three years. This expectation should be expressed in the strategic plan as a desired longer-term outcome, though the action plan should be capable of translating the vision into achievable and measurable outcomes.

Key point: The idea is to develop action plans that allow reporting year on year, demonstrating progress and creating a momentum for change.

BUDGET SETTING

Any initiative will require some degree of resourcing. Most budgets in organisations grow each year as the benefits of an initiative are realised. Setting realistic solutions in the action plan can strengthen the annual budget claim.

It should be possible to work with the finance director in order to seek creative solutions for funding. For example, money may be sourced from the charity budget if an organisation regularly donates money. Diversity is about the social model of inclusion, which does not necessarily support the charitable model of giving money away. It would be useful to examine instances where the organisation has 'given' money to good causes, and also what it is planning to do in the future. Often the diversity action plan will require outreach work in the community. It may be that the charitable budget can be diverted to this partnership building. Similarly it would be useful to look at what the CSR department is planning to do over the coming year and identify synergies amongst stakeholders.

If the diversity action plan has been written as a cost/benefit to the business, the budget needs to be advanced within this framework. For example, if a cost saving of £30,000 per year is predicted from an increase of women employees returning to work following maternity leave, the budget should show the return on investment made from the initial costs against the savings.

Following below is an example of a diversity position paper.

Example 12

The problem: We do not provide access to our customer complaints procedure for visually-impaired and hearing-impaired customers. The potential financial risk to the organisation, if there was one claim per store under the *DDA 1995, Part III* for a failure to provide alternative media in our stores, is £20,000. In addition, there is a potential for negative impact upon our brand reputation from media reports. We are also failing to attract the potential spending power of disabled people, which is estimated to be around £10 million based on a 20% market share of some five million economically-active disabled adults.

The cause: We do not have access to a translation service for Braille, audiotape and large print. The customer service help line is telephone operated and we do not use a minicom or e-mail alternative.

The solution: Form a partnership with a translation service for Braille, audiotape and large print. Install a minicom and subscribe to type talk. Also, offer e-mail with complete disability awareness training for all operators.

The resource: Providing a translation service costs a minimum fee of £3,000, plus a charge each time the service is used. Type talk is free and then pay as you go. Minicom and e-mail solutions cost £1,500 and the disability awareness training programme costs £5,000. Total budget required is £9,500. Potential saving is £11,500 year on year.

Key point: By presenting arguments based on real costs, the finance director will be able to help identify where cost savings can be found elsewhere in the business.

Example 13

In 1998, the then managing director of B&Q, Martin Toogood, was quoted as saying, 'if we can get customer service right for disabled people then we can get it right for everyone'. By exploring the use of distance learning, B&Q developed a disability awareness programme for 23,000 employees. This programme was all about customer service and it was funded by the agreed budget for general customer service training. This enabled both disability awareness training and an exciting new customer service training programme to be delivered cost effectively utilising just one budget.

IMPLEMENTING THE ACTION PLAN

If a diversity strategy is going to achieve its vision, there needs to be a change in behaviour at all levels of the organisation. Once the strategic plan and the business plan have been agreed, the next step is to actually manage the diversity. This means communicating clearly to people what is expected of them either as a manager, champion or individual. This understanding and accountability must spread across the whole organisation and be capable of being linked to measurement and identified with success. Distance learning enables training and communication to be delivered to all employees at the same time, creativity in how the communication plan is implemented can save the organisation time and duplicated effort.

The organisations which are most successful in managing diversity tend to have two things in common; clear accountability for diversity management and an experienced diversity manager who drives forward change. A retail organisation, for example, would not introduce a new product range without first having in place a chain of support processes, ranging from the supplier, buyer, marketing and advertising. Why, therefore, do some organisations still expect diversity to be managed by an individual in addition to his or her usual role?

The lessons of the Stephen Lawrence Enquiry should also be remembered. It is not only the people who should be accountable but also the organisation and its system processes. Long-standing methods of doing things can contain hidden barriers and discriminatory processes. The public sector is being forced to recognise this aspect of managing diversity within RESs. The requirement to assess all functions and processes for more subtle forms of discrimination should be recognised in the private sector too.

Key point: It will not matter how impressive the action plan looks if there is no one to manage the processes through to conclusion and report on progress.

Engaging Staff with the Action Plan

Securing top-level commitment is vital in the early success of managing diversity. However, this is not the only factor in determining success.

- Lasting change can only be achieved through a well-informed workforce.

- A receptive environment needs to be created in which to introduce change.

- There needs to be a critical mass of knowledge within the organisation in order to trigger change.

The communication strategy needs to inform staff of the diversity strategy and achieve the three points listed above. It also needs to develop an awareness-raising programme which will inspire all employees. When enough people are committed to change, the programme starts to gain a momentum, which in turn creates a sustainable behaviour change in people.

It is important that staff at all levels become involved in the diversity evolutionary process. Staff teams should be encouraged to help in the development of action plans. For example, it may be appropriate to use staff in focus groups, which also helps create feelings of involvement and influence. It is important that the majority of employees within the organisation are aware of the diversity strategy. If the organisation has 10,000 employees and it conducts a quick survey in the canteen asking 200 people if they know about the diversity action plan, at least 45% of the employees should respond positively. This critical mass of knowledge will help sustain change. The old style equality plans are somewhat like the Highway Code; something people read once and think they know about. The diversity action plan, however, needs to be embedded in everyday work and constantly referred to.

Key point: Unlike equality policies, action plans cannot be filed away as a completed piece of work.

Diversity awareness is a two-way process of communication and staff must to be able to offer input into the development of any action plan. There was always a finality implied in an equality policy that something had already been achieved. The diversity action plan conveys the message that there is no end state for diversity management, only progress and an understanding of the anticipatory duty to a proactive approach.

DIVERSITY CHAMPIONS

Key point: Diversity management is an issue which is personal to people's quality of life and it links directly with people's own sets of values.

By involving people in the process, those who feel moved by the issue will want to become even more involved. For example, B&Q has been extremely successful in using champions in store for a whole range of issues, from health and safety to the environment to disability.

This system of champions is useful for engaging multi-site organisations and helps corporate plans take on a locally-driven focus. It also helps to involve all departments in contributing to the success of the action plan. B&Q effectively had a diversity team of 321 people; 318 champions and three people at the centre. Champions are very effective at generating new ideas and sharing best practice, and at ensuring that there is a wave of commitment to diversity. This 'bottom up' approach of generating commitment is just as effective as 'top down' management. The use of champions allows for more internal recognition, which in turns sustains the communication plan. Good news stories are inspirational and the Army, for example, has opted for its own newsletter on equality and diversity.

COMMUNICATION PLAN

The diversity strategic plan and the business plan need to be translated into everyday language which can be communicated to all staff. They also need to be communicated externally to all stakeholders. This process should be slow and gradual in building up the message and managing people's expectations. Members of staff must 'own' the messages that are communicated. An organisation does not want to boast flexible working arrangements in an article on HR if staff feel that some managers discourage applications for such arrangements. There must be honesty in the communication of diversity initiatives, which helps to manage people's expectations.

Research by Bartlett Scott Edgar, *Diversity. Big Difference or Indifference?*,[4] highlighted that key decision-makers and managers talked about the business benefits of diversity as the reason for doing it, but staff in general believed that organisations should embrace diversity as it was the right thing to do. It is important that the key drivers throughout the business are identified and are used to inform people of the communication strategy.

A consistent and constant message is needed on diversity both to staff and service users. Timing is very important when considering when to launch a communication initiative. All branches of HSBC have leaflets available which explain the services on offer to customers with disabilities. It makes sense to ensure that all staff training is completed and all the services are in place before communicating this information to customers. However, some organisations do not tell customers at all that they have a service available, and they wonder why the service is not then used. Other organisations put a service in place but fail to maintain it.

The communication message must extend across all that the organisation does. It is not sufficient, for example, to only have a welcoming statement on job adverts. In fact, this is probably the least effective action which could be taken to encourage more job applicants. B&Q featured a disabled person in a mainstream advert. That one action probably communicated more on what B&Q was doing for disabled people than all the other actions put together. Conversely, Marks & Spencer suffered from adverse publicity on a race issue following an employment tribunal case. Marks & Spencer subsequently won the case, but the damaging publicity in the press must have had an impact on its reputation in the Asian community.

Membership of external organisations helps a business to network, and often provides an organisation with a forum to share best practice. Delivering keynote-speaking roles at conferences by using the organisation as a case study is an excellent way of raising its profile within a small but influential network. As the diversity story matures, articles may be used in the personnel and business press, which in turn generates internal interest.

Throughout the process of implementing diversity, it is worth reflecting on the developments as they occur and writing down the organisation's story of diversity. These stories are easy to communicate and can be used as great PR documents. These documents can be used to support recruitment and also help new employees understand how far the organisation has come in terms of diversity management.

In-house magazines and notice boards are an excellent way of generating human interests stories and sharing what staff are doing to get involved. The best way to publicise a job-share scheme is to highlight the success stories of the people already involved. Trials and pilot schemes are also good tools to use in generating interest in a scheme.

Political influence is important in the field of diversity. Ministers are always pleased to be involved with organisations and councils are often keen to work with businesses on local schemes, such as shop mobility and 'park and ride'. Local Members of Parliament often wish to follow up press opportunities highlighting successful employment ventures. For example, Centrica achieved considerable recognition for a call centre programme which involved the employment of disabled people.

The communication plan will have greater influence if it is recognisable and understandable. This will be helped by an organisation developing a clear branding for its message and ensuring that the language is in plain English, and indeed other languages where appropriate.

CONCLUSION

The role of the diversity manager is to be able to present a persuasive argument for diversity to the key decision-makers within the organisation to convince them of the benefits of managing diversity within a strategic framework. The objective of working through a process of vision setting and agreeing an action plan is to engage staff at all levels in the diversity programme, thereby overcoming scepticism, 'lip service' and passive reluctance. It is essential to drive ownership and involvement in diversity across the organisation. However, the influence of the diversity manager in achieving this aim is paramount. The diversity manager is responsible for steering the diversity agenda and cascading knowledge across all stakeholders.

With diversity management, progress needs to be sustained as the benefits will evolve over time. Many people will have a role to play in this, including senior managers and champions, and mainstreaming ownership is the ultimate aim. However, mainstreaming still needs to be sustained and the diversity manager is responsible for continuing to inspire and drive change, and for keeping diversity issues high on the business agenda.

Managing diversity requires an internal partnership between all departments if the potential benefits of diversity are to be explored beyond the employment relationship. By setting out clear actions, the aims of the diversity process can be clearly communicated to all staff.

When used as an effective management tool, diversity can make a real impact upon the success of mainstream business objectives. For example, if the organisation needs to secure a 10% year-on-year growth in customer sales, diversity can add value by understanding the different needs of customers. Understanding diversity can help managers make the difference between a good organisation and a great organisation.

CHECKLIST

✔ Is the role of the diversity manager positioned effectively within your organisation?

✔ Have the steps that need to be worked through, in developing the strategic plan and the business plan, been identified?

✔ Can you present a persuasive argument for the wider remit of diversity management?

✔ Have senior managers been prepared for a change in approach to diversity?

✔ Have you ensured commitment from senior management?

✔ Has a strategic plan for diversity been developed?

✔ Has the business plan for diversity been agreed?

✔ Are you ready to communicate the diversity plan to all staff?

✔ Have you ensured that people at all levels have been involved with the business plan?

✔ Can you sustain the momentum of diversity evolution?

✔ Can you demonstrate how diversity can be used as an effective management tool to help realise the full impact of existing business objectives and present a robust financial argument for developing a strategic framework for diversity management?

References

1. McEnrue M P, *Managing Diversity*, Winter (1993).
2. Thiederman S, *Staff Diversity*, Associate Management (1994).
3. Ross R and Schneider R, *From Equality to Diversity*, Pitman Publishing (1992).
4. Bartlett Scott Edgar, *Diversity. Big Difference or Indifference?*, A Bartlett Scott Edgar insight study (2002).

Chapter Four

Measuring the Success of a Diversity Strategy

OVERVIEW

This chapter covers the following issues.

- The role of monitoring and target setting (see p **78**).

- The problems and benefits of setting equality targets (see p **81**).

- Setting the right equality target (see p **82**).

- Assessing the impact of positive action (see p **88**).

- How to develop intelligent diversity measurement (see p **83** and p **92**).

- Reporting on the success of the business plan in the annual report (see p **96**).

- Measuring corporate knowledge and employee understanding (see p **97**).

INTRODUCTION

If directors from the top 100 companies in the UK were asked 'is diversity management and equality of opportunity important for your company?', no doubt they would answer a resounding yes. Companies seem to be taking diversity management more seriously, and most have policy statements and defined diversity within the context of their business. Yet despite this growing interest in diversity management, there is still little hard evidence of the impact it can have upon the overall success of a company, and the whole issue of measurement remains the weakest link in the organisational case for diversity.

In the past, equality measurement has been synonymous with employment monitoring. Although it is not required by law, the Commission for Racial Equality (CRE) and the Equal Opportunities Commission (EOC) are very keen to encourage organisations to actively demonstrate what they are doing by monitoring data and setting definable targets for employment figures. The whole issue of monitoring is essential if organisations are going to bring about real change within employment profiles. However, the monitoring debate brings with it perceptions of externally-demanded quotas and positive action, which can generate a resistance in management to introducing diversity measurement.

Key point: The widening remit of diversity needs a broader and more intelligent measurement process which goes beyond employment monitoring if the link between diversity and organisational performance is to be made clear.

Reliance on employment monitoring alone will not allow the full impact of diversity management for all the stakeholders to be measured, and it does not help build credibility for diversity as a management tool.

This chapter discusses the traditional requirement for equality monitoring within the context of target setting and positive action, and explores alternative performance indicators which help meet the new demands expected of diversity management from a wider business perspective. It examines the difference between monitoring and intelligent diversity measurement and explores the link between diversity and organisational performance.

In addition, it discusses how organisations can increase their corporate knowledge on diversity and measure the participation and understanding of employees in diversity learning programmes.

The overall aim of this chapter is to explore how intelligent diversity measurement can start to provide robust, actionable information on the impact of diversity management. It discusses the practical steps which can be taken to benchmark an organisation and considers what areas can be measured for performance against diversity targets within the diversity business plan.

THE ROLE OF MONITORING AND TARGET SETTING

This section explores the use of employment monitoring and the use of target setting as a means of measuring the success of diversity management. The advantages and disadvantages of targets are discussed in relation to achieving change. It is important that those people who are responsible for implementing the diversity strategy understand these arguments. A failure to set the right measures for success will ultimately weaken the organisational case for diversity.

Monitoring Information

The legal impetus for equality and fairness has been with business for some time. Change, however, has often been slow to materialise and the frustration of the campaign organisations has led to demands that targets be set and positive actions be put in place to help disadvantaged people into employment. There is a strong argument which suggests that leaving organisations to their own devices does not encourage a move towards greater equality. For example, more than 30 years after the

Equal Pay Act 1970 (EPA 1970), we are still experiencing a pay gap between men and women. Women in full-time work earn, on average, 82% of male full-time employees' pay.[1]

Monitoring information on employment data is a powerful method of revealing where inequalities exist, especially in the management structures of an organisation and in pay scales. The monitoring argument has been given a further boost by changes introduced by the *Race Relations (Amendment) Act 2000 (RR(A)A 2000)*, which demands that monitoring is carried out within the public sector on a whole range of issues which could affect racial equality. What is interesting about the Act is that monitoring is starting to venture outside pure employment data and is encouraging public sector organisations to monitor all their services.

Equalities monitoring, however, is much more than just collecting data. It requires both an understanding of the context in which the data is collected and an analysis of the information. Many organisations collect data but then fail to understand what this data is telling them, and many fail to conduct trend analysis and carry out further research to explain the reasons for the data.

Monitoring is mostly used to present a snapshot of what the current employment profile looks like. In most organisations information is input into a payroll or HR (human resources) system as new employees join the business; monthly or quarterly reports are then produced to give the number of employees in posts by age, gender, disability and race. In many cases this information is not robust and it is common to see a large percentage of 'unknowns' entered into the categories. The production of the monitoring report is often seen as a routine job lacking any credibility within the business.

The role of monitoring needs to become much more sophisticated and take centre stage in a diversity strategy if it is to realise the aspirations of equalities legislation. Monitoring needs to become much more capable of demonstrating its ability to measure the performance of the diversity business plan.

Key point: Monitoring should be to tell a story of what is happening in an organisation and provide robust employee intelligence. It should not simply provide pure statistical data reflecting a static position.

Monitoring in Relation to Demographics

In the UK only gender has been researched at a corporate level through the FTSE Female Index, which was launched in 2000, whereas in the USA there is data on disability and ethnicity. The FTSE Female Index highlighted the lack of women in senior roles, where they account for only 2% of the female directors.[2] Women were more widely represented by non-executive directors, accounting for 8% of the total.

When the chief executive of Debenhams (a FTSE 300 company) took maternity leave, she hit the headlines as though she was the first woman to take such leave! A recent study by the Cabinet Office showed that ethnic minorities were also absent from the management of organisations and that there is a great deal of evidence of payroll inequalities.[3]

Good data is available on UK demographics. The information from the most recent census will be available in 2002. It is not difficult to research local populations and gain an understanding of community concerns. There are changes taking place in demographics which diversity managers must be aware of. They include the following.

- Of the 60 million people living in the UK, five million are from a black or Asian background. Over half of the ethnic minority population was born in Britain and they represent a significant number of graduates leaving university. The average profile of the ethnic minority community is younger than the white population. By 2005 it is estimated that some towns and cities will have a majority population of black and Asian people. The estimated spending power of this section of the population is in excess of £60 billion.

- The white population in the UK and across Europe is ageing. Most people who are approaching the age of 60 are still economically active and have financial dependants. The failure of pension funds is driving the need to remain in work for longer.

- More women are delaying having children until age 35, and they are much more likely to want to return to work within eight months of childbirth. Women now make up 45.6% of the available labour force but are still poorly represented in senior roles.[4]

- Most disabled people become disabled during their working lives. The spending power of disabled people in the UK is estimated to be between £45 and £50 billion. Ninety-three per cent of disabled people live in their own homes and two million disabled people are looking for employment.[5]

It is clear that the UK is changing and organisations need to be prepared to listen and respond to the needs of people. When used in relation to employment monitoring, demographic evidence is usually taken as numerical fact with little or no reference to local issues, the needs of people or the available employment pool. A proper understanding of local and UK demographics is an important piece of research evidence for the diversity strategy. However, it is dangerous to use pure demographic information to set employment targets.

Key point: Demographic information should be used to highlight what diversity solutions should be put in place and to draw attention to areas of potential inequality.

The Problems and Benefits of Equality Targets

There is no doubt that a target can be a powerful motivator. Performance targets and business measures serve to focus the mind on what needs to be done to achieve a future goal and, by implication, help move the organisation forward. However, when it comes to managing equality and diversity, targets and measurement are a source of contention and confusion.

There is a compelling argument for having clear monitoring information, both on employee data and employee perception.

This would appear to be a simple concept.

- If an organisation fails to measure and understand where it stands in relation to diversity, it will have no benchmark against which to show improvement.

- If an organisation cannot demonstrate its improvement, it will have no defence against criticism.

- If an organisation cannot show it is moving forward, it cannot convey a sense of commitment to employees and the outside world.

There is, however, a more complex debate which needs to take place on the question of measurement and target setting for equality and diversity. Clearly, organisations need to make progress on diversity issues by setting a target; this shows that the organisation has both the desire and determination to bring about change.

However, there is concern about the use of the term 'targets' when attached to equality and diversity; and yet 'targets' for sales performance are fully accepted and expected. The definition and implications of targets need to be understood in order to see why they cause anxiety when used as equality measures.

Explaining the Conflict between Equality Targets and Diversity

Targets are difficult to explain in relation to diversity and they create a totally different expectation to sales targets. The main differences include the following.

- Performance targets and sales targets are internally driven, understood and owned by the management, but there is a perception that equality targets are externally imposed and will be open, therefore, to external criticism.

- Sales targets are impersonal and it is accepted that external factors can legitimately influence poor performance. Equality targets allow for an interpretation which can imply personal failure, and accusations of discrimination and unfair treatment of people. This can create tension and a fear of criticism.

- Sales targets can be revised downwards as well as upwards. Equality targets are less easy to revise downwards.

- Equality of opportunity is based on giving opportunity to disadvantaged groups. Diversity is an evolving subject which is creating an understanding of the value of individuals. It is hard to explain to senior managers the definition of diversity and its values based on the needs of the individual if, at the same time, positive action based on someone's group membership is advocated.

This is where the difference in definition between equality and diversity becomes most evident and causes the most problems. Most explanations of the two terms suggest that equal opportunities is about the collective rights of disadvantaged groups of people, and that diversity management is about being able to respond to, and capitalise on, the value that individual difference brings. Employment monitoring sits firmly with the definition of equal opportunities but appears to be counter-productive to diversity management.

The setting of employment targets has another serious drawback. Sales targets can easily be revised downwards in poor years. This is accepted practice in business. However, the revising downwards of equality targets is not so easy to accomplish. Demographics are unlikely to show a decrease in the numbers of disabled people, black and Asian people, older people or women available to work. Therefore, any revising downwards of equality targets is likely to be criticised.

This problem of definition needs to be resolved within the diversity strategy of an organisation. Employment monitoring clearly conforms to the equal opportunities definition; therefore, what is needed is a new style of intelligent measurement to support diversity management. Equal opportunities and diversity management form a strong partnership and all diversity strategies will require a robust foundation in equal opportunities. Monitoring has a role to play but the move to embrace the 'business case' for diversity has proved problematic for the monitoring argument.

Setting the Right Target

Example 1

A typical response for an organisation operating in an area which has an ethnic minority of 6.2% of the community, is to set an employment target of employing an ethnic minority of 6.2% of the total staff. This is typical of the policy in, for example, the police force and the fire service, where they are trying to respond to Home Office targets which have been set based on demographics of ethnic minorities in the UK.

Targets are usually set to reflect demographics rather than in response to the needs of the community. The demographics are being used as the visible indicator. Targets are often set without much thought as to the implications of achieving or failing to achieve those targets, and often organisations are chasing an unrealistic target.

In order to set the right target, it would be more intelligent to research why an organisation such as that in Example 1 above does not already employ an ethnic minority of 6.2% of the total staff, and to look at what it must do to do to bring about change. The organisation should then measure the success of the diversity initiatives which are put in place by tracking trends within the data gathered. If, for example, the research indicates that it is the recruitment source which is preventing ethnic minorities from applying, measures should be put in place to change recruitment processes and to influence the available recruitment pool. Efforts should then be made to assess the impact of the changes made.

Targets in relation to diversity fall a long way short of bringing about equality. Equality targets are often set in isolation from other information and do not help managers understand the benefits of diversity. Monitoring reports tend to consist of complex numerical spreadsheets with vast columns of numbers purporting to be an accurate reflection of what is happening within the organisation. These monitoring reports are occasionally read, rarely understood and never responded to by managers in the organisation; the monitoring report remains in the domain of the equality department.

DIVERSITY MEASUREMENT

The challenge for the diversity manager is to be able to set the right target and present intelligent diversity measurement in a style and language which is understood by the business.

When employment data gathered reveals an imbalance, organisations often react by feeling compelled to set targets in order to prove their commitment to equality of opportunity. However, target setting can create more problems than it solves and is not always the right response.

Key point: Diversity is really about change management and it is important to look for performance indicators which measure the desired change.

A Model for Diversity Measurement

It would be more useful to position diversity measurement within the organisational case for diversity, which is comprised of the legal, moral and business case. Data gathered for equality tends to be narrowly defined within employment and tracked in isolation, with little or no understanding of the wider issues that exert an effect on that target.

Organisations should be asking the following intelligent questions about their monitoring information.

- Why are we not better than we are?

- What do we need to do to bring about change?

- What information do we need in order to be able to measure change?

- What demographic information do we need to understand?

The problem with targets is knowing how to set the right target and communicate progress.

CHAPTER THREE – DEVELOPING THE STRATEGIC PLAN AND BUSINESS OBJECTIVES FOR DIVERSITY, discusses managing expectations and outlines four basic principles which should be followed (see p **53**). These principles help organisations to manage any scepticism and 'lip service', and to overcome the barriers of managers' passive reluctance to accept diversity as a business benefit. These principles should also be followed when setting equality and diversity targets.

- *Basic principle:* Use the same rationale, language and format as the strategic plan to underpin the diversity strategy.

  The same language and style should be used as those used by the business for all the other performance indicators. If the organisation uses a balance scorecard, for example, the diversity strategy should use the same technique. Language is important; if the term 'equality targets' is causing anxiety, performance indicators should be used to measure the impact of changes as opposed to end results on employment figures.

- *Basic principal:* Link the diversity action plan to issues which are important to managers. Demonstrate how diversity management can help achieve the overall business aims.

  Managers need to be able to link the diversity measures to other business measures. For example, if the business objective is to reduce costs by 25%, the diversity strategy should be looking for the same savings on turnover, recruitment and employment tribunal costs.

- *Basic principle:* Demonstrate robust, intelligent diversity measurement which is capable of reporting success.

  The performance indicators chosen for diversity must have credible criteria for success and be capable of demonstrating their impact on the business.

- *Basic principle:* Ensure that that there is a common understanding of diversity and equality of opportunity amongst managers in order to secure ownership and commitment.

  The diversity definition offered to managers must not conflict with the messages that employment monitoring sends out. If the diversity definition talks of valuing difference and the individual, there is a need to reconcile the language on measurement if measurement indicators report on groups.

Key point: Using these four principles will help change the language and emphasis in order to help managers understand how to use data on employment in a positive rather than accusatory way, and to overcome any negative backlash. The employment monitoring information should be seen as a performance indicator, which demonstrates the collective success of the diversity business plan, and not as a target.

Example 2

In 1997 B&Q were about to embark on a five-year diversity strategy. However, at this time the employee monitoring information lacked credibility and was out of date in relation to changes in legislation; there was little customer information collated in respect of diversity. This lack of information posed a potential problem. How would B&Q know if its diversity initiatives had really been successful and what should it be measuring? This led the business to debate the use of targets and positive action for employment.

CASE STUDY: Diversity strategy

In 1998 B&Q held a series of focus groups with disabled people revealing that employing disabled people through positive action could have been a premature move resulting in some disabled people being employed in a culture which did not understand disability. By developing a more intelligent approach to data gathering, B&Q debated the issue of an employment target.

B&Q deliberately did not seek to employ more disabled people. Instead, it embarked on a three-year journey to increase its own awareness of disability. Slowly, over two years, B&Q positioned itself as the DIY (do-it-yourself) retailer most able to meet the needs of disabled people. As the culture and credibility moved forward, the monitoring information started to reflect an upward trend in the number of disabled people applying for, and being appointed to, mainstream jobs.

The monitoring reports indicate that the number of disabled people employed by B&Q has increased by 300% since monitoring started. Monitoring has, therefore, allowed B&Q to observe changes in the employment profile and thereby determine the success of the diversity strategy. This increase was not solely due to more disabled people being employed but also to a change in culture which encouraged employees to declare hidden disabilities.

Key point: The driving force behind the improvement was the desire to be the best organisation for understanding the needs of disabled people, not to achieve an employment target. This change in emphasis determined the solutions which should be put in place. The business measured the effect that the solutions had in order to ensure that the solutions chosen were in fact the right ones. Employing more disabled people was only one output from the actions put in place.

Language and Management Commitment

Diversity measurement should be approached in the same way as any other business objective, in order to measure the results of a diversity initiative.

CASE STUDY: Evidence of improvement

Evidence of improvement, as opposed to defined targets, helped senior managers in B&Q to see the benefits of diversity. Real information which was observable and measurable, and that could be shown to make a difference, caught the imagination of the boardroom.

B&Q's targets were internally driven and fully understood by managers, and there was never an issue of potential failure. The business did not see the changes as being externally demanded by legislation but as a business benefit.

The employment monitoring information became the improvement indicator for the diversity department and was read as closely, and with the same importance, as the monthly business report. Varying levels of improvement allowed the business to question the effectiveness of specific aspects of the diversity strategy, thereby improving its learning on diversity solutions.

Evidence of improvement was not limited to employee data but covered a range of business measures, including:

- corporate reputation;
- PR;
- customer and employee satisfaction; and
- employee retention.

All these indicators measured the success of the diversity goal, which was to be the employer of first choice and retailer for disabled people.

B&Q made the decision not to use the language of targets, preferring to focus on creating an inclusive environment. The diversity team was concerned that, although a target-driven approach may result in increased appointments from under-represented groups, this approach would not solve problems with retention, bullying, employee dissatisfaction or customer complaints. By using the language of performance instead of targets, the measurement indicators are more readily accepted by managers.

Do Targets Help Solve the Problem of Inequality?

The drive to achieve targets should not take precedence over tackling the causes of the problems. When an organisation puts a strategy in place it will have gone through the process of understanding where its business stands and what it wants its business to look like in relation to diversity. The business plan is designed to bring about change but this change must be of benefit to the business and the results should be measured.

Organisations have to understand that equality issues cannot be resolved simply by recruiting a more diverse workforce. Recruiting more black and Asian employees does not explain why the numbers are low in the first place or give reasons for the problems. Every organisation will benefit from diversity in the workforce but this only comes from understanding diversity, not from simply setting a target and achieving it at all costs.

There is also a danger that too much emphasis is placed on employment targets when these are merely the visible issue. This criticism demands exploration of how an organisation functions and what lies behind the visible employment figures. Employment targets for ethnic minorities take the spotlight off an organisation which has 50% of its employees from different racial backgrounds and yet has higher disciplinary levels, poor performance, lower pay scales and high dissatisfaction amongst ethnic minority employees. The 'tick-box compliance' mentality is evident in many busy departments and targets are an easy option.

There are a number of fundamental errors made by organisations when setting targets for equality.

- Targets are often unrealistic and poorly researched and do not reflect the relevant labour market.

- Targets do not take into account attrition and organisational change which creates vacancies.

- Once set, targets are difficult to draw back from, as this can be perceived as a decrease in commitment to equality of opportunity.

- Failure to achieve targets generates anxiety and accusations of discrimination.

- Blame can occur without understanding why the targets have not been achieved.

Each organisation must research why it is facing a particular set of problems and then set about implementing the appropriate solutions. Intelligent data gathering should be capable of informing the organisation of its issues, and also driving the solutions which can be measured for their effectiveness and to demonstrate change.

Example 3

A local authority, according to its monitoring report, was able to show statistical evidence that 10.9% of its employees were black and Asian employees, which was a reasonable

> reflection of its community. If the employee monitoring exercise stopped with the reporting of the statistics, it would be unaware of a deeper-rooted problem, especially as a credible employment target of ethnic minorities could always be shown. However, upon further investigation, an age analysis and an attitude survey revealed that the black and Asian employees were all over the age of 40. The findings of a focus group revealed that, whilst they felt they had to maintain their employment, older people were taking the message back to their communities that the organisation was racist and they did not recommend it to younger people.

Key point: Within a diversity strategy there is never an 'end state', only a journey of continual improvement. Equal opportunities, monitoring and targets can imply that there is an end goal.

POSITIVE ACTION

One concern for diversity managers in pursuing the concept of the value of an individual, as opposed to the disadvantaged group, is the historical picture of positive action which grew out of the inequalities in employment monitoring data. Positive action has had a role to play in evolving equality debate and it is important that an organisation understands the implications of any diversity solutions it is proposing within its business plan.

Assessing the Impact of Positive Action

Positive action is grounded in the moral and social responsibility remit of diversity. It is derived from numerical measures which are designed to increase the representation of a group of people in employment. The idea of positive action comes from the civil rights campaign of the 1960s in America aimed at encouraging positive effort to overcome discrimination. It was surmised that creating such initiatives would overcome social injustice. In the UK this idea is again based on 'groups' of disadvantaged people and fits with the equal opportunities argument.

The idea of positive action takes a quantitative approach (it measures success by numbers employed), but there seems to be little evidence of the impact that positive action can have. Furthermore, positive action techniques can often produce a backlash, which can in turn generate more hidden barriers to discrimination.

In 1994 Heilman[6] wrote that if a person is selected or promoted for a job on criteria other than his or her competence, he or she would feel undermined and lose self-confidence. In addition, preferential selection will lead to feelings of alienation from other colleagues. Heilman also pointed to the increased level of stress felt by people who been promoted in such circumstances.

Example 4

In 2001 this notion was clearly seen when Asian policeman Anil Patani, who was promoted in order to achieve targets set by the Home Office for more Asian policemen, made the headlines. He believed his promotion left colleagues feeling that he had been promoted ahead of more deserving colleagues and that he had only been promoted so that the force was able to meet employment targets, which it was under pressure to do.

It should be a point of concern for all diversity managers that although Heilman warned of this problem back in 1994, in 2002 use of his study still does not appear to have been made. There has been a strong shift in favour of target setting in the public sector and in education, and this is being accompanied by an increase in press reports of bias and backlash.

Example 5

There has been anger in the Essex fire brigade over the decision to employ women who have failed part of the entrance test for the brigade. The equipment has long been designed around height restrictions that accompanied applications. In an attempt to attract more women the height restrictions have been relaxed. However, changes in the equipment design have not followed so quickly. The result is that, in an attempt to encourage more women into the fire service, the men feel standards are being lowered and that safety is being put at risk.

Key point: Implementing positive action without analysing the causes of the inequalities will result in a random series of short-term, quick fixes, which invariably rely on the enthusiasm of an individual and rarely become embedded in the culture of an organisation. Ad hoc initiatives will produce selective results which will fail to change the collective behaviour of an organisation.

An Alternative to Positive Action

Diversity management should not be confused with positive action. Diversity management is a more strategic approach which contributes to profitability and the goals of an organisation, not just on employment. Positive action tends to concentrate on getting people into an organisation, whilst diversity management is more about culture change and how people are treated once they are in employment.

Example 6

A monitoring exercise revealed that a police force does not have a high enough representation of women at middle and senior management grades. At the same time, the organisation lost a high profile sex discrimination case that received a lot of media attention. It has a reputation for being a difficult environment for women to work in, with stories of bullying and harassment.

A positive action campaign might focus on recruitment. An alternative to positive action would be for the organisation to understand the cause of its problems and to put in place effective solutions. Positive action techniques would have traditionally sought to employ more women. However, diversity management should look at the causes of the inequality.

The diversity solutions for the organisation in Example 6 above could include the following actions.

- Counselling services for officers who are experiencing bullying.

- Raising awareness of harassment amongst police officers.

- A new complaints procedure for fast-tracking harassment complaints.

- Recognition of the seriousness of complaints.

- A mentoring scheme.

- The use of role models for recruitment.

The diversity performance indicators in Example 6 above could include the following.

- The number of grievances brought by women police officers.

- The time taken to deal with complaints from women compared to complaints from male officers.

- The turnover rates of women police officers.

- The length of time taken to receive promotion.

- Results of attitude surveys on job satisfaction by gender.

- The publicity received in the press.

- The recorded instances of bullying and harassment.

- The number of female recruits applying and being appointed.

- The number of requests for flexible working.

- The age profile of women in the police force.

Ultimately, the police force would expect to see more women enjoying longer and more successful careers. If this was not reflected in the employment profile then the causes of inequality may not have been identified correctly or may have changed over time. This kind of approach is likely to cause the male police officers concern.

Key point: An alternative to positive action is to develop diversity solutions with performance indicators which measure the results and the changes brought about by the solutions. It is important that the driving force for change is the cause of the inequality and not the targets.

The argument put forward in favour of positive action is that it helps create equality of chance for those people who come from a disadvantaged background or who are under-represented in the workforce. Again, for any organisation with a diversity strategy the problem with trying to put forward such action is one of definition. Positive action fits well with equal opportunities as it defines people by group. Diversity management is about creating an environment where everyone feels valued and that they are able to make a contribution; any action should be targeted to the individual who has a developmental need and not restricted to a particular group. If positive action is taken to help ethnic minorities, what about disabled people, and gay men and women for example? The argument for positive action becomes too restrictive for diversity. Diversity solutions would be more inclusive. If flexible working is introduced, it should be introduced to help all employees enjoy a work-life balance and not just targeted at women.

In developing a diversity strategy the research will have highlighted any inequalities and, more importantly, the reasons why the inequalities exist. The diversity strategy should be working towards the removal of the barriers and cause of the problems.

Example 7

In 1993 a high street bank knew that it was not attracting any ethnic minority employees. It decided to set a pre-recruitment training session which was only open to ethnic minorities, and ran an advertising campaign to attract people from certain communities. Initially the bank appeared to have some success and the numbers of ethnic minority employees appointed increased. However, once in employment, these new recruits quickly left the bank. A subsequent review highlighted a lack of management ownership for the scheme and a strong feeling of preferential treatment which caused resentment. The new recruits who chose to leave felt this.

The kind of limited positive action highlighted in Example 7 above does not address the wider problem of why ethnic minorities were not applying for vacancies in the first place.

Following are suggestions for a diversity solution for the bank.

- An investigation into whether the brand is seen as an employer of choice with ethnic minority graduates using a series of focus groups.

- Discussions with community leaders and leading families in order to understand how graduates from ethnic minority backgrounds make career decisions within the family.

- A repositioning of the brand within the community looking at customer services for ethnic minorities, perhaps the introduction of translation services, Halal bank accounts, varying opening hours, etc.

- An examination of the selection methods.

- Ownership of the solution by managers by encouraging them to be involved in considering the reasons why it was important to widen the recruitment pool, as opposed to just employing more ethnic minorities.

The success of the holistic programme should be reflected by an increase in the number of ethnic minorities applying for jobs, being appointed, remaining with the bank and enjoying successful careers. There should be no pressure placed on managers to achieve a target; there should simply be an appraisal of progress.

Key point: Limited positive action will only produce short–term and selective results. The diversity strategy should be seeking long–term sustainable change.

SUMMARY OF THE ARGUMENT FOR MONITORING AND TARGET SETTING

- The use of equality targets is problematic and their use does not fit easily with the definition of diversity.

- Employment monitoring is only the starting point in measuring diversity.

- The challenge is to really understand what lies behind the causes of discrimination and to introduce intelligent measurement of the solutions.

- The organisation should be seeking to develop a range of performance indicators to measure the success of diversity initiatives.

INTELLIGENT DIVERSITY MEASUREMENT

There are four main areas listed below that a diversity manager should be interested in measuring. Each of these areas provides a source of intelligence on what is happening within an organisation.

- *Culture change:* Diversity management is about change management and communication, and its goal is to mainstream change throughout the organisation. Therefore, it would make sense to begin measuring the success of any diversity strategy by looking for changes in the culture of an organisation. IBM, for example, regularly conducts attitude surveys, including questions on equality and diversity. By tracking changes over time it should be possible to link changes to the introduction of new diversity initiatives. Measuring changes in employee culture will indicate the extent of ownership and mainstreaming of diversity.

- *Business performance indicators:* Nearly all organisations measure their performance, whether this is sales, share price, customer satisfaction, employee turnover, profit or loss. Most will have indicators which change in importance depending on the fortunes or type of organisation. It is important that diversity managers know what the key decision-makers are interested in measuring and that the diversity indicators are geared towards supporting that measure.

- *Specific diversity indicators:* The diversity business plan must have specific diversity indicators against each of the actions in order to justify budget and resource costs and to measure sustainability. These measures must be used to produce the annual diversity report, which will include information on customers and the community.

- *Employment data:* Monitoring will always have an important role to play. However, this should be in trend analysis and should be used to highlight potential problem areas. The employment monitoring should not be presented as a 'snapshot' of the organisation but as a source of information and analysis. Change is important but the employee profile should be used as an indicator and not as a target. Demographic information should be used to support the understanding of employment data.

How to Measure Diversity

Within the four areas listed above, various methods can be used to produce intelligent diversity measures.

Culture change

Focus groups are a good way of checking change. If one of the original action plans was to understand why women fail to achieve promotion, focus groups used over time can measure whether the reasons change. Focus groups help to highlight changes in attitude and understanding. They also help generate new ideas.

Employee attitude surveys provide information on overall changes taking place within an organisation. Questions on diversity should be built into the data which can be tracked over time.

External focus groups can be used to see if there has been any change in how the brand is positioned as an employer of first choice. Graduates are an excellent source of information for measuring how the brand is perceived as a fair employer.

Business performance indicators

The business will have performance indicators which the senior managers pay attention to. These could include:

- sales;

- profit and loss;

- share price;

- customer satisfaction;

- costs; and

- job performance.

Whatever business indicators are used to measure overall business performance, they should be built into the diversity business plan.

Specific diversity indicators

Each action which is detailed in the diversity business plan should have an expected outcome identified with specific diversity measures in order to report on the success of the strategy.

Employment data

Monitoring can reveal a great deal of information by highlighting trends in:

- employee complaints;

- sickness absence;

- turnover;

- recruitment;

- employee profile; and

- local demographics.

Establishing the Link between Diversity and Organisational Performance

CASE STUDY: Example of diversity measurement

A retail organisation selling food has set a business objective of realising a 10% growth in market share year on year.

In researching the potential impact of diversity management on this business objective, a series of customer focus groups and mystery shopping exercises were conducted and the employment data was analysed. In addition, the UK demographics were compared to the postcodes and profitability of the retail network.

Results of the research

- The feedback from the mystery shopping revealed that black and Asian women were twice as likely to be dissatisfied with the customer service than white women were.

- On average, more store complaints were received in areas of high ethnicity.

- On average, if a store was located in an area which had an ethnic minority representation in the community of more than 10%, profitability of the stores was down by 4%.

- Market research revealed that most black and Asian women could not find the products they wanted.

- Communication and language was proving a problem in areas which had a high proportion of Asian women as residents.

- Employment of black and Asian people was not reflective of local demographics, and there was clear evidence of inequality in management positions.

- The stores were not regarded as an employer of choice by the Asian community.

- Two stories had been reported in national papers about the mistreatment of black staff.

Diversity solutions

- Training for customer services staff on cultural awareness and appropriate behaviour.

- Greater store recognition of local community demographics and religious festivals.

- Trialing of new products which reflect local needs.

- Involvement with local community groups to offer work experience to young people from different community backgrounds.

- Translation service via a help line.

- Greater understanding of the barriers to recruitment and promotion.

Diversity measures

- The employment profile would be tracked over time to look for any changes which would indicate an improvement in the brand as an employer of choice. This would include tracking applications, appointments and promotions. This improvement in brand reputation should be a result of a range of actions.

- Distance learning on diversity would be introduced on a voluntary basis, but with an expected indicator of 50% of employees wanting to take part.

- Each store would be expected to be able to show what it was doing to reach out to local communities.

- A decrease in the overall number of complaints.

- A 25% increase in customer satisfaction rates for black and Asian customers.

- Take up rates of the translation service.

- Product sales of the niche products targeted at the local community.

This holistic model of diversity will start to realise benefits across the business as diversity managers understand that success and change is rarely the result of one isolated diversity action.

Reporting on Success

It is important that diversity managers report on the year's progress in the organisation's annual report. In doing so it will start to communicate to the external audience the importance the organisation places on the value of respect for people and diversity. It positions diversity management as a business issue which has an impact on brand reputation and one which can influence share price. This annual reporting process will help sustain momentum and reinforce to managers that diversity is a long-term commitment and not just topic of the moment.

The main advantage of the annual report is that it ensures that the diversity strategy is reviewed annually and that, each year, Step 1 (see **CHAPTER TWO – UNDERSTANDING THE ORGANISATIONAL CASE FOR DIVERSITY**, p **42**) can be re-visited with the board. The question posed by Step 1 becomes a report of progress made and an understanding of the current position of the organisation. The vision setting of Step 2 (see **CHAPTER TWO**, p **40** and **CHAPTER THREE**, p **64**) need not change the actual vision statement, but the process allows the board to reaffirm its commitment. What will change and evolve each year, however, is the diversity action plan, as this must continue to reflect progress made.

Honest and accurate reporting is important for keeping people's attention and inspiring new ideas. If an organisation uses champions to drive forward communication on diversity, an annual conference for all the champions provides a useful opportunity for networking and sharing good practice.

Summary of the Key Elements of Measuring Diversity

- The wider remit of diversity brings in more stakeholder groups. Information will be needed on customers and the community.

- Qualitative information on people's perceptions is just as valid as quantitative employment data.

- Diversity measurement should use language which is relevant to the organisation and should seek to measure issues which are important to organisational success.

- Progress on diversity should be included in the annual report.

The following questions should be considered when the business case for diversity is prepared.

- What are the demographics of the customers?

- How much does employee turnover cost the business?

- How much is spent on recruitment?

- How much has been spent on discrimination and harassment (both in terms of legal fees and management time)?

- Do current policies attract the right candidates?

- Do employee attitude surveys reveal that staff feel valued?

- Is career advancement favouring one group of individuals?

- Is diversity reflected in procurement contracts?

Measurement needs to be an integral part of a diversity process, not just a check at the end of an initiative.

MEASURING CORPORATE KNOWLEDGE

It has been argued that diversity must have a strategy and a business plan which deliver sustainable change. It is not enough to put in place specific actions and have a vision statement that is only owned and understood by a few people in the organisation. It is vital that the whole organisation understands the values and objectives of the diversity strategy.

Achieving mainstreaming of diversity will require some creative application of communication and learning programmes which are capable of reaching every employee in the organisation. This process is greatly assisted by the development of intranet sites, CD–ROM learning and improved distance learning techniques.

If diversity is going to be mainstreamed, methods of communication must change to reflect this. In the past, the equal opportunities policy was the only source of communication which the organisation used to explain the expected behaviour of staff. However, this does not communicate progress or recognise success. Furthermore, it is not capable of measuring employee understanding.

Diversity managers need to think about how they could measure corporate knowledge on diversity. There are several reasons for doing this:

- to communicate a sense of progress;

- to mainstream diversity across the organisation;

- to recognise success; and

- to help sustain change.

Distance learning techniques are now becoming sophisticated in measurement and much easier to administer.

CASE STUDY: B&Q

When B&Q embarked upon its journey to accessibility, it piloted a training session in a new store in Norwich. All 250 new members of staff were trained by Churchill and Friend in customer service and disability awareness. The results of the training were excellent; however, replicating this across 200 B&Q stores would have been expensive. The main opposition to rolling out the training was the time it would take to take people out of stores in order to deliver face-to-face training. B&Q wanted to ensure that all 23,000 members of its staff knew about the *Disability Discrimination Act 1995* (*DDA 1995*) and understood the values of 'Respect for People'. In partnership with diversity consultants, the Grass Roots Group (GRG), and Churchill and Friend, B&Q developed a distance learning workbook which was distributed to every member of staff via an extensive communication process including posters and team briefs. A workbook was chosen as not all staff had access to a computer. (However, B&Q is now developing an on-line version.)

The idea was that every member of staff would work through the distance learning programme and, at some point during a six-week period, they would ring a free phone number and take part in an 'interactive voice response' question and answer session. In order to pass, each person had to score ten out of a possible twelve points. The system was able to tell people immediately if they had passed or failed.

The advantage of using such a system was that each week a report could be generated highlighting the number of people who had taken part and passed/failed. Because each person keyed in a PIN number, which was his or her employee number, the information in the report could be analysed by the store. This enabled B&Q to capitalise on the competitive spirit which existed between stores by running a competition for participation. In this way B&Q was able to recognise store commitment and success. Eventually the process was built into the overall store standards, which meant that all stores had to be able to show that 75% of their teams had passed the training.

Recognition was also given to each individual in the form of a badge to wear. This badge slowly began the process of communicating to customers the existence of the disability awareness campaign. The badge used the Leonard Cheshire symbol. (Leonard Cheshire is a charity whichhelps provide independent living for disabled people.) This was linked to the Corporate Social Responsibility (CSR) programme, as an amount of money was set aside each time an employee passed the training. In this way B&Q was able to donate a significant amount to Leonard Cheshire. The donations were then given to named disabled people living independently to help them decorate their homes and, at the same time, enable them to gain work experience in B&Q. This in turn kept the diversity story alive; internal public relations (PR) stories were generated as more stores became involved with their local Leonard Cheshire Home and helped to employ more disabled people. This kind of holistic approach to diversity helps sustain change.

By being able to measure corporate knowledge on disability, B&Q was able to show:

- compliance with the *DDA 1995*;

- participation rates of employees;

- sustainability of knowledge by involving 12,000 new employees per year; and

- individual store knowledge on disability.

The distance learning measurement also enabled people to say whether they had enjoyed the training and how much they had learnt. This is far more effective than launching a video or written policy.

DIVERSITY AND THE LEARNING ORGANISATION

This idea of measuring corporate knowledge is linked to the model of the 'learning organisation'. In his book, *The Learning Organisation*,[7] Bob Garratt says that success depends on two key skills; learning continuously and giving direction. B&Q was able to achieve both by using the workbook to explain the vision and values for disability, and by giving knowledge to individuals. This concept of learning continuously is an important one for the equality and diversity debate.

Theories of equal opportunities in the 1990s focused on behaviour which would not be tolerated. This was especially evident in areas of harassment and bullying. This is still important within policies and procedures today but the definition of diversity allows learning to re-focus training on what can be achieved and what can be done to ensure equity and fairness.

The learning organisation focuses on realising the potential of all employees and the capacity of individuals to learn. Both these principles underpin the more sophisticated diversity strategy. The diversity strategy must build a learning and communication campaign as part of its annual process.

CONCLUSION

Measuring the impact of diversity remains the weakest link in the argument for diversity being able to deliver change. As the debate evolves from equal opportunities to diversity, the use of targets and employment monitoring must become more sophisticated to embrace a wider remit beyond pure employment. The role of the diversity manager must be to understand performance measurement and research analysis of all the stakeholder groups and to be able to identify diversity measures.

Diversity management must be about respecting the quality of life of *all* the people who come into contact with an organisation. Measurement of the success of a diversity strategy must be able to understand customer issues, the employment relationship and the community impact that an organisation has. This will mean forming internal partnerships between CSR, brand reputation and HR.

An organisation should be able to gather intelligent data which enables it to:

- understand the implication of demographics;
- ensure integrity of employee data;
- capture people's perception and views;
- analyse appraisals and competency ratings;
- examine pay scales;
- monitor employee stability rates, promotion and absence;
- record instances of discipline and grievance and the cost of complaints;
- track applicants against appointment; and
- understand customer perceptions.

Once an organisation understands what the data is telling it, informed decisions can be made. Solutions can be put into place and the impact of diversity can be analysed by tracking changes in the data. If the solutions are the right ones an improvement will be seen in the measures as the organisation progresses in its diversity strategy.

The starting point for a strategy should not be to set a target but to understand why there is a problem in the first place and to start the process of change management.

CHECKLIST

✔ Can you explain how your organisation will measure the success of the diversity strategy?

✔ Has the most appropriate language for your organisation in relation to targets and measurement been agreed?

✔ Do you understand that business performance indicators are important to the organisation, and are you aware of how diversity could have an impact upon these?

✔ Have you developed a series of intelligent diversity measures for your organisation?

✔ Have senior managers agreed to include diversity in the annual report?

✔ Have you put in place methods to measure corporate knowledge on diversity?

References

1. Equal Pay Task Force, *Just Pay*, Equal Opportunities Commission (2001).
2. www.busygirl.co.uk, FTSE Female Index launch (2000).
3. Cabinet Office, *Ethnic Minorities and the Labour Market*, interim analytical report (2002).
4. www.employersforwork–lifebalance.org.uk.
5. Employers' Forum on Disability, *Promoting Change* (2002).
6. Heilman, *Affirmative Action, Research in Organizational Behavior*, Volume 16, pp 125–169 (1994).
7. Garratt B, *The Learning Organisation*, Director Books (1990).

Chapter Five

Implementing and Managing Diversity

OVERVIEW

This chapter covers the following issues.

- The employment relationship and the impact of terms and conditions on diversity (see p **103**).

- Factors which can affect the implementation and management of diversity (see p **105**).

- Becoming an employer of first choice for a diverse range of applicants (see p **107**).

- Managing the impact of an organisation's procedures on equality and diversity (see p **118**).

- Work-life balance practices (see p **135**).

- The impact of pay and benefits on diversity (see p **139**).

- Delivering training and development of a diverse work force (see p **149**).

- Effective communication of diversity values within policies and practices (see p **151**).

INTRODUCTION

Diversity needs a shared vision which is inextricably linked to the business strategy (see **CHAPTER TWO – UNDERSTANDING THE ORGANISATIONAL CASE FOR DIVERSITY** and **CHAPTER THREE – DEVELOPING THE STRATEGIC PLAN AND BUSINESS OBJECTIVES FOR DIVERSITY**). However, just as important are those processes of an organisation which govern how decisions are made that can impact upon the employment relationship. The way an organisation implements its policies and procedures obviously plays a crucial role in embedding diversity into operational activities.

Managing diversity cannot be achieved over night; it requires continuous and co-ordinated effort. There is no single way of ensuring success in managing diversity; however, the combined effort of:

- leadership and clear values communicated in a diversity strategy;

- agreeing an agenda for action linked to the business objectives;

- embedding diversity into policies and practices;

- effective and sustained communication; and

- measuring, reporting and reviewing diversity;

will all help an organisation to move forward on its diversity agenda.

If the diversity strategic plan and business plan are to be translated into effective actions they will need to be embedded into all HR (human resources) management procedures. This chapter looks at the procedures and policies which govern who gets a job and how people are treated once they are employed. It considers how diversity can be managed through these employment policies and practices. Concentrating specifically on the employment relationship, it examines how terms and conditions of the contract of employment can have either a positive or negative impact on the diversity management of the workforce.

The chapter also considers who should manage the processes and policies which can influence the outcome of a diversity strategy. In recent times there has been a change in the HR function. Some organisations maintain a central function whilst others have decentralised to move decision-making and accountability to line managers. Some organisations, such as BP, have even chosen to outsource their HR function altogether. Throughout this chapter attention is given to the diversity indicators which can be used to monitor the effectiveness of the HR policies, whether these are devolved to line management or controlled centrally. Those factors which can hinder or help the successful implementation of a diversity strategy are also considered.

THE EMPLOYMENT RELATIONSHIP

The terms and conditions governing the employment relationship can have a negative or positive impact on the diversity management of the workforce. It is important that the contract of employment is reviewed and 'diversity proofed' to ensure that it does not contain any unnecessary or restrictive clauses. If the organisation is unionised and recognises a collective agreement, the union will have to be involved in the commitment to diversity from the beginning and must agree to any changes that might be introduced to the contractual agreement.

The *Employment Rights Act 1996 (ERA 1996)* gives employees the right to receive the main terms and conditions of their employment in writing. Certain terms have to be contained in one document, called the 'Principal Statement'. Additional terms also have to be in writing, but these can be contained in additional documents, most commonly the staff handbook.

A contract of employment is made up of express terms, implied terms and statutory terms (also called imposed terms). The contract of employment governs the expected behaviour of both the employer and the employee.

- Express terms are contractual obligations which exist and determine the basic rights and conditions of employment. They are specifically mentioned and agreed.

- Implied terms cover accepted and reasonable conditions which are not specifically stated but which could be expected to be covered by the contract.

- Statutory terms are those which refer to compliance with employment legislation. These are imposed on a contract.

The biggest impact in recent times on the contract of employment has come from statutory conditions being imposed on the employment relationship, most of which affect diversity management.

For example, working time, maternity and parental leave, time off for dependants, disability discrimination and equal pay are all areas covered by legislation, and there are several more changes to come, such as religious observance (see **CHAPTER SIX – DIVERSITY AND THE LAW**, p **191**). These changes may impact upon the terms and conditions of employment. It is important that, as part of the diversity research which forms Step 1 of the organisation's strategy (see **CHAPTER TWO**, p **30**), a review is made of legal compliance. This should include a forecast of future legislation. All terms and conditions must be compliant with employment law.

In addition to being legally compliant, the contract of employment should be examined to ascertain if there are any practices which are unnecessary and which could have an adverse affect on diversity management. For example, conditions in the employment contract which are no longer relevant, such as:

- specifying the place of work;

- specifying the requirement to drive; or

- demanding a medical examination.

The contract of employment should not be so restrictive that it prevents the introduction of flexible working and reasonable adjustment.

Example 1

Terms and conditions regarding holiday and holiday pay entitlement must be included, but consideration of religious observance should also be given. Some contracts provide for a shut-down period during Christmas when specifying holiday entitlement, which may not be welcomed by people who do not observe this holiday.

> **Example 2**
>
> A public sector authority wanted to give work experience to its large traveller community and to give the community members access to services such as the library. Both the contract of employment and the library membership required a permanent address to be given. In overcoming this problem some creative thinking was needed. A local hostel was involved to provide an address.

It is not uncommon to have a statement of equal opportunities in the contract of employment and a referral to a more comprehensive policy in a staff handbook. If a policy is stated to be a contractual term, failure to adhere to it will give rise to a breach of contract. If, however, the policy is non-contractual, it cannot give rise to a claim of breach of contract. Some equality policies already go further than the law currently demands such as by recognising sexual orientation. Organisations should decide whether they mean to make this term contractual or whether they merely wish to observe this policy as good practice, outside of the legal employment relationship.

Key point: It is sensible to consider making the equal opportunities policy contractual, as a statement in the contract of employment will reinforce an organisation's commitment to equality and diversity, and will help clarify possible areas of confusion.

There are Codes of Practice from the Commission for Racial Equality (CRE), the Equal Opportunities Commission (EOC) and the Disability Rights Commission (DRC) which offer guidance on the implementation of discrimination law. These codes are not legally binding in themselves, but they will be taken into account by an employment tribunal in any claim alleging unlawful discrimination. In reality, there are many policies and practices, covered in the handbook on employment policies, which will have an impact on equality. Any failure by the organisation to have in place a comprehensive set of policies and practices is likely to mean that the organisation is in a much weaker position should a claim be brought before the tribunal.

Although an equality term in the employment contract strengthens the commitment to equality, it also makes that term a contractual obligation, which can make it difficult to change terms in the future.

Key point: The terms and conditions of employment must reflect current employment legislation, but the specific requirements should enable an organisation to achieve its diversity objectives on flexibility. The terms and conditions can only be changed later if both the employer and the employee agree.

FACTORS WHICH CAN AFFECT THE IMPLEMENTATION AND MANAGEMENT OF DIVERSITY

Most organisations will have a centrally-defined diversity strategy which explains key values and principles, while line managers are expected to make day-to-day decisions on issues such as recruitment, selection, promotion and dismissal. Whether a fully-centralised function or a structure that devolves accountability for diversity, there is a still a need to ensure commitment to the principles of equality of opportunity within the employment relationship. A central policy does not guarantee practical implementation of procedures which will impact upon diversity, and mainstreaming does not always equate to ownership.

Two issues need careful attention when implementing and managing diversity.

Firstly, organisations should be aware of, and seek to minimise the effect of, those factors which can have an adverse impact on diversity.

In 1997 the Wainwright Trust commissioned a report by Alan Fowler, *The Decentralisation and Devolution of Equal Opportunities*.[1] Fowler's research in the private sector highlighted a number of factors that detracted from the effective implementation of equal opportunities policies. These factors included the following.

- No accountability for equality in managers' job descriptions.

- Inadequate monitoring information and no performance measures.

- Poor communication of corporate policy.

- Poor/inadequate training on policies which impacted upon equal opportunities.

- Poor recruitment practices, such as 'word of mouth', still being used.

Fowler described three major points arising from the research.

- Key decision-makers must be determined to see the vision and values fully implemented throughout the organisation.

- There needs to be a co-ordinated and comprehensive approach to training on policies which have equality implications; ie recruitment, selection and promotion, discipline and harassment, appraisal and remuneration.

- Equality practices must be integrated into broad-based business objectives and strategy, instead of being treated as a separate unrelated issues.

These factors are discussed throughout this chapter in relation to policies and procedures which affect the successful implementation of diversity action plans.

Secondly, organisations need to identify a range of diversity performance indicators which, when tracked over a period of time, can reveal if the commitment to equality and diversity is being carried out in practice.

Measurement of outcomes is an integral part of most management processes, and yet organisations are relatively unsophisticated at identifying diversity performance indicators which can be tracked over a period of time in order to reveal progress in the commitment to diversity. There are three areas where diversity can be subject to this kind of observation.

- Measuring the success of broad diversity outcomes as defined in the business plan (see **CHAPTER FOUR – MEASURING THE SUCCESS OF A DIVERSITY STRATEGY**).

- Identifying individual areas of accountability.

- Tracking and analysing a range of statistical indicators which monitor employment.

If diversity management is going to be mainstreamed across the organisation, an explicit requirement to be accountable for equal opportunities has to be built into the performance measures for both the organisation and the individual manager. It is important that measurable objectives are set in the business plan (see **CHAPTER THREE**); however, it is also important to focus attention on measuring individual accountability for diversity.

By making a provision for equal opportunities within the employment relationship, a clear signal is given that there is a requirement to provide a working environment which is free from discrimination. This should be included in all job descriptions and reinforced in the contract of employment. It is not enough to draw up policies which affect equality and diversity, an employment tribunal will also want to see evidence of custom and practice, how these policies have been communicated and what training has been provided. As Fowler indicated,[2] training and communication are the weakest factors affecting the successful implementation of diversity policies.

The remainder of this chapter provides a framework and practical guidance on what to do within each of the policy areas which impact on equality prior to employment, during employment and at termination. Each area is discussed in terms of identifying diversity performance indicators. The point made by Fowler is also examined. He said 'there needs to be a co-ordinated and comprehensive approach to training on policies which have equality implications: recruitment, selection, induction, promotion, discipline and harassment, appraisal and remuneration'.[3]

RECRUITMENT AND SELECTION

The aim of an organisation is to become an employer of first choice for a diverse range of applicants. It will, therefore want to attract a diverse range of candidates.

Diversity Strategy

The objective of a diversity strategy on recruitment and selection is to ensure that an employer has the widest possible pool of talent from which to select and recruit the best employees. To implement an effective strategy, the organisation must have information on how the recruitment and selection process works, along with outcomes to identify gaps and target improvements.

Key point: While the development of appropriate policies and procedures is essential, it is also important to ensure that these are seen as a practical tool and as a means to deliver a diversity strategy in practice.

Core demands include the following areas.

Image of the organisation

What image does the employer portray in recruitment literature and advertising? It is very important that the right messages are sent out at the beginning of the recruitment process. The recruitment literature may be the potential candidates' first contact with the organisation. Increasingly, applicants are not just looking for information about salary, job content and location; they want to know how they can expect to be treated by a prospective employer and they want to decide whether this is the type of organisation they would like to work for.

The employment market is becoming an increasingly competitive place for employers. There are skills shortages in some areas, a declining birth rate and an ageing population. Significant problems, for example, are currently encountered in parts of the public sector in recruiting staff at all levels. Public authorities are now increasingly seeing the advantage of selling their 'terms and conditions', areas that had previously been taken for granted. Such factors dictate that employers must make sure they are in a position, when recruiting, to attract and select employees from the widest possible pool of talent.

The expression 'employer of choice' is now common currency. Employers recognise that they have to sell themselves to potential employees as never before. Selling points include advertising flexible working practices, adopting the 'two ticks' symbol indicating that the organisation is 'positive about disabled people', making sure that any images of the workforce reflect its diversity and advertising the organisation's diversity policy and strategy.

As well as striving to convey positive messages in recruitment advertising, care must also be taken to ensure that advertisements do not contain negative messages, which may deter qualified people from applying. Advertisements need to be checked for language which may make assumptions about the type of person able to do the job, ie 'salesman', 'manageress', 'young person wanted', 'energetic person required'. In some instances, where advertisements indicate an intention to discriminate they are unlawful and may lead to action by the EOC or CRE.

Widening the pool: attracting all the talent

Attracting applicants from a wide range of backgrounds is an essential part of a successful diversity recruitment policy. Relevant issues which need to be addressed include the following.

- Does the organisation have an advertising strategy on recruitment?

- Is one of the objectives of such a strategy to attract as wide a range of suitably-qualified candidates as possible?

- Does the recruitment system rely on one source of applications?

- Does the organisation recruit by using 'word of mouth' among existing employees, with a disproportionate impact on other methods?

- What message does the publicity material send out about the company? Are all the images of a particular type of person or customer?

- Are 'family friendly', or flexible working arrangements part of the recruitment package?

- Are job-share arrangements considered?

- Have outreach and related approaches been explored to attract applications from a range of communities and groups?

- Have managers and staff involved in the recruitment process been involved with the development of, and been trained on, diversity approaches?

- Have disability considerations been taken into account?

The issue of attracting and appointing people from all backgrounds, reflecting diverse Britain today is a continuing challenge. For example, obtaining sufficient numbers of ethnic minority applicants, reflecting local communities and populations, is a problem for many organisations. They find that even though they are operating in areas of high ethnic minority populations, despite feeling they have taken all the correct steps they consistently fail to obtain sufficient applications from ethnic minorities.

Example 3

This has been a particular problem for the voluntary and charitable sector where, despite being generally unprejudiced at staff level, these organisations often fail to attract ethnic minority applications. The National Council for Voluntary Organisations (NCVO), a representative body for the sector, is now developing guidelines for members as well as providing examples of good practice. Part of the strategy is to bring organisations together to explore problems, challenges and also solutions within a diversity context.

> ## Example 4
>
> One organisation faced with small numbers of ethnic minority applications was a major international record company, with its headquarters in central London. The organisation was particularly concerned, not only because it operated in an area with a large ethnic minority population, but also because of the large list of black artists and the organisation's customer base. The company was challenged to use its innovative techniques in selling records to instead attract ethnic minority applicants. The company responded by reviewing and changing recruitment practices, which had previously been ad hoc and frequently based on 'who you knew' (ie 'word of mouth') practices. The company also developed mentoring and trainee schemes, along with other outreach work in the local community. It has learnt to sell itself better to its target audience. Inevitably, success breeds success and, as the organisation's profile in appointing ethnic minority applicants has met with some success, more applications and subsequent appointments are being generated.

A key starting point is how candidates find out about vacancies. If traditional methods of recruitment (for example, professional magazines, national or local newspapers, university 'milk rounds' etc) are not reaching certain groups, organisations need to be more innovative and look at ways of widening the net. Organisations, and managers within them, will need to examine their own behaviour, styles, beliefs and attitudes, and any assumptions about the 'type' of people they want to attract. Looking at things in new ways, questioning stereotypes, challenging their own feelings and views about people all form part of an organisation's diversity perspective.

Non-traditional recruitment strategies

The Internet is becoming an increasingly popular source of information for job seekers. Evidence in the UK also shows that people with certain types of disabilities make greater use of new technology, including the Internet, to search for jobs. Employers who want to attract applications from people with disabilities should advertise jobs and on-line applications on their website, after first ensuring it is accessible to people with certain disabilities, such as impaired vision.

Other ways of circulating and advertising job opportunities include, for example, advertising on Ceefax and local radio, at career fairs and through links with local networks, or pressure groups (for example, Age Concern to attract older recruits) and disability networks. If graduates are needed, an organisation must consider whether recruitment campaigns concentrate on particular universities or colleges which do not have a representative student population.

Other examples of initiatives that have been taken include the following.

(*a*) A major manufacturing company employed high numbers of technical and scientific staff. However, once the company started looking at diversity issues, perhaps unsurprisingly, it was discovered that women formed a low proportion of the workforce at all levels. This was especially the case at more senior levels. Initially, a convenient explanation for this was that women were less likely to qualify in the relevant subject areas. While this in part explained the situation, it was found overall to be inadequate. Other companies operating in similar areas were observed as having significantly higher numbers of women employees. Women were also found to form a higher proportion of the labour market than originally thought. The company has subsequently developed closer work with colleges and universities to target and attract women graduates. It has also developed specific schemes, including trainee schemes and secondments aimed at women with science degrees.

(*b*) BP has started a high profile campaign to target gay men and lesbians. The company says that this is part of its aim to rid itself of the 'golf club culture' which it views as encouraging only white Anglo-Saxon men. The company is planning to attract more gay and lesbian applicants by offering equal benefits for partners in same-sex relationships. This will ensure that the offer to spouses and heterosexual partners of pension rights, death benefit provision and relocation allowances is also extended to partners in gay relationships.

(*c*) Reaching out locally, regionally and nationally with relevant minority networks is important. For example, recruitment fairs can be a potentially useful source of attracting minority groups. The Afro-Caribbean Finance Forum (ACFF) arranges regular career fairs targeted at black students and graduates, with significant numbers of companies from all sectors in attendance. ACFF also runs seminars and trainee schemes along with input from major companies. This initiative has been especially successful with a range of city companies.

(*d*) Mentoring schemes developed locally can encourage applications from minority groups. The Windsor Fellowship supports a national mentoring scheme for ethnic minority potential employees. *Project Fullemploy* specialises in training and developing ethnic minority young people and placing them with employers. The Employers' Forum on Disability also developed a number of initiatives.

(*e*) Asda has adopted a 'Goldies' campaign to recruit older (over 50s) workers for its business. The supermarket is convinced of the business benefits of employing older people in its stores. A survey carried out showed that stores with higher numbers of older workers had a staff turnover rate below the group's average. and absenteeism had dropped to one third of Asda's national average. Over 16% of Asda's current workforce are now over 50 years of age, and the company is looking to increase this figure. Asda has recruitment teams visiting bingo halls, coffee mornings and pension queues advertising the benefits of returning to work after 50. The campaign includes in-store promotions using posters and shelf labels encouraging its customers aged over 50 to join as members of staff.

(f) Use of the 'two ticks' indicates an organisation's commitment to equality for people with disabilities. This symbol enables employers to demonstrate their willingness to recruit disabled people. To qualify to use the symbol, employers must do the following.

(i) Offer an interview to any disabled job applicant who meets the basic criteria for a particular job, and consider him or her for employment on his or her abilities.

(ii) Consult all disabled employees about their career development at least once a year.

(iii) Do everything possible to retain employees who become disabled.

(iv) Review their own action and achievements annually and, at the same time, plan future measures.

(v) Encourage and develop awareness about disability within the organisation to ensure that all commitments are fulfilled. (Information about the symbol can be obtained from Disability Employment Advisers who are based at job centres.)

Key point: Recruitment innovation customised to the company's profile and area of operation can be an important start in attracting a diverse range of candidates. Such initiatives can begin to produce a profile for a company of being an attractive place to work for all diverse groups.

Flexibility in Working Arrangements

There are a number of flexible working arrangements which will help attract and retain a range of applicants. Important arrangements include job shares and part-time working.

Job shares and part-time working

Job sharing is where two or more people share the responsibility for one full-time job. The pay and benefits of the full-time job are shared on a pro rata basis. Jobs can be shared on a daily basis (with one partner working mornings and the other working afternoons) or on a weekly basis (with partners working half a week each). Another option would be for partners to work alternate weeks. There is often a changeover period when both are present.

Key point: Through job sharing an employer can obtain a wider range of skills and experience than would be possible with a single employee.

Importantly, job sharing can increase access to more skilled and rewarding work for people who are only able, or who only wish, to work reduced hours. For example, single parents, people with disabilities, those caring for dependants and those nearing retirement age.

Job sharing is distinct from part-time work. Part-time work occurs when a particular function which the employer requires to be carried out does not amount to full-time work, and one person is employed on reduced hours to undertake the whole job. Salary, leave and benefits are calculated on a pro rata basis. Part-time work should be equally available to both men and women. Part-time staff (including those who work as job sharers) have the same rights as full-time staff and should be offered the same terms, conditions and access to training and promotion.

The Department of Trade and Industry (DTI) provides guidance for employers on part-time work and job-share arrangements.[4] Employers need to ask the following questions.

- Does someone need to be present in the post during all hours of work?

- Can the post be filled by a job share?

- Is there a suitable candidate for a job share or could someone be recruited?

- Can all the work be done in the hours requested?

- Can the work be re-defined to make it easier to do on a part-time basis? Is there another job at a similar level which the worker can do part time?

- How much will it cost to recruit and train a replacement if the worker leaves?

- What benefits would the organisation obtain from a part-time arrangement (for example, more commitment, retaining a valued member of staff, a better-skilled worker, a lower wage bill, staff cover for peak periods)?

- What is the effect of such an arrangement upon morale and commitment of other members of staff?

- Can other forms of flexible working (for example, term-time working or working from home) be introduced?

More generally, however, it is suggested that employers do the following.

- Maximise the range of posts designated as suitable for part-time working or job share.

- Effectively circulate information about vacancies.

- Consider measures through which transfers between part-time and full-time work can be facilitated.

- Monitor the organisation's use of part-time workers where possible.

- Ensure that training has been arranged in a way that is convenient to part-time workers and those on job shares. For example, it may be difficult for such staff to attend training courses if they have other commitments.

- For larger organisations where it is cost effective, consider providing childcare facilities on site.

It is essential that those applying for job shares or part-time work are not discriminated against and that an organisation's recruitment policies are used in the normal way.

Job Descriptions and Person Specifications

An important part of employing the right person for a job depends on having a clear definition of the job and the skills involved. A good person specification should also be concise and straightforward and link directly to the job description. A specification should define the knowledge, skills and experience a person will need, or be able to acquire, to meet the requirements of the job. It is important to spend time drawing up job descriptions and specifications as it will make comparison between candidates easier. It will also make it easier to develop effective advertisements, and can be used as a basis for the selection.

It is important that only requirements necessary to do the job are included, and this is particularly relevant in terms of disability considerations. For example, the requirement for a driving licence would exclude people with certain disabilities from applying, eg people with cerebral palsy or epilepsy. If driving is only a small part of the proposed job, and the prospective employee could travel by public transport when necessary, such a requirement might not be justified.

Recruitment Agencies and Head-Hunters

Many organisations use employment agencies and head-hunters to assist in the recruitment of staff.

It is important to ensure that any agency used is aware of, and understands and can act upon, the diversity approach and policy of an organisation utilising its services. Some head-hunting agencies may only use relatively restricted networks and contacts to attract candidates. Organisations need, therefore, to discuss their requirements and expectations in detail with such agencies, and to obtain evidence that these can be met in practice.

Summary and Checklist

Recruitment is an essential part of a diversity policy and approach. It is important that clear procedures are in place and, at the same time, are understood. It is also necessary to have the active involvement of staff. While this area will inevitably include detailed procedures and advice, this should not detract from it being seen as a practical part of a vibrant diversity approach and strategy.

- Review the range of publications or other media used to place job advertisements to make sure that they are reaching the widest pool of potential applicants for the jobs on offer. Ensure that the advert includes a reference to the organisation's diversity policy.

- Review the avenues used to recruit employees. Can they be widened to include non-traditional channels in order to attract a larger range of candidates?

- Monitor the success of an advertising and recruitment system. What is working and what is not?

- Following monitoring and review, explore innovative ways of recruiting. Exchange examples of good practice wherever possible with similar organisations and companies.

- Sign up to the 'two ticks: positive about disabled people' initiative.

- When drafting job descriptions and the type of person required to fill them, only include requirements necessary to do the jobs.

- Have a clear policy and approach in dealing with employment agencies and head-hunters. Ensure that they fully understand and follow the diversity policy and approach.

- Include a question on the application form asking applicants with disabilities whether they have any special requirements to facilitate the selection process.

The Selection Process

Success in tapping the widest pool of applicants must be consolidated by a fair and open selection process designed to select the best person for the job, irrespective of background, sex, race, age, sexual orientation and disability.

By ensuring that the recruitment process is fair and does not discriminate, employers can avoid the cost and bad publicity caused by employment tribunal cases. It also ensures that the diversity strategy is implemented in practice.

The process of selection is a crucial part of the recruitment procedure and also the stage where things can go wrong. Bias can creep in, as highlighted below.

- Standardised or agreed questions may not be followed, creating problems in comparing interviews. Where interviews are carried out inconsistently, more subjectivity will be encouraged and possible prejudiced decisions made.

- Some staff holding interviews may be unaware of, or not sensitive to, cultural differences or disability requirements and implications. They may fail to communicate with an applicant or interpret responses wrongly or unfairly.

- Interviewers may favour candidates who mirror themselves, and who have a similar social, educational and cultural background.

Dealing with stereotypes

Avoiding stereotypes is important, as is an awareness that everyone uses stereotype to one degree or another. Being aware of this and taking account of it is what matters. In one race case brought against a company it was found that Irish applicants, as opposed to others, had been asked questions about Guinness beer. The tribunal held that this would be interpreted as racial stereotyping in relation to alcoholism.

Dealing with such stereotypes is one of the major challenges in managing diversity in any workforce. As Daniel Goleman writes, 'Negative stereotypes can cripple (sic) work performance. To be successful in a job, people need to feel they belong there and are accepted and valued, and that they have the skills and inner resources to achieve, and even prosper. When negative stereotypes undermine these assumptions, they hamper performance.'[5]

Stereotypes can create an expectation of low performance which, though unspoken, permeates an organisation, creating an atmosphere which negatively affects someone's work abilities. Such expectations have the potential to cause levels of anxiety which seriously impair cognitive ability.

Some groups may be treated differently in what appears to be a positive way but is in fact negative, reflecting a manager's lack of confidence in dealing with diversity. For example, a black member of staff whose performance is not up to standard may not be questioned or 'pulled up' as a white member of staff would be. Different rules begin to operate in the way members of staff are treated by the manager. The manager may be embarrassed about dealing with performance issues with some black staff but perfectly confident in dealing with such issues with white staff.

Dealing with stereotypes is an important part of the diversity equation, and especially relevant with respect to the selection process. Stereotypes and views on differences between groups are usually based more on imagined characteristics than anything real. In fact, diversity is concerned with respecting and acknowledging differences, but not necessarily emphasising them. There is a danger that emphasising and exaggerating difference can lead to more stereotyping, not less.

Therefore, dealing with stereotypes should form part of a diversity training programme. The example set by managers and staff is also important. Their behaviour will reflect organisational priorities and the importance given to diversity. Core behaviours (and competencies) will include areas such as respecting, and relating to, people from all backgrounds, having sensitivity to group differences, and challenging intolerance and potential bias.

Short-listing and interviewing

Short-listing and interviewing should be undertaken by the same people. Short-listing procedure should include the following elements.

- A simple marking system to gauge how far each candidate has presented their skills and abilities to meet the job requirements.

- Consideration of each application against the requirements, in order of importance, and a mark/grade awarded accordingly.

- A brief review at the end of the exercise to ensure that marks have been given rationally and consistently, based on the evidence contained in the application. Skills and abilities can also be shown by experience gained outside the workplace.

- Open-mindedness. There should be no stereotyping or judgement of people by an interviewer in terms of himself or herself, or favoured image.

- Adjustments required for a disabled applicant to meet job requirements.

- Consideration of evidence directly related to the job and referred to in the job specification. The requirements must not be changed to ensure that someone who is favoured gets short-listed.

The job description, person specification and short-listing process provide a good framework for interviews. However, simply relying on interviews alone may not provide the candidates with the best opportunity to sell themselves, or for interviewers to assess them. Other methods of selection may be more appropriate; for example, the use of presentations, 'tests' and group discussions should be explored. However, it is important that steps are taken to ensure that these are not culturally biased.

Interviews

- It is reasonable to explore particular points with candidates and ask follow-up questions if an interviewer is unsure of answers given. However, it is important that the same topics and areas are dealt with by each of the candidates.

- A candidate's experience outside his or her workplace may be discussed but it must relate to the job. Candidates should be encouraged to give a wide range of different examples which show they can meet the requirements of the job. However, exploration of the candidate's personal circumstances, for example questions about marital status, is unlikely to be relevant to the post and can be unlawful.

- Unlike questions relating to a candidate's gender or race, questions about a person's disability are reasonable and not unlawful. Applicants can, and should, be asked direct questions about their disability, though this should not be used to discriminate against the person. Talking about the effects of a disability can help a panel to consider whether reasonable adjustments can be made, which may then help them to appoint the best person for the job.

Audit trail

It is important that, throughout the process, a clear audit trail is established and notes are kept of interviews, along with assessment decisions and sheets. By keeping such records, employers can ensure that they are making objective decisions based on demonstrable competency to do the job. It is suggested that records should be kept for a year after the appointment is made. In the event of a claim of discrimination being made, employers have the necessary information available to defend themselves. Lack of such material to back up the recruitment process does not impress tribunals. Absence of evidence to the contrary can lead them to infer that discrimination may have occurred.

It is also important that proper feedback is given to candidates, especially internal candidates. This should be seen as part of a continuing career and staff development programme. Above all, in implementing recruitment and selection processes, employers need to be confident that the following core areas are taken into account.

- Staff involved in the recruitment process should have been trained on the diversity/equality implications of the process, including potential bias.

- The selection process, including interviews, should be documented.

- Interviews and/or tests should relate to the job description and specification.

- The selection and interview process should take account of disability considerations.

- The results of the process should be monitored, and the process reviewed from time to time. This should include feedback from staff involved in the process.

MANAGING THE IMPACT OF AN ORGANISATION'S POLICIES AND PROCEDURES ON EQUALITY AND DIVERSITY

The following section discusses the impact policies and procedures can have on the successful implementation of the diversity strategy. One of the results of the Stephen Lawrence Enquiry was that organisations should examine their processes to identify areas of race discrimination. This concept can be applied to all areas of discrimination, across both public and private sector organisations.

This section does not describe how to conduct a procedure, instead it discusses how to identify areas of institutional discrimination within a procedure, and how to measure its impact on diversity.

Much discrimination can result from long-standing ways of implementing an organisation's processes, even though it may be believed that they are consistently applied to all employees. The implementation of the diversity strategy should allow for a review of all policies, procedures and processes which can affect the employment relationship.

Induction

The induction process is important in forming first impressions. It does much more than give information and training on the organisation; it is, in addition, a socialisation process. If the culture of an organisation is immediately hostile to women or ethnic minorities it can have an impact upon a new starter. Pranks or jokes can cause offence and it is important that awareness training covers this point. All team members are involved in the induction process, not just the line manager who has responsibility for covering job training. Training on the induction process should be communicated to all members of staff as part of their commitment to treating colleagues with respect.

A useful diversity indicator for the effectiveness of the induction process is to analyse the leavers' profile of an organisation and to track the length of service by age, gender, race and disability. Often, high turnover is attributed to poor selection; however, if the induction process is poor this could also be a factor. The statistics should reveal if certain groups of people are not staying very long. If the average length of service of young Asian people is only twelve months, compared to an average length of service of five years for young white people, the socialisation process of induction may need attention.

Example 5

If it is custom and practice for new starters to go to the pub for lunch to meet colleagues, managers should be made aware of cultural sensitivities on alcohol or dietary requirements. An exit interview for a local authority recorded one employee's reason for leaving as a feeling of exclusion from the team because everyone always went to the pub for lunch at least twice a week. The pub they went to, however, did not serve Halal food and, therefore, the individual did not go with them.

It is often these informal aspects of an induction process which can make a person feel uncomfortable. A useful part of the diversity research is to hold a series of focus groups to discover how different people feel about the induction experience. If the company consists predominantly of white males, such as the police force, it may be necessary to consider the use of mentors so that new people can have access to experienced people able to give them appropriate guidance and support. This information can help determine who is the most appropriate person to actually carry out the induction process. It may be necessary to choose a mentor who is sympathetic to a person's background or someone who has been suitably trained in the induction process. It does not, however, have to be a line manager.

Induction is not necessarily only for the new recruit. If a person has declared a disability at the recruitment stage, part of that person's strategy for coping with their own disability will be how they want to manage other people's understanding of their impairment and how they want to be treated. For example, if a new recruit has diabetes, this should be discussed in a confidential manner with the individual. If the individual wants to inform colleagues of his or her diabetes, the most appropriate way of doing this should be agreed. This might include the provision of information on diabetes and management of the condition.

Example 6

Marks & Spencer recruited a transgender person without discussing this with the team. Whilst the confidence and dignity of the individual must always be respected, the team should be prepared. It is better to proactively manage the situation rather than suffer the consequences of a staff backlash. Marks & Spencer suffered at the hands of *The Sun Newspaper* with headlines of 'Gender Bender', which damaged Marks & Spencer's reputation and were undoubtedly hurtful to the individual.

Example 7

B&Q employed a person who was recovering from chemotherapy, which had caused hair loss. The individual had chosen to wear a wig for a period of time. The first team brief was handled sensitively and the individual's circumstances were explained to the team. Within days the individual was so confident and at ease with the team that, in the staff areas, she removed her wig as it was hot and this caused some discomfort. With the full consent of the individual the store raised money for the cancer research department.

When organising meetings for new employees, timing, accessibility, food and dietary requirements, and language should all be considered. There is usually a requirement for new people to read all about the organisation. The induction process should ensure that everyone can access the information. It should also allow for a two-way communication process giving new employees the opportunity to share information on their needs. It is a good idea to have a feedback interview at the end of the first month, conducted by a person who is not perceived to be a line manager with influence over job security.

Key point: The induction process must be accessible and relevant, and should take account of an individual's needs. It should not be confined just to learning about procedures and job processes but should enable the individual to be welcomed into the organisation.

Managing the Appraisal Process

A powerful motivator for achieving success in diversity is determining individual accountability using performance appraisal. However, before doing this, it should be remembered that lasting change and commitment is only going to happen if managers are involved in identifying areas for change and in planning the changes needed. Furthermore, a term cannot be imposed on a contract of employment without ensuring training and guidance is given on equality and diversity.

There are two aspects to the appraisal process which can influence the success of the diversity strategy.

Firstly, by including diversity as a core component of personal development against achieving agreed diversity objectives, the appraisal process can begin to influence management attitude towards diversity.

Example 8

A B&Q store manager has the objective of ensuring that diversity awareness training is delivered to all people in the team. This measure is built into store standards which measure a whole range of performance indicators for the store.

Secondly, the appraisal can in itself affect the ability of an individual to progress if the process is potentially discriminatory.

Example 9

The performance appraisal may be used to rate an individual's ability to do the job and offer opportunities for promotion. If the process takes into account factors such as mobility and working hours, the process may be discriminatory towards women.

Used effectively, the appraisal process can be an excellent tool for mainstreaming diversity into an organisation. By including equality objectives into people's job descriptions, organisations can begin to develop systems for measuring managers' performance on delivering equality.

Example 10

Littlewoods managers are appraised on several equality objectives, including employee grievances, customer complaints and employee profile.

Example 11

The Sainsbury's employee attitude survey includes questions on equality and diversity. A manager's performance appraisal refers to these questions to ensure that people are managed with dignity and respect.

Specific objectives can be built into team objectives. If the diversity business plan has identified an action to recruit and develop more women into management, this action should be built into the appraisal process of all those people who influence the recruitment and selection process.

Appraisals can also be badly managed and build in stereotypes and discrimination. The *Race Relations (Amendment) Act 2000 (RR(A)A 2000)* recognised the appraisal process as a potential area for race discrimination, and part of the public duty is to monitor the effects of appraisal by ethnic origin. The private sector could learn from this example and ensure that there is effective monitoring of the outcomes of appraisals, especially if these outcomes affect pay and promotion criteria.

A number of tribunal awards have recently highlighted discrimination in bonus payments for women which were based on appraisal of performance, identifying a lack of transparency in the procedure which led to the discrimination. It is important that people's perceptions are taken into account when using performance appraisals to influence employment prospects. Negative perceptions can include the following.

- It is perceived as a top-down process.

- The process emphasises assessment rather than feedback.

- The process is not transparent.

- It tends to be an annual process rather than ongoing one.

- Managers are often poorly trained in appraisal techniques.

Often, monitoring statistics reveals an imbalance in the management profile of an organisation. If, for example, the majority of managers are white and male, it may not be appropriate for them to conduct the performance appraisals of a largely female workforce. Questions need to be asked about role models and reference groups. Managers in these situations may feel nervous about addressing potentially difficult situations which are outside their usual terms of reference.

Example 12

A white male manager in a local authority wished to address an attendance issue with a black member of staff. However, this issue was avoided by the manager for fear of saying or doing something that could be misinterpreted as racism. This scenario can result in problems being compounded and the appraisal being confined to safe areas only.

Alternative methods of managing the appraisal meeting could be considered; for example, using peers or specially-trained independent work colleagues from other departments.

Training must be given on how to assess the results of performance. For example, in some organisations a culture of 'presenteeism' exists. If working late is perceived to be an indication of dedication and degree of commitment, this may impact on women who are more likely to need routine working hours in order to balance family commitments.

The appraisal should be monitored in order to establish whether:

- appraisals are actually being carried out;

- there is a disproportionate number of women, disabled people, older people or ethnic minorities being excluded from training and promotion opportunities; and

- the outcome of the process is perceived to be transparent and fair.

Phrases such as the 'sticky floor' and 'glass ceiling' (see **CHAPTER ONE – WHAT IS DIVERSITY?**, p **15**) have in the past been associated with the appraisal process. The employee attitude survey should be looking for any indicators which might suggest this is happening. Succession planning schemes which operate by nomination and recommendation are clearly open to bias and allegations of discrimination. Even apparently objective methods, such as psychometric testing, can create a barrier where language, literacy and culture can influence the outcome.

Key point: Effective monitoring and feedback from the appraisal process is vital to the credibility of the process. Staff attitude surveys and focus groups should be used to gather information on how the appraisal is perceived. The outcome of the process should be free from discrimination.

Religious Observance

An employer's equal opportunities policy may include a statement that the employer will not allow discrimination against employees on the grounds of religion. According to a Labour Research Department (LRD) survey,[6] 15% of workplaces had a local agreement on religious observance.

For some people religion is a very important part of their life, whilst for others it may be less important. Employers need to make sure that they place an appropriate level of importance on a person's religious beliefs or practices. The induction process is a useful way of determining this. Examples of discrimination on religious grounds can include:

- dress restrictions;

- working on religious holidays;

- lack of respect for, or ignorance of, religious customs;

- lack of prayer facilities; and

- discriminatory practices during recruitment (for example, holding interviews only on a Friday).

Time away from work may be needed by employees whose religious duties are not covered by Saturday, Sundays and bank holidays. This can include days off for religious festivals and time away from work during the day for prayer, or it may involve adjusting the working day to accommodate periods of fasting.

Consideration must be given as to how to manage the requirement for time off. For organisations operating seven days a week and 365 days a year, this is relatively easy to manage simply by giving an annual holiday allowance.

It is more difficult, however, to manage the weekly requirement for prayer.

Example 13

The Jewish members of staff will require flexibility on a Friday, especially when they have to be home before dusk in the winter.

Observant Muslims pray five times a day, and that may impact on work scheduling and meetings This prayer may only last five minutes but meetings should be planned with sensitivity.

Many problems to do with managing religion arise from a lack of knowledge. Raising awareness within teams can often help people find local solutions to managing time off. This knowledge will allow greater understanding in the management of policies. For example, an Orthodox Jew will need to take a week off work in the case of bereavement. The standard bereavement leave policy may only allow for two or three days.

Where accountability is devolved in an organisation and procedural compliance is less restrictive, it will allow managers greater flexibility in managing the needs of a team. Consideration should be given to building in optional, unpaid, leave days, which can help ease tensions on holiday requirements.

Key point: Knowledge and awareness training on religion will help managers to understand the reasons for requests for time off. Flexibility should be built into contracts to include procedures which accommodate individual needs, whilst ensuring equity in benefits concerning leave.

Dress Code

Dress codes can have an impact upon diversity management. Where health and safety is an obligation and employees are required to wear, for example, goggles, ear protection, hard hats, steel toecap boots, etc, employees are expected to comply with the requirement. However, there are exceptions to this. For example, a Sikh may choose not to wear a hard hat in observance of the requirement to wear a turban.

It would be sensible for an employer to ensure that when safety is called into question they investigate any possible reasonable adjustment. In the case of *BAC Ltd v Austin [1978] IRLR 322*, Austin was dismissed for not wearing safety goggles. She argued that they would not fit over her glasses. The employment tribunal held that this amounted to unfair dismissal.

There also needs to be sensitivity regarding jewellery. Married Hindu women may wish to wear a nose stud to signify their married status, and Sikhs, for example, may wear a metal bangle called a Kara or a dagger called a Kirpan under their clothing. Knowledge of such issues will help managers to respect this requirement.

In certain circumstances the *Disability Discrimination Act 1995* (*DDA 1995*) may also be a consideration. The Code of Practice on Rights of Access to Goods, Facilities, Services and Premises gives the example of a person who has a skin complaint which is aggravated by wearing a collar and tie.

A potential area of confusion could arise in the case of an individual who is going through the process of gender reassignment, or if a person is a transvestite. Under the *Sex Discrimination Act 1975* (*SDA 1975*) it is unlawful to discriminate on the grounds of gender reassignment, including when a person is undergoing gender reassignment. Part of this process involves the person living and dressing as a member of their chosen gender for two years before surgery can be agreed. This is known as the 'real life' test and will impact upon work. Organisations will need to approach this issue sensitively, especially if uniforms are worn or if the individual would prefer to continue to wear trousers.

In many cases, rules regarding dress and appearance are not based on any legal requirement. Instead they relate to what organisations consider is appropriate to both the business and the role of the individual. However, if a dress code is to be enforceable it should be part of the terms and conditions of employment. As with all such procedures it must be unambiguous and clearly communicated to all staff.

Key point: If the dress code is going to be enforceable it needs to be part of the contract of employment. This should be an express term and the policy should be written out in full within the staff handbook to avoid any misunderstanding.

Disciplinary Procedures

The disciplinary procedure can impact upon diversity by:

- reinforcing what behaviour is acceptable;

- dealing with discrimination effectively; and

- treating all people fairly and equally.

Enforcement of the diversity objectives through a disciplinary process is a visible test of how seriously the organisation takes its commitment to providing a fair and equitable employment relationship.

However, this must be balanced with an understanding of when to use counselling as a first step to invoking the disciplinary procedure. For example, if an employee appears to have repeated unexplained absence it may be sensible to explore the reasons for this before the disciplinary hearing. And, if an employee is experiencing depression or problems at home, the organisation may wish to accommodate these reasons.

The disciplinary procedure must have an appeal process. This process is likely to have more credibility if the appeal is heard by a panel of people who reflect, and understand, the individual's circumstances. This is especially important where translation or interpretation is required.

Organisations need to provide effective training on the diversity implications of disciplinary proceedings.

Example 14

A black employee of Pizzaland complained of racist and derogatory remarks which were made against her by colleagues. She complained to her line manager and no action was apparently taken. The employee experienced depression and subsequently took sick leave. Whilst onleave she made a further complaint which resulted in an investigation, but no formal action was taken against the staff. An employment tribunal upheld her claim for constructive dismissal and race discrimination.

Research by the Institute for Employment Studies (IES)[7] found that some racial bias can result from lack of confidence and experience by managers. They found that the following two approaches existed:

- avoiding the issue of discipline; and

- recording everything in a highly formal way to avoid allegation of bias.

In managing disciplinary procedures, it is important that the process is monitored for any adverse impact on equality. The *RR(A)A 2000* requires that the public sector monitors the use of disciplinary hearings by ethnicity. The private sector can learn from this example.

It is important that the disciplinary procedure is monitored to understand whether:

- appropriate action is taken against individuals who are guilty of inappropriate behaviour;

- a disproportionate number of a particular section of the workforce has been subject to the disciplinary procedure;

- managers who are enforcing the procedure have received training; and

- the appeals procedure is accessible.

Key point: Clear guidelines and training must be given on how and when to use counselling or a disciplinary hearing. Managers should not be expected to do this in isolation and a panel of people who are representative of the workforce provides for a fairer, more transparent approach to managing issues of discrimination.

Grievance Procedures

The grievance procedure is the formal method by which employees can raise complaints. This can be difficult for employees to do, especially on issues relating to discrimination, bullying, harassment and victimisation.

Many organisations have a well-written grievance procedure contained within the staff handbook. However, people may be reluctant to use the process if:

- they do not get immediate attention;

- no action is taken; or

- it is perceived to affect their career or job security.

In cases of harassment, it is important to make sure that managers who are likely to handle a grievance hearing are aware that it is the individual's perceptions which determine whether behaviour is offensive. This means that there is a subjective element to investigating allegations of inappropriate behaviour in relation to discrimination.

Example 15

An Asian female member of staff walked into a staff rest room to find her colleagues watching a comic video during a lunch break which contained offensive racist and sexist jokes. The TV and video were provided for the use of training material but it was accepted custom and practice that staff could bring in material to watch for recreation. This video, however, caused offence to the individual and therefore the matter should be taken seriously.

In some cases the procedure for raising a grievance can compound the problem. For example, if the procedure requires that the grievance be raised with the line manager in the first instance, this will not be appropriate if it is the line manager who is doing the harassing. Consideration needs to be given to allow a 'bypass' situation to occur which enables an individual to approach an appropriate person.

Harassment and Bullying

Harassment and bullying policies go to the core of a diversity approach and strategy. They cover how people treat each other on a daily basis, how they interact and whether they treat each other with courtesy and respect. Harassment and bullying in any workplace, if they are accepted or tolerated, constitute a negation of all the diversity approach stands for.

Sexual harassment in the workplace is already a well-established concept in the European Union (EU), with the European Community (EC) Code of Practice on the Dignity of Women and Men at Work defining sexual harassment. The code concentrates on 'dignity at work' and, as pointed out above, this is central to a successful diversity strategy.

Furthermore, change to UK legislation is imminent; harassment in the workplace will, for the first time, be explicitly outlawed under UK law. The revised Equal Treatment Directive (Directive 76/207/EEC), which will have to be implemented by 2005, defines sexual harassment and will require changes to UK law.

This is an important area where managers need to play a clear leadership role, develop confidence in dealing with cases, apply consistent standards and support staff who are potential victims of harassment and bullying.

All employers must make it clear to employees that harassment and bullying behaviour is unacceptable. Effective procedures must also be established to deal quickly and effectively with any allegations of harassment and bullying. A clear policy and approach needs to be agreed and members of staff should be made aware of their responsibilities within this policy. Often, in such a procedure, there will be an informal and a formal stage, with action being taken based on the seriousness of the case. Core areas for development include the following.

- A harassment/bullying policy which is understood by all employees and which is seen as an integral part of the organisation's diversity policy and approach.

- Employees' understanding of what is acceptable and unacceptable behaviour.

- Following up complaints of harassment/bullying quickly and confidentially.

- The need to train managers to enable them to identify and deal effectively with cases of harassment and bullying.

Example 16

The 'insignificant event': A small and perhaps even insignificant event caused a complaint to be made to a manager. The complainant did not perceive it as a major matter but felt that the behaviour was unacceptable and should be drawn to the attention of the member of staff. However, nothing happened. The manager might have even trivialised the matter and joked to other staff about it.

In the meantime, aggrieved by the lack of notice being taken of the complaint, the complainant began to notice other incidents and behaviour at work. Banter by colleagues, previously considered to be something which was put up with, or even joined in with, was seen to be offensive. Further complaints were made, but still no action was taken. The complainant began to be the subject of comment and innuendo and started to take notes of occurrences in the workplace. At this point the complainant spoke to the union representative.

Background work on the preparation of a possible legal case was begun, and only at this point was action taken.

A small, 'insignificant' case which was not immediately dealt with effectively by the manager had suddenly multiplied into a potentially major case, a 'cause celebre'. In this example, the company could not afford the bad publicity and the case was settled at a cost of £30,000.

Example 17

Racist graffiti: In a more serious case, racist graffiti was sprayed across part of a production line where predominantly Asian staff worked. Management arranged for the graffiti to be removed, but no action was taken in order to locate the possible culprits. No warnings were given about the unacceptability of the behaviour. The case hit the headlines, generating enormous bad publicity. The company, belatedly, began to explore a 'zero tolerance' approach to such harassment.

Example 18

Racist banter: In another case, a company had allowed a culture of banter and racism to develop, with managers of the section being unaware of, or choosing to ignore, what was happening.

A new chief executive was appointed, who was convinced by the business arguments for a diversity approach and wanted a policy developed in this area. A diversity review was commissioned where the views of staff formed an integral part of the work. The situation in the section was exposed, as were similar problems throughout the company. Management problems were highlighted, and many left their jobs. A comprehensive diversity programme was developed along with training programmes. However, it was recognised that it would take some years for any change to have a tangible effect on the entrenched old culture in some parts of the organisation.

Definition of harassment

Harassment is generally defined as:

'Unwanted conduct of a racial or sexual nature ... affecting the dignity of men and women at work.'[8]

Harassment can take many forms. Following are some examples.

- Verbal or written forms of harassment through crude language, offensive jokes, pranks, uneducated stereotyping, suggestive remarks, innuendoes, lewd comments, wolf whistles, gossip, offensive letters and offensive songs.

- Physical contact, ranging from unnecessary touching, patting, pinching or brushing against another person, to assault and physical coercion.

- Display of posters or pornographic material, obscene gestures, graffiti and offensive objects.

- Coercion, ranging from pressure for sexual favours to pressure to participate in political, religious or trade union groups.

- Intrusion by following, pestering, or spying.

Harassment is usually associated with race and sex, and most of the high profile media cases have been concerned with these areas. However, harassment also relates to issues of age, sexual orientation and disability.

In terms of disability, behaviour such as staring and/or uninvited touching, exclusion from social events, speaking to others rather than the disabled person directly, asking intimate questions about an individual's impairment and making assumptions about disabled people (eg that they do not have a social, sexual or private life) would be unacceptable. The following would also be unacceptable: physical abuse or intimidation, unreasonably questioning a disabled person's work capacity or ability by making inappropriate demands or requirements, and jokes and mimicry of the particular disability.

Definition of bullying

Bullying gradually makes an individual feel demeaned and inadequate. In order to solve the problem of bullying in the workplace it has to be recognised. Bullying can be described as:

'Any unsolicited or unwelcome act which humiliates, intimidates or undermines the individual involved and which is aimed at making the person feel worthless.'

Bullying is a sustained form of psychological abuse, which often emanates from a senior person taking what he or she feels is a strong management line with employees. There is, however, a fine line between strong management and bullying. That line is crossed when the target of the bullying is persistently downgraded by the person in a position of power, with the result that they begin to show signs of distress, and become physically or psychologically hurt.

Bullying in the workplace can take many forms, including:

- verbal insults or ridicule;
- direct verbal aggression and bad language;
- teasing or humiliation;
- physical assault;
- imposing unrealistic targets or excessive workloads;
- sabotaging a person's work results or deliberately impeding his or her progress at work;
- sending rude or intimidating e-mail messages;
- deliberately withholding work-related information, or supplying incorrect information;
- ostracising or deliberately ignoring someone;
- allocating menial or unpleasant tasks;
- blocking requests for leave or training/promotion opportunities; and
- unfair and excessive criticism from work colleagues.

The duty of mutual trust and confidence implied in the contract of employment obliges employers to treat employees in a reasonable manner, and to provide reasonable support to enable them to perform their duties. Placing unreasonable work demands on an employee, permitting bullying behaviour or failing to provide support could all amount to unreasonable behaviour in this context. Indeed, any behaviour that causes stress-related symptoms, or which has a serious negative effect on an employee's morale, confidence or self-esteem, is likely to fall into the category of unreasonable behaviour to the extent that the working environment becomes intolerable and the conduct amounts to breach of the employment contract. Such behaviour entitles the employee to resign and claim unfair constructive dismissal. If the behaviour also amounts to sexual or racial harassment, the employee may also have a discrimination claim and may win unlimited damages as a result.

Dealing with the problems of harassment and bullying in the workplace

A clear policy statement is an important first sign of an organisation's commitment to preventing harassment and bullying. The aim is to make sure that everyone understands the type of behaviour that is unacceptable and knows that effective remedies are provided. Such a policy may include the following.

- A clear statement of purpose and top-level commitment.

- Examples of unacceptable behaviour.

- Explanations of the damaging effects that unacceptable behaviour can have on the individual and the company as a whole, and why it will not be tolerated.

- A statement that harassment and bullying will be treated as a disciplinary offence with appropriate remedies, as will any false allegation of harassment and bullying.

- An explanation that such behaviour may be unlawful.

- The method an individual can use to get help and, where necessary, deal with the situation either informally or by making a formal complaint.

- An undertaking that allegations will be dealt with seriously and confidentially, and that employees will be protected against victimisation for making, or being involved in, a complaint as long as it is made in good faith.

- A declaration that it is the duty of managers and supervisors to implement the policy and bring it to the attention of their staff.

- A statement that every employee carries a responsibility for his or her behaviour under the policy.

- A statement that malicious complaints will not be tolerated.

Many organisations have now produced detailed policies on harassment and bullying. An example of such a policy is that of Harrogate Borough Council, which states:

'Harrogate Borough Council believes that all of its employees have the right to be treated with dignity and respect and that harassment and bullying is totally unacceptable. It will deal effectively with any form of harassment or bullying and take any steps it sees fit to either stop or prevent it.'

(For the full policy, see **CHAPTER EIGHT – MODEL POLICIES**.)

The policy goes on to provide details in respect of:

- the definition of harassment and bullying;

- the legal framework;

- providing a supportive culture;

- responsibilities under the policy;

- detailed procedures, including formal and informal action; and

- monitoring and review.

Dealing with complaints

The biggest challenge is getting those who are genuinely being harassed or bullied to deal with the situation. There must be a strong message that the organisation will take genuine allegations about harassment seriously.

Informal solutions

It is possible for some complaints of unacceptable behaviour to be dealt with informally. This can produce solutions which are speedy and effective. Whether or not the informal route can be used depends on the individual involved and the seriousness of the situation.

The decision as to how to move forward with a complaint rests with the individual; dignity at work is an individual right.

The attractions of the informal route should not be used to discourage employees from instigating formal action where it is the preferred option.

If the informal route is the chosen option, the employee has three possible approaches.

- The employee can raise the matter directly with the person who is creating the problem, and explain that the behaviour is offensive and making him or her feel uncomfortable.

- If the employee would find it difficult or embarrassing to raise the issue directly with the person creating the problem, he or she may wish to be accompanied by a colleague or trade union representative when speaking to the harasser or bully.

- The employee may wish to express his or her feelings in writing to the person who is causing offence.

Formal complaints

Formal complaints will normally be appropriate where the behaviour is totally unacceptable and the informal route would be inappropriate, or where previous informal attempts to resolve the problem have failed.

The individual should be assured that complaints will be handled professionally and with the seriousness they deserve. He or she must also be assured that complaints will be investigated thoroughly and quickly, at the same time ensuring that the rights of the alleged harasser or bully are protected, as well as those of the complainant.

Once the complaint has been put in writing, formal mechanisms for investigating the complaint, usually by an independent manager unconnected with the allegations, should be put into motion.

Checklist for investigating a complaint

- To ensure fairness the manager must not have had any previous involvement in the circumstances leading up to the complaint being made.

- The basis of the complaint must be examined to identify the issues being raised.

- Any written documentation provided by the complainant in support of the complaint should be examined. Details of incidents, informal approaches to stop the unacceptable behaviour and statements from other employees should all be recorded.

- The employee's personnel file and training record should be examined to obtain an overall picture of the individual, in particular reviewing any previous complaints concerning harassment issues.

- If the alleged harasser is named by the complainant, that person's personnel file and training records should be examined to gain an overall view of the individual and any previous complaints.

In making a decision, the manager or 'investigator' must, on the balance of evidence, decide if the harassment and bullying is genuinely believed to have taken place. If this is the case, an outline of the facts which have led to this conclusion is required. If it is believed that an act of harassment has been committed, an assessment of the seriousness of the case is required, and the damage it has caused, along with recommendations on sanctions to be made. If there are no grounds for upholding the complaint, the facts again need to be set out.

The key issue throughout is to deal with allegations speedily, objectively and effectively. Many cases also need to be monitored and data on this should be included in annual reports on the diversity strategy. Finally, training on harassment and bullying (covering, for example, what it is, what it means and how to deal with it) needs to be an integral part of a company's strategic training programme on diversity.

Key point: Dealing with harassment and bullying, and creating a culture where this is unacceptable, is a key part of a successful diversity strategy.

Work-Life Balance Practices

The Chartered Institute of Personnel and Development (CIPD) recently reported that three out of five employers have experienced difficulty in recruiting and retaining talent in the past year.[9] On average, labour turnover in the UK was 17.9% in 2000. Ernst & Young recently calculated that the cost of replacing a member of staff should be estimated at four times that employee's salary. This means that the annual profits of a company could be seriously reduced by failing to retain staff. In addition, a high staff turnover is likely to add to problems of staff workload and absenteeism.

If the diversity research for an organisation shows that labour turnover is a serious issue which needs to be addressed, further analysis needs to be carried out looking at why someone is likely to stay or leave employment. An increasing number of companies are asking these types of questions (such as Lloyds TSB, Barclays Bank plc and Nationwide) in order to try to understand the real cost benefit of having flexible working.

Graduates are a good litmus test for how the recruitment market is behaving. A recent survey of Master of Business Administration (MBA) final year students indicated that the ability to achieve work–life balance in their lifestyle would influence their choice of job; 90% identified work–life balance as a key factor in being committed to an employer.[10] A recent survey of 200 managers found that 70% of managers who already have flexible working policies scored higher marks on issues such as leadership, commitment and resilience.[11]

The following section looks at the cost benefit for organisations of having work–life balance practices and discusses the practical implementation of such policies.

The potential cost of not having flexible working practices

The Confederation of British Industry (CBI) believes that the cost to British business of employee absence is over £10 billion per year, or an average of £434 per employee in one year.[12] Employers believe that genuine sickness is the most common reason for absence but, increasingly, issues such as carer responsibilities, poor morale, personal problems and childcare are being cited as reasons for absence.

The Trades Union Congress (TUC) reported[13] that workplace stress caused by shift patterns, bullying and long hours is now one of the biggest health hazards in UK workplaces, and this is now a main cause of absence from work. Also, 70% of respondents to the then Industrial Society's survey[14] cited that a lack of balance between work and personal life is a major factor in occupational stress.

The Industrial Society (now the Work Foundation) reported in its manual, *Work-life Balance*, details of case studies which all indicate that flexible working practices have an impact on absenteeism rates. Lloyds TSB is a leading organisation in the field of flexible working. The organisation has a large workforce, which is mainly female, and an average rate of absence which is lower than the national average. It is estimated that achieving a 1% reduction in absence saves the business £10 million a year.

The UK has the longest working hours, especially for men, than any other country in Europe. A quarter of fathers work more than 50 hours per week.[15] A whole range of new legislation has been imposed on the employment relationship in order to help address this problem; including:

- the right to four weeks' holiday;

- the Part-Time Work Directive (Directive 97/81/EC);

- the right to maternity and paternity leave; and

- the Working Time Directive (Directive 93/104/EC).

Furthermore, the *Employment Act 2002* (*EA 2002*) provides parents with the right to request to work flexible working hours.

The above evidence is a compelling argument that inflexibility in people's working life is definitely leading to stress, absenteeism and resignation, and is frustrating efforts to recruit the best people. Yet cost is still cited as the barrier for almost three quarters of big organisations wishing to introduce flexible benefits, especially in the area of childcare.

The potential benefits of having flexible working practices

Whilst it is possible to cite the costs to a business of not having flexibility in lifestyle policies, it is also possible to find evidence of the benefits which such policies can bring. Lloyds TSB reported that the number of women returning to work after maternity leave has risen by 10%, saving the company £1.4 million a year in turnover costs; and yet cost is perceived to be a barrier according to a new survey published by the Daycare Trust.[16]

Nationwide Building Society has an average turnover cost of £5,000 for every employee who leaves. This cost is calculated from the training and recruitment costs for replacement staff. The company estimates that the 30% increase in women returning to work from maternity leave over the last ten years has saved the business

£3 million. Currently, 91% of women return to work after maternity leave. When constructing an argument for how much money to invest in such benefits, it is possible to calculate a virtually cost–neutral scheme.

As well as the direct cost savings there is an indirect benefit to the business. Lloyds TSB estimates that it has reaped the benefits worth £350,000 of good publicity from its approach to flexible working. BT was awarded the top prize at the *Parents at Work Awards* in 2001. The rate of women returning to work from maternity leave for the organisation had increased from 84% to 96%, because mothers knew that their family commitments would be taken into account.

Implementing flexible policies

Employers need to be more open and creative when responding to requests for flexible working. The gradual movement towards work–life policies and flexibility within legislation means that organisations are having to look more closely at working at home, job shares and flexible hours. However, organisations should be taking a more measurable approach to flexible working.

Example 19

Sainsbury's offers a range of contracts for its retail staff which helps students, for example, balance their need to work with the requirement to study.

Example 20

Asda introduced a revolutionary 'grandparent contract' to allow grandparents more time off for their family when a baby is born. The scheme allows grandparents seven days off following the birth of a grandchild; thus, recognising the growing role of grandparents in the childcare provisions of the UK.

A weakness of some work–life practices is that they still tend to infer that work–life balance is something only needed by women. However, the case of *Walkingshaw v The John Martin Group (15 November 2001) Case No S/401126/00* demonstrated that men too need access to flexible work–life practices. Mr Walkingshaw successfully argued the need to work reduced hours because of childcare needs.

In a survey of senior male managers a high proportion of respondents said that they felt unappreciated and resented the sacrifices demanded by the 'long hours' culture. Almost 30% reported problems at home and 20% said they turned to alcohol to ease the pressure of work.[17]

CASE STUDY: Assistance with the cost of childcare

The Government currently allows a net saving on National Insurance contributions (NICs) if the cost of childcare is paid as a salary sacrifice before tax and National

---

> Insurance is deducted. Few organisations, however, have been creative enough to take advantage of this scheme.
>
> | | |
> |---|---:|
> | If the purchase price of childcare is: | £3,820 |
> | National Insurance savings at 9% would be: | £344 |
> | Net cost of childcare vouchers would be: | £3,476 |
> | There would be a benefit in kind tax of: | £75 |
> | Overall cost of childcare would be: | £3,551 |
>
> This simple process would save an employee nearly £450 a year, which is equivalent to nearly five weeks' free care.[18]

Schemes like the 'Care4 system', offered by the Grass Roots Group (GRG), are virtually cost-neutral to the employer but can make a significant difference to the employee.

Work-life balance is simply about encouraging the employment relationship to become more flexible so that everyone can find the right balance for them to combine the need to work with their other aspirations and responsibilities. Organisations will need to look at implementing a portfolio of initiatives which will help overcome the problems of turnover and absenteeism highlighted above. These may include:

- part-time working;
- flexible hours;
- job sharing;
- paid family leave;
- returners' schemes;
- 'keeping in touch' schemes during absence;
- working from home;
- childcare support;
- weekly hours which can be condensed into four days;
- annualised hours;
- enhanced maternity and paternity leave;
- study leave;
- dependency leave; and
- religious observance.

The starting point for any arrangement is that any provision which retains staff is likely to save money. This should be costed to give an indication of likely budget spend.

Pay and Benefits

Equal pay and benefits are now a central part of the diversity agenda. There are good business case reasons for ensuring that pay (and other relevant benefits) is delivered on an equitable basis. These include, appointment and retention issues, impact on staff morale and the negative impact on organisations which have equal pay, or sex discrimination, cases taken against them. A number of global city companies have experienced bad publicity and high compensation awards due to lack of transparency in their reward systems. For example, in *Bower v Schroder Securities Ltd, EAT 678/01* a city analyst, Ms Julie Bower, was awarded £1.4 million in a sex discrimination claim.

Legislation

Equal pay legislation was introduced in the UK as long ago as 1970, in the form of the *Equal Pay Act 1970 (EPA 1970)*. EC law also covers equal pay, and Article 141 of the EC Treaty requires that men and women should receive equal pay for equal work.

The legislation applies only to inequality in pay between women and men. There is currently no equivalent legislation applying to other disadvantaged groups. However, there is evidence of pay and benefits inequality in relation to other groups. A TUC report, *Black and Underpaid* (available on the TUC website at www.tuc.org.uk), highlights that black and Asian male workers are earning up to £150 a week less than their white counterparts. The TUC believes that employers should be encouraged to use equal pay reviews to monitor pay data for black workers. It also wants the law changed to allow trade unions and the CRE to take collective cases in relation to pay, as it believes that group action would speed up the legal process.

In relation to lesbians and gay men, there is widespread discrimination in the way in which benefits, such a pensions and travel concessions, are offered as they are available only to partners of the opposite sex.

However, it is still sex discrimination which has attracted much attention. The TUC has mounted a continuing campaign to educate members about evaluating equal pay by running equal pay seminars around the country for trade union officials. This followed on from the report, *Just Pay*, by the EOC's Task Force on Equal Pay published in February in 2001. It recommended that employers, large and small, should be required to conduct compulsory pay reviews in order to establish whether there are gender pay inequalities and to adopt an action plan to deal with any such inequality. The Government refused to legislate in response to the recommendations of this report, but set up its own inquiry into women's pay and employment, the *Kingsmill Review*. The brief for this review was to find 'non-legislative and cost-effective' ways of delivering equal pay. Despite this brief, however, the *Kingsmill Review* does state that systematic employment and pay reviews are 'an essential first step' to improving women's pay.

The Government has supported a number of voluntary measures to tackle inequality in pay between women and men, including:

- allowing groups of workers involved in the same equal pay case to make a single claim;

- introducing a new questionnaire to enable women to obtain key information from their employers when deciding whether to bring an equal pay claim;

- training trade union officials to carry out equal pay reviews at companies;

- the introduction of the *Castle Awards* for employers who undertake and act on voluntary pay reviews;

- the creation of 'fair pay champions' who will publicly promote the benefits of equality; and

- government departments and agencies reviewing their pay systems by April 2003 and preparing action plans to reduce any gender pay gaps.

Furthermore, the Government made additional funding available to the EOC. The EOC developed an Equal Pay Kit, which is a tool to be used by employers in order to facilitate equal pay reviews.

What do employers need to do?

Assessing the area of equal pay, especially when comparing a range of jobs, is potentially complex and challenging. However, the work of the Equal Pay Task Force has helped to define the relevant issues and factors, and has also very usefully outlined a tiered, or phased, approach to carrying out pay reviews. This has now been backed up by the EOC's Equal Pay Kit.

The Task Force found that there were three main factors contributing to the gender pay gap:

- discrimination in pay;

- occupational segregation; and

- the unequal impact of women's family responsibilities.

The focus of the Task Force was that part of the pay gap which is caused by pay discrimination. It is believed that this amounts to 25% to 50% of the pay gap.

The Task Force concluded that with a concerted effort by all key players, it is feasible that the gender gap caused by discrimination in the workplace could be reduced by 25% over five years, and eliminated entirely within eight years.

Key initiatives put forward by the Task Force to help achieve tangible changes include:

- raising levels of awareness and developing a common understanding of what pay gap means;

- reforming and modernising the equal pay legislation;

- capacity building to ensure that employees and trade unions know how to implement equal pay;

- enhancing transparency and developing accountability for delivering pay equality; and

- amending social, economic and labour market policies to complement equal pay measures.

The Task Force also provided an outline for carrying out equal pay reviews. The two stages are detailed below (Stage One is divided into two steps).

The initial part of any review, however, should be a simple and efficient check to assist employers in establishing whether or not they have a potential pay gap. The following questions need to be asked and answered with a 'Yes' or 'No'.

- Does your organisation have a stated policy on equal pay?

- Has the equal pay policy been communicated to employees and recognised trade unions?

- Has responsibility for the implementation of the policy been clearly assigned?

- Has a pay systems review been carried out, to establish whether there is a gender pay gap, in line with the EOC's Code of Practice on Equal Pay.

- Does the organisation use a single job-evaluation system covering all employees to determine who is performing equal work?

If the answer is 'Yes' to all the above questions, the key steps have been taken to address the matter of equal pay. However, if any questions are answered 'No', the organisation cannot be confident that it is an equal pay employer.

Stage one: is there a gap?

The Stage One review aims to provide a speedy check allowing employers to begin to establish whether they have a gender pay gap. This first stage is broken down into two key steps.

Step One: Check equal pay for men and women doing 'like work'.

Organisations should look at the jobs which are carried out by both men and women. They should:

- calculate the average basic pay and average earnings of (a) the men doing each job, and (b) the women doing the same job (if the hours worked are different, for example when comparing part-time workers with full-time workers, the average hourly basic pay and average hourly earnings should be calculated); and

- compare the average (hourly) basic pay and average (hourly) earnings of men and women doing the same job.

This process allows employers to see if they are awarding equal pay where men and women are performing 'like work'. Any pay differences must be based on facts that are free from sex bias, or employers may be vulnerable to equal pay claims.

Step Two: Check equal pay for work of 'equal value'.

If employers operate a grading system they need to:

- identify the grades of work being carried out by both men and women;

- calculate the average basic pay and average earnings of (a) the men in each grade, and (b) the women in each grade (where hours worked are different, the average hourly basic pay and average hourly earnings should be calculated); and

- compare the average (hourly) basic pay and average (hourly) earnings of men and women in the same grade.

Undertaking these comparisons allows employers to see if they are paying men and women equally for performing 'work rated as equivalent' or for work of broadly 'equal value'. For simplicity, averages are used to compare pay rates, although these may conceal inequalities between individual men and women performing different jobs, which are, nonetheless, 'equal work'. If employers wish to avoid equal pay claims, any pay differences must be based on factors which are 'free from sex bias'.

The Task Force recommends communicating the results of the Stage One review to employees and recognised trade unions. This information should be accompanied by a declaration from the employer stating whether or not he or she believes there is a gender pay gap, and signed by the chief executive. Once a Stage One review has been undertaken, the Task Force says it should be easy to repeat the exercise annually to allow trends to be monitored.

The Task Force recommends that an organisation should move to Stage Two of an equal pay review when, either:

- half or more of the comparisons undertaken in Stage One reveal gender pay gaps of 5% or more; or

- the review reveals any gender pay gaps in excess of 10%.

Stage two: equal pay review

The main purpose of a Stage Two review is to find the reasons for any gender pay gap and to identify how to close it. The diversity of pay systems in operation means it is not feasible to specify all the details of a Stage Two review; that will depend on the particular features of an organisation's pay system. However, the Task Force says that a full equal pay audit will involve 'detailed analysis of all aspects of an organisation's payment system'.

Differences in the average pay of men and women for like work, or within a pay grade or band, must be explained, and there may be a problem if the employer cannot give an objective justification for any pay differentials. Particular areas to watch for include the following.

- *Pay on recruitment or assimilation into a pay scale following a restructuring or regrading exercise:* Are new starters given a clearly-understood, consistent rate for the job, and are women recruited or assimilated into pay grades at the same points as men?

- *Red-circling* (to protect an employee's pay after he or she has been transferred to a job with a lower rate of pay, or where a job evaluation system has shown that an employee's pay is higher than other comparable workers): This can be a defence to an equal pay claim, but are men and women equally affected by red-circling? Is the period of time for red-circling reasonable and is the element of pay protection still a justifiable reason for the red-circling?

- *Incremental progression:* Progression through pay bands is often a factor in unequal pay. Where are men and women within the bands and are they progressing at the same speed? A cohort sample of graduates with five years' service may identify emerging differences in men and women's pay.

- *Market rates:* Market forces can be a valid defence to an equal pay claim, but do the premiums apply equally to men and women? Do they have a disproportionate impact on one group of workers and can the premiums be justified?

Equal pay is not just about wages, it covers an employee's total reward package. In addition to basic pay, employers will need to equality-proof all elements of reward, including bonuses, performance and competency-based pay, all benefits (such as enhanced pensions, company cars, medical insurance and childcare assistance), premium payments (for overtime, shift working, call-out), and broadbanding.

In considering these other elements of reward, employers are encouraged to ask the following:

- Do men and women have equal access to all these pay elements, and if not, can this be justified? If these elements do apply equally across the sexes, employers should then also consider whether they have a different impact.

- Do elements of the pay system disadvantage part-time workers, those on maternity leave or any other predominantly female group?

- Were the design and implementation of the pay system, and the associated criteria and rules, checked for potential bias?

- Has the pay system been communicated to employees and understood? Are rules applied consistently or is there an element of managerial discretion?

The above steps also apply to reviewing pay systems for potential racial discrimination, or discrimination against gay men and lesbians and other disadvantaged groups.

The EOC report says that answers to the Stage Two review will highlight the nature and extent of any gender pay gaps, and an action plan should be drawn up to eliminate discrimination within a 'reasonable timescale'. In all but the most complex of cases, it says that equal pay should be put in place within three years.

Increasing litigation

Given the activity by the EOC and trade unions in this area, an increasing number of test cases can be expected. While 'class actions', as such, cannot be taken, cases can be 'joined together' as test cases. This is undoubtedly an area for increasing litigation, and yet another reason why organisations should be carrying out pay reviews as part of their diversity strategy.

Other benefit issues

Apart from the issue of equal pay, there are a number of related benefit issues which are relevant. The range of benefits which form an effective part of a worker's 'wage' can vary from bonuses to car allowances, to leave arrangements, etc.

Other issues which need to be taken into account in this area include, for example, the following.

Performance-related pay and appraisals

It is important that there are well-designed and transparent schemes in place. Differential appraisal markings and their impact on pay are an increasing source of tribunal cases. Following are key issues which have been developed by the EOC but are relevant to all equality areas.

(*a*) Regularly monitor the distribution of appraisal ratings and subsequent allocation of performance pay increases by gender, ethnic group, job level (particularly female and male-dominated areas) and length of service.

(*b*) Make the results of the monitoring available to managers, employees and their representatives. This is likely to increase trust and transparency.

(*c*) Where monitoring results indicate possible discrimination, it is necessary to investigate the system to identify the source of bias.

(*d*) Regularly train managers in basic appraisal techniques, objective setting and sources of bias in performance evaluation.

(*e*) Ensure where possible that performance criteria are measurable and there is a balance between quantitative and qualitative measures.

(*f*) Ensure that criteria are not based on, and do not perpetuate, gender, race, disability, or other stereotypes.

(*g*) Include a formal appeals procedure for evidence of bias.

(*h*) Undertake a formal and comprehensive review of the performance pay and appraisal system at least every three years. This may include:

    (i)   statistical analysis of payroll data;

    (ii)   an employee attitude survey;

    (iii)   interviews with managers and employers;

    (iv)   making the results available to managers, employees and their representatives; and

    (v)   reviewing pay systems by conducting an analysis of employee's pay and other elements of remuneration with reference to sex, marital status, number of hours worked, grade, etc.

(*j*) Set up a system of regular monitoring to check pay practices and their impact on groups of employees.

(*k*) Provide guidance to managers and supervisors involved in decisions on pay and benefits.

(*l*) Formulate and communicate an equal pay policy in conjunction with employees and, where appropriate, trade unions.

Pensions

Ensuring that all employees have equal access to pension schemes and pension benefits is increasingly important, especially in the light of forthcoming legislation on age. It is also an especially relevant factor in relation to gender and disability. In respect of disability the *DDA 1995* provides that every occupational pension scheme is deemed to include an equality provision with regard to people with disabilities. Trustees or managers of schemes are required not to discriminate against disabled people either in the way they are given access to schemes or in the way they are treated as members of a scheme.

Conditions of employment: same-sex partners

Employers need to review their policies governing employee benefits. Where benefits, such as pensions for surviving partners of employees, health or life insurance cover, private medical care, relocation expenses, discounts and loans, are made available to unmarried opposite-sex partners of employees, such benefits should also be offered on the same terms to employee's 'same-sex' partners. Employers should also examine their policies on special leave to care for dependants and bereavement leave, to ensure that they do not exclude employees who have gay or lesbian partners.

Where such benefits are available only to married partners of employees, this could be unlawful discrimination against gay and lesbian employees, unless such a policy can be justified.

Termination of Employment

Managing diversity is just as important in the termination of a contact of employment, although typically this might not be seen as an area associated with diversity. However, there are two issues which should be considered:

- the effect dismissal will have on the employee profile, especially where large numbers of employees are concerned (in redundancy cases, for example); and

- discrimination in the process of dismissal.

Redundancy

The impact of diversity on managing a redundancy situation can be wide, not just from the risk of discrimination claims but also from the loss of expertise from staff. In some cases, the contractual rules governing the selection criteria for redundancy can actually work against the diversity strategy.

Example 21

The 'last in first out' policy at Consignia may undo much of the recent work to recruit more women and ethnic minority staff if this policy is applied in the expected downsizing of the organisation.

During the economic downturn in the 1970s and 1980s, many organisations opted to use age as a criteria for redundancy. The result was that many industries saw an exodus of knowledge which was difficult to replace (see CHAPTER SEVEN – CASE STUDIES ON DIVERSITY).

Any redundancy situation, especially those involving high numbers, should be assessed to see if it affects employees predominately of one group, which could be disproportionate and unjustifiable; for example, only selecting part-time employees, or selecting people on a 'last in first out' basis. The selection of part-time workers may be discriminatory on the grounds of sex, as most part-time workers are likely to be women. Employees who are made redundant for reasons connected to pregnancy, parental leave or for time off for dependants are now afforded protection under the *ERA 1996*. Selection criteria for redundancy must be carefully thought through and applied consistently to a pool of employees.

The process should:

- warn staff of the possibility of redundancy;

- choose a pool of employees for selection;

- agree criteria for redundancy;

- assess the criteria and ensure that they are objective and do not have an adverse impact on a particular group of employees;

- produce a profile of all the employees who would be made redundant, should the decision go ahead (to be assessed in terms of age, gender, ethnicity and disability);

- consider suitable alternative employment, including for those staff on maternity leave;

- include proper consultation;

- ensure that managers who are carrying out selection for redundancy are trained and understand the diversity implications of their decisions; and

- ensure an appeals procedure is put in place.

The criteria used should be made known to staff so that the process is transparent. It is important to show that alternatives have been discussed, such as part-time work, flexible working and voluntary selection. Evidence of barriers and discrimination should be assessed with the same vigour as the selection process. If, for example, a redundancy situation does occur and one of the staff selected is pregnant, the redundancy will still be fair providing the proper selection process and consultation has been carried out.

Dismissal

The tests for unfair dismissal and discrimination are different.

- In unfair dismissal claims, the tribunal will consider the reasonableness of the employer's actions.

- For race and sex discrimination claims the difference in treatment is critical. It is this comparison which determines if discrimination has occurred.

If the reason for dismissal constitutes less favourable treatment, a claim can be brought under the discrimination legislation. This is important because a claim under this legislation allows a questionnaire to be served on an employer which can be very searching. There is also no upper limit on compensation claims, unlike unfair dismissal claims which carry a statutory cap. In addition, compensation for injury to feelings and aggravated damages are also available under discrimination law.

The only way to safeguard against this is to ensure that effective training on diversity is put in place for all those managers who have the authority to dismiss. Managers must understand that dismissals on grounds of race, gender or disability cannot be made.

Claims under the *DDA 1995* differ from the *Race Relations Act 1976* (*RRA 1976*) and *SDA 1975* in that:

- there is no provision for indirect discrimination under the *DDA 1995*;

- discrimination can be justified in certain circumstances; and

- there is a positive obligation to make reasonable adjustment.

Where an employee does have a disability and this is known to the employer, all aspects of reasonable adjustment must be considered, especially where the person's ability to do the job is being called into question.

Constructive dismissal is not unusual in discrimination cases. Discriminatory conduct is invariably hurtful to an employee and can often lead to a situation where an employee would rather resign than continue in employment, especially if the grievance procedure has not helped resolve the problem.

Maternity dismissal

Some reasons for dismissal are automatically unfair under the *ERA 1996*. This includes dismissal on the grounds of pregnancy. Claims are, therefore, brought under the *ERA 1996* although the complainant can claim sex discrimination as well. For a dismissal to be fair, the employer would have to prove that the reason for dismissal was completely unconnected with the pregnancy.

Exit interview

Whatever the reason for dismissal, an exit interview is an important, but poorly-utilised, method of gaining feedback which will provide anecdotal information to help analyse statistical data about leavers. It can be useful to have an external consultant, or person who is perceived to be impartial, conducting the exit interview. Information which helps to explain why people are leaving the organisation will also help to decide what diversity solutions would be most effective in reducing labour turnover costs. The employee's reason for leaving should be categorised, recorded and analysed against the employment profile.

DELIVERING TRAINING TO ENSURE COMMITMENT TO A DIVERSE WORKFORCE

Diversity training is a fundamental part of delivering the diversity strategy. It has several functions.

- It provides an opportunity to communicate, inform and educate employees at all levels.

- Training increases knowledge and awareness, which can prevent problems from arising.

- It allows skills to be developed at all levels, which ensure the effective implementation of the diversity action plans.

When designing the training it is important that the reasons for the training are thoroughly worked out and that measurable outcomes are identified. One weakness with training is that it is often delivered in an ad hoc fashion, with little thought to the sustainability of knowledge levels. Training must also be given in order to back up the knowledge needed to implement those policies and practices which impact upon diversity, such as recruitment, performance appraisals and dismissals.

For example, if an organisation has had an issue with sexual harassment and dignity at work, there are clear reasons for implementing specific training and these reasons can be communicated. The measurable outcome would be a decrease in the number of complaints of sexual harassment. However, more generic awareness training will need a more generic communication campaign.

The following guidelines should be used when designing diversity training.

- Determine the training objectives – What do people need to know and why?

- Conduct a training needs analysis – What knowledge exists and where are the gaps?

- Make sure the timing is right – Will the training be given the profile it needs?

- Test the initiative before rolling it out – Has the administrative process been thought out?

- Decide who should receive the training – Beware of selective training.

- Measure the outcomes – Validation will help sustain change.

Diversity awareness training should be delivered in steps. It should be seen as an ongoing process to change the behaviour of an organisation. A continuous message is better than delivering all the knowledge in one go.

Example 22

The Army conducted a training needs analysis, and reviewed all its equality training. A fundamental conclusion was that a progressive learning approach was needed for new recruits who should be able to recognise what they had to do during their first training year through to an annual refresher course which moved the knowledge of new recruits from recognition of what diversity means to being able to explain and understand how diversity can impact upon combat effectiveness once they are trained soldiers. This will enable the Army to constantly update and reinforce the diversity message.

When designing course content the first step should be to deliver knowledge and facts on diversity to all staff. This initial step serves as a foundation which can be built upon. If it is assumed that most discrimination takes place because of lack of knowledge, or incorrect assumptions, this raising of awareness can help to stimulate thought and discussion. This step is as much about communication and language as it is about training.

The second step is to deliver specific training designed to improve certain processes of an organisation; for example, more in-depth awareness of the recruitment and selection process. This can be targeted at smaller groups of people.

There are some basic issues which can have a negative impact on diversity awareness training.

- *Poor timing:* The training must not clash with more urgent training or busy periods. Nor should it be launched during periods of redundancy because of fears and anxiety which may exist in the workforce.

- *Objection:* If it is known that a backlash might occur, people should be involved in the design of the training. Focus groups could be used to understand people's views and opinions.

- *Reasons for the training:* The perception that training is something which the organisation has to do, and that it is simply 'lip service' to pacify the legal department or external pressure, should be avoided if possible.

- *Training approach:* The training should be delivered in a method which most people will enjoy. Distance learning and use of the intranet can help alleviate problems caused by taking people out of the workplace for training.

A whole range of creative learning techniques is available, such as:

- distance learning (workbooks, CD–ROM, intranet);
- classroom style teaching; and
- awareness debates.

The method of training chosen should be capable of delivering the training objectives. By delivering knowledge to the whole organisation, distance learning, 'desk drops', team briefings and newsletters can all help start the process of raising awareness.

Validation should be built into the training methodology. This can be done by measuring a range of benchmarks before the diversity training is launched and tracking any change as the training moves forward.

For example, a range of issues, which can indicate the effectiveness of diversity management, can be measured, such as:

- responses from staff attitude surveys on issues of respect and dignity at work;
- number of staff complaints;
- staff turnover;
- problems arising from recruitment;
- changes to the staff profile; and
- customer feedback.

Key point: The training objectives should help to identify the measurable outcomes. Training should be linked to the business plan and be able to demonstrate a benefit.

EFFECTIVE COMMUNICATION

Effective communication of the diversity strategy and business plan to all employees has to be the starting point for the implementation of diversity, as this raises expectations, increases employee knowledge and demands certain standards from the employment relationship. Communication is central to the success of the diversity strategy as it is the means of engaging staff at all levels to embrace diversity. How the messages are reinforced is very important.

When designing a communication campaign it is important to find out why people in the target audience think diversity is important. This will help determine the main messages. For example, if it is the moral case which is important to people in frontline roles, this should be the message which drives the communication strategy. There is little point in listing the business case benefits to all staff if this is not the key issue for people. The style of communication will have to be varied for each target audience.

Sustainability is also crucial when developing the communication strategy. Thought should be given as to how the key message can be regularly communicated in a way which reinforces the main messages and objectives of the diversity strategy. However, it is not just the main communication drive which is important. The key messages of diversity should start to influence all the communication media. Employees will see external advertising which is aimed at customers. If the same message of respect for people and diversity is not evident in the external adverts, employees may develop a sense of 'lip service' to diversity.

Example 23

The B&Q TV adverts for products convey the same images of respect for diversity in people that its internal messages convey.

Example 24

HSBC has an advertising campaign which recognises the 'local community' aspect of its global network.

It is also important to determine the most effective communication channels for launching the internal campaign. Some organisations already have effective team briefings organised, or have internal magazines or the intranet. It is important not to assume which channels will be effective. During the research phase of the diversity strategy, people should be given the opportunity to offer feedback as to how they like to receive information. The most effective strategies will use more than one method to constantly communicate information.

An important part of the communication strategy on diversity will be awareness training. Often the budget for communication and training can be combined to make one sustained campaign on diversity.

Example 25

ABN AMBRO have launched a 'desk drop' and poster campaign, designed to raise awareness of facts surrounding diversity as well as communicate the organisation's values on diversity.

In communicating policies and practices which impact on diversity, issues will be dealt with that can be personal and emotive. It is vital that key messages are reinforced with action and commitment. A policy statement on harassment and bullying, for example, must be backed up with a commitment to enforce the policy, should an instance of bullying occur.

CONCLUSION

The contract of employment defines the parameters of the employment relationship and sets expectations of behaviour. The terms of a contract can have a restrictive affect on the objectives of a diversity strategy if they are not written so as to accommodate the varied needs of employees.

The processes of an organisation serve to reinforce the commitment to diversity set out in the diversity strategy and business plan. It is essential that the diversity implication of all processes are assessed for discrimination and accessibility. If problems occur in recruitment, employment or termination which undermine the diversity objectives, the values of respect for people are likely to be viewed with indifference.

Organisations which have embedded diversity into all their policies, and adopted more flexible approaches to work–life balance, are more likely to gain a reputation as an employer of first choice.

- Recruitment will benefit from an organisation being able to attract a wider talent pool.

- Employees who are treated with respect are more likely to be loyal.

- Being able to respond to individual needs will impact on turnover rates as staff can be encouraged to stay in employment.

- Less time and money will be spent managing damaging discrimination claims.

CHECKLIST

✔ Do you understand the factors which can affect the implementation and management of diversity?

✔ Can you identify performance indicators for diversity?

✔ Do you understand the employment relationship and the impact of terms and conditions on diversity?

✔ Do you know how to be an employer of first choice for a diverse range of applicants?

✔ Can you identify the role of an organisation's processes in managing diversity?

✔ Do you recognise the impact of pay and benefits on diversity?

✔ Do you appreciate the need for work–life balance practices?

✔ Can you deliver training and development for a diverse workforce?

✔ Do you know how to effectively communicate the values of diversity?

References

1. Fowler A, Decentralisation and Devolution: The Impact on Equal opportunities at Work of Equal Opportunities, Wainwright Trust (June 1997).
2. See 1.
3. See 1.
4. Department of Trade and Industry website, www.dti.gov.uk/er/inform.htm.
5. Goleman D, *Emotional Intelligence*, Bloomsbury Publishing plc (1996).
6. *Finding the Balance*, National Joint Council for Local Government (September 2001).
7. Institute for Employment Studies, Institutional Racism: Where's the Prejudice in Organisations?, Brighton (January 2000).
8. Government Consultation Document, Towards Equality and Diversity: Implementing the Employment and Race Directive (December 2001)
9. Chartered Institute of Personnel and Development, *Labour Turnover 2000*, London (2001).
10. PricewaterhouseCoopers, *International Student Survey Report*, (1997).
11. Knell J and Savage, *Desperately Seeking Flexibility*, The Industrial Society (2001).
12. Confederation of British Industry, *Pulling Together: 2001 Absence and Labour Turnover Survey*, London CBI (2001).
13. Trades Union Congress, *Focus on Health and Safety*, London, TUC (2000).
14. The Industrial Society, *Managing Best Practice Occupational Stress*, London, Industrial Society (2001).
15. Office for National Statistics, *Social Trends 30*, London, The Stationery Office (2000).
16. www.employersforwork-lifebalance.org.uk/docs/case_studies/cs_hsbc.htm
17. Trades Union Congress. *Focus on Health and Safety*, London, TUC (2000).
18. CARE4 product, The Grass Roots Group PLC, www.grg.com

Chapter Six
Diversity and the Law

OVERVIEW

This chapter covers the following issues.

- The main legal requirements which employers need to be aware of when implementing a diversity strategy (see p **155** et seq).

- Diversity measures in UK law (see p **159**).

- Sex and race discrimination (see p **160**).

- Equal pay (see p **173**).

- Disability discrimination (see p **175**).

- Adopting good practice (see p **182**).

- Work-life balance (see p **183**).

- Future developments in the law (see p **189**).

INTRODUCTION

When agreeing and implementing a diversity strategy and policy, employers need to be aware of the legal requirements in relation to a number of disadvantaged groups. Although diversity means looking beyond the separate groups, and ensuring that diversity is valued regardless of individual differences, the legal framework is, however, aimed at particular groups. The law sets out the minimum requirements which apply to the groups identified as needing the protection of the law.

SCOPE OF THE LAW

The law prohibiting discrimination is laid down in Acts of Parliament. The Acts define the grounds upon which discrimination is prohibited and provide a definition of discrimination. The legislation also deals with enforcement and remedies which are available to people who have been subjected to discrimination.

The Sex Discrimination Act 1975 and the Equal Pay Act 1970

The *Sex Discrimination Act 1975* (*SDA 1975*) and the *Equal Pay Act 1970* (*EPA 1970*) both deal with gender, while the *SDA 1975* also deals with marital status and gender reassignment.

Gender

Gender discrimination applies to both women and men (see *SDA 1975, s 2* and *EPA 1970, s 1(13)*). The *SDA 1975* does not apply to discrimination on grounds of sexual orientation, although this has been opened up to doubt following the implementation of the *Human Rights Act 1998* (*HRA 1998*).

KEY CASE SUMMARY: Gender

Pearce v Governing Body of Mayfield School [2001] IRLR 669

A lesbian teacher who was subjected to gender-specific homophobic abuse was not discriminated against on grounds of sex because she was not treated less favourably than a male teacher subjected to homophobic abuse would have been treated.

However, Hale LJ stated that had the *HRA 1998* been in effect at the time, the outcome of the case could well have been different. The *HRA 1998* could not, however, be applied retrospectively.

Marital status

Discrimination on grounds of marital status can apply to both women and men who are married. It is unlawful to discriminate against married men and women in favour of single men and women (see *SDA 1975, s 3*).

KEY CASE SUMMARY: Marital status

Hurley v Mustoe (No 2) [1983] ICR 422, EAT

An employer cannot rule out a class of employees (eg, women with children, married persons) because of a stereotypical view that members of such a class are unreliable. The policy in this case of not employing people, of either sex, who had young children was held to be indirect discrimination against married persons.

Bedfordshire Constabulary v Graham [2002] IRLR 239

Ms Graham's appointment as an Inspector was rescinded on grounds that her husband was the Divisional Commander. The Chief Constable took the view that she should not work in the same division as her spouse because she would not be a competent and compellable witness against her spouse in any criminal proceedings. The Employment Appeal Tribunal (EAT) upheld the original decision that this was both directly and indirectly discriminatory on grounds of marital status. The major reason for the decision to rescind the appointment was based on the fact that Ms Graham was married. She was treated less favourably on grounds of her marital status than an unmarried person of the same sex would have been.

As far as indirect discrimination is concerned, the proportion of married officers of the same sex, who could comply with a policy on conflicts of interest involving partnerships and relationships, was considerably smaller than the proportion of unmarried officers.

> From a policy perspective, the lesson here is that there must be compelling reasons to justify a policy which prohibits partners from working together.

Gender reassignment

The *Sex Discrimination (Gender Reassignment) Regulations 1999 (SI 1999 No 1102)* extended the scope of the *SDA 1975* to include discrimination against transsexuals (see *SDA 1975, s 2A*).

KEY CASE SUMMARY: Gender reassignment

P v S and another [1996] ALL ER (EC) 397

The European Court of Justice (ECJ) held that discrimination on grounds of gender reassignment amounted to sex discrimination. The *SDA 1975* was amended by *SI 1999 No 1102* to include discrimination on the grounds that a person has undergone, or is about to undergo, gender reassignment.

The Race Relations Act 1976 and the Race Relations (Amendment) Act 2000

The main piece of legislation is the *Race Relations Act 1976 (RRA 1976)*. It applies to discrimination on racial grounds. The *Race Relations (Amendment) Act 2000 (RR(A)A 2000)* places a duty upon specified public authorities to promote racial equality.

Racial grounds

Racial grounds are defined in *RRA 1976, s 3* as 'colour, race nationality or ethnic or national origins'. The wide definition given to 'ethnic origins' means that some religious groups have been brought within the ambit of the definition.

KEY CASE SUMMARY: Racial grounds

Mandla v Dowell Lee [1983] 1 ALL ER 1062

A group can be defined by its 'ethnic origins' where it constitutes a separate and distinct community by virtue of characteristics which are commonly associated with racial origin.

In this case, the House of Lords held that Sikhs are a group of people defined by ethnic origins.

Commission for Racial Equality v Dutton [1989] IRLR 8

Gypsies are an identifiable group defined by ethnic origins and, therefore, fall within the scope of the *RRA 1976*.

Seide v Gillette Industries Ltd [1980] IRLR 427

> Jewish people fall within the scope of the *RRA 1976* as they are members of a particular group of people defined by ethnic origins, as well as being members of a particular religious faith.
>
> *Dawkins v Department of the Environment [1993] IRLR 284*
>
> Rastafarians are not a separate racial group within the meaning of the *RRA 1976*.

The Disability Discrimination Act 1995

The *Disability Discrimination Act 1995 (DDA 1995)* prohibits discrimination on grounds of a person's disability. The meaning of disability is set out in the Act and applies a medical model of disability rather than a social model. The application of this definition is discussed below in the section '*What is the law?*' (see p **160**).

The Fair Employment and Treatment (Northern Ireland) Order 1998

The *Fair Employment and Treatment (Northern Ireland) Order 1998 (SI 1998 No 3162 (NI 21))* applies only in Northern Ireland and prohibits discrimination on grounds of religious belief or political opinion (see p **183**).

The Employment Rights Act 1996

The *Employment Rights Act 1996 (ERA 1996)* provides rights relating to work–life balance. It covers rights for women relating to maternity, including the right not to be unfairly dismissed on grounds of pregnancy. The Act also includes rights for parents relating to time off (ie paternity leave and parental leave). These help to provide a framework for work–life balance initiatives but, as in other areas of the law, they provide the minimum protection which can be improved by employers who wish to implement a diversity strategy.

The Employment Act 2002

The provisions of the *ERA 1996* have been amended by the *Employment Act 2002 (EA 2002)*. Most of the provisions are due to come into force by April 2003. The amendments include the right to request a change in working hours, improvement to the maternity leave provisions and the right to paid paternity leave.

DIVERSITY AND THE LAW

The law does not recognise 'diversity' as a concept, and the legal framework does not, on the whole, promote diversity. However, as has been seen, compliance with legal requirements is one of the arguments for an organisation to adopt a diversity policy.

Valuing diversity ensures that employers comply with the various statutes which prohibit discrimination.

Complaints verses Human Rights Model

Discrimination law in the UK prohibits discrimination and provides redress for individuals whose rights have been infringed. Enforcement of the law, on the whole, relies upon individual complainants taking their case to an employment tribunal. (This is subject to the powers of the enforcement agencies to carry out investigations into particular organisations/industries/professions and issue a non-discrimination notice where appropriate.) This can be contrasted with other jurisdictions (eg USA/Canada) where a human rights approach is taken. The right not be discriminated against is treated as a basic human right and can be enforced via the relevant human rights agency.

Despite the introduction of the *HRA 1998*, which incorporates rights from the European Convention of Human Rights (ECHR) into UK law, the right not be discriminated against is not protected unless there has been an infringement of one of the other rights in the Convention. This is set to change in the future, as the Council of Europe has agreed Protocol 12 to the Convention which will, when formally adopted, provide a free-standing right against discrimination.

Diversity Measures in UK Law

As stated, there is no law which *requires* a diversity policy. However, recent developments in the law show that there is increasing recognition of the need to value diversity. There are now areas of legislation which place a positive duty upon employers and service providers in relation to promoting equality.

The *RR(A)A 2000* places a positive duty upon specified public sector bodies to 'promote racial equality', not just in employment but in all aspects of the work of the organisation. An organisation which is covered by the Act must draw up a race equality scheme (RES), which demonstrates how the organisation is going to ensure that racial groups are treated equally. There are specific requirements relating to monitoring and reviewing the workforce (see CHAPTER FOUR – MEASURING THE SUCCESS OF A DIVERSITY STRATEGY, p **78**).

The *DDA 1995* requires employers and (from 2004) service providers to make reasonable adjustments to ensure that people with disabilities are not subjected to a disadvantage.

Future legislation is likely to follow this lead. The revised Equal Treatment Directive (Directive 76/207/EEC), which will have to be implemented into UK law by 2005, contains provisions relating to 'equality plans'; employers are being encouraged to review their workforce for gender inequality and to draw up appropriate action plans.

Key point: Employers who have adopted a diversity strategy which is properly implemented will be well placed to deal with all these aspects of legislation and to comply with the legal requirements.

WHAT IS THE LAW?

The *SDA 1975* and *RRA 1976* are very similar in their wording and approach to anti-discrimination, although the *RRA 1976* has been recently amended (by the *RR(A)A 2000*) to incorporate a more positive approach by public authorities.

As the *SDA 1975* and the *RRA 1976* are identical in many respects, these are considered together. The *SDA 1975* does not apply to discrimination in pay, however, and the *EPA 1970* is considered separately therefore. Discrimination against people with disabilities raises different issues from sex and race, therefore the *DDA 1995* is looked at separately. Religious discrimination is restricted to Northern Ireland and this is also considered.

The Codes of Practice issued by the Equal Opportunities Commission (EOC) and the Commission for Racial Equality (CRE) contain recommendations and guidance to prevent discrimination. They also recommend a number of ways in which to promote equality. These are highlighted where appropriate. The Codes are not enforceable but provide guidance as to good practice, and they may be used in evidence in cases brought before employment tribunals. Examples of good practice and sample employment policies can be found on the CRE and EOC websites (www.cre.gov.uk/ and www.eoc.org.uk/).

Sex and Race Discrimination

The similarities between the *SDA 1975* and the *RRA 1976* has resulted in employment tribunal decisions, and decisions by the courts, made under one Act being used to interpret the other, and comments made on one Act applying to the other, unless otherwise indicated. (The European Union (EU) law on sex discrimination has, therefore, indirectly influenced race discrimination laws in Britain.) There are, however, a number of differences between the two statutes, such as the scope of the legislation as defined in *section 1(1)(a)* of both Acts.

The *SDA 1975* refers to less favourable treatment 'on the grounds of *her* sex' (author emphasis), whereas the *RRA 1976* refers to less favourable treatment 'on racial grounds'. This has been interpreted in such a way that the *SDA 1975* is only applicable to the applicant herself, whereas this is not the case with the *RRA 1976*.

KEY CASE SUMMARY: Discrimination

Showboat Entertainment Centre Ltd v Owens [1984] 1 ALL ER 836

In this case it was decided that a white employee had been discriminated against following his dismissal for refusing to carry out an instruction to exclude black youths from an amusement arcade.

The definition of discrimination and the duty on public authorities to promote race equality

Historically, the legislative approach has generally been one of reacting to discrimination rather than promoting equality, and the legislation has adopted a complaints-based culture, requiring individuals to pursue complaints of discrimination rather than imposing any duty on employers to prevent discrimination or promote equality. Recent equality legislation has taken a more positive approach, however, with the *DDA 1995* placing a duty on employers to make reasonable adjustments for disabled workers (see p **180**), and the *RR(A)A 2000* recognising that steps should be taken to eliminate discrimination and promote equal opportunities. The *RR(A)A 2000* imposes a general duty on all public authorities listed in *Schedule 1A* of the Act to promote racial equality and prevent unlawful discrimination. All public authorities covered by the general duty must:

- carry out ethnic monitoring of applicants and existing staff for jobs, promotion and training;

- publish the monitoring results annually; and

- train staff in the new duties.

In addition, authorities with 150 or more staff must ethnically monitor:

- disciplinary action taken;

- grievances registered;

- training provided;

- performance appraisals, where these exist; and

- dismissals.

There are two main forms of discrimination recognised by the *SDA 1975* and *RRA 1976*; direct and indirect discrimination. Another form of discrimination is victimisation.

Direct discrimination

This is where a person from one group is *treated less favourably* than people who are not in that group, on grounds of sex (as defined in the *SDA 1975, ss 1(1)(a), 3(1)(a)* and

2A) and race (as defined in the *RRA 1976, s 1(1)(a)*). This is the most blatant form of discrimination.

The employment tribunal must decide whether an employee has received 'less favourable' treatment in cases such as those following.

- *Owen & Briggs v James [1982] IRLR 502*: An employer stated that he would not 'take on a coloured girl when English girls are available'. This was held to be direct discrimination.

- *Wylie v Dee & Co (Menswear) Ltd [1978] IRLR 103*: A woman was refused employment in a men's tailoring shop. This was found to be direct discrimination.

- *Etam plc v Rowan [1989] IRLR 150*: A man was not considered for a vacancy for a position as a sales assistant in a womenswear shop. This was also held to be direct discrimination.

Employers should avoid using ethnic or gender-based criterion in their employment practice as this will amount to direct discrimination, unless there is a *genuine occupational requirement* for a particular ethnic background or sex (see p **168** below).

When determining whether different treatment has resulted because of sex or race, the tribunals and courts apply the 'but for' test; ie would the complainant not have been treated differently *but for* his or her sex.

KEY CASE SUMMARY: The 'but for' test

James v Eastleigh Borough Council [1990] 2 ALL ER 607

A local authority allowed free admission to a swimming pool for people of pensionable age (ie 60 for women and 65 for men). This was found to be discriminatory as Mrs James, aged 61, was admitted free whereas Mr James, who was also 61, was required to pay. *But for* his sex, Mr James would also have been admitted free.

This leading case concerned the provision of services, but the test must also be applied to employment cases. Tribunals will ask whether the employee would have been treated differently *but for* his or her sex, marital status, race or ethnic origin.

Sections 1(1)(a) of the *SDA 1975* and the *RRA 1976* refer to a comparator. However, the phrase 'treats or would treat' means that a hypothetical comparator can be used. The comparison must be made with someone in a similar position to the complainant, as the Act seeks to compare like with like. The law recognises that some situations are incapable of comparison, such as pregnancy.

KEY CASE SUMMARY: Inappropriate comparisons

Webb v EMO Air Cargo (UK) Ltd (No 2) [1995] IRLR 645

Mrs Webb had been employed to cover for an employee who was on maternity leave. She was dismissed when she became pregnant herself. The employer sought to justify the dismissal by comparing Mrs Webb with a man on sick leave who would similarly have been dismissed. It was held that such a comparison was inappropriate, as pregnancy only affects women.

Indirect discrimination

This occurs where an apparently neutral employment practice has a disproportionately disadvantageous effect upon a particular group. Indirect discrimination is more covert than the direct form of discrimination and is intended to cover those situations where discrimination is institutionalised. The *SDA 1975* and *RRA 1976* provide that indirect discrimination occurs where an employer imposes a requirement or condition which applies equally to all groups but can be met only by a considerably smaller proportion of a particular group than the proportion of those not of that group. Statistical evidence is not required unless the employment tribunal would find it impossible to reach a decision without such evidence.

An individual member of the disadvantaged group who suffers as a consequence of the requirement or condition can claim indirect discrimination where he or she has suffered a disproportionate impact; unless the employer can objectively justify the requirement or condition on other grounds.

KEY CASE SUMMARY: Indirect discrimination

Mandla v Dowell Lee [1983] 1 ALL ER 1062

A school required boys to have short haircuts and applied a 'no turbans' rule. It was held that this requirement had a disproportionate effect upon Sikhs, as the number of Sikhs who could comply with the rule was considerably smaller than the number of non-Sikhs who could comply.

London Underground Ltd v Edwards (No 2) [1998] IRLR 364

In this case, changes to the rostering system resulted in all the male drivers (2,000 drivers) and 20 out of 21 female drivers being able to comply with the new rosters. The female driver who could not comply with the new rosters mounted a challenge. Ms Edwards, a single parent, was unable to comply with the rosters due to her childcare commitment. The Court of Appeal decided that the new system had indirectly discriminated against women, even though around 95% of the female drivers were able to comply with the system. The Court of Appeal took a wider view of Ms Edwards' position and held that, as it was generally accepted that women were more likely than

> men to be single parents, a smaller number of women would be able to comply with the new rosters.
>
> The definition of indirect discrimination has been subject to recent amendments. A definition of indirect sex discrimination was recently included in the European Union (EU) Burden of Proof Directive (Directive 97/80/EC); and the *RR(A)A 2000* includes the word '*practices*', which will allow a much looser test of disadvantage to be applied.

Discrimination by way of victimisation

Victimisation of individuals who complain of discrimination is a risk recognised by the law (it is defined in *SDA 1975, s 4* and *RRA 1976, s 2*). The legislation seeks to protect complainants from suffering *less favourable treatment*. This would include, for example, being dismissed, being subjected to disciplinary action or being denied opportunities for promotion. Valuable protection is provided for employees who may be in a difficult position making a complaint or bringing a legal action against their employer. Tribunals tend to award higher amounts of damages in cases where victimisation is proven.

Key point: A diversity policy should ensure that employment practices do not discriminate either directly or indirectly.

Who does the law apply to?

The definition of employment under the *SDA 1975* and *RRA 1976* is broader than other definitions and includes:

- employees and self-employed persons;
- agency workers;
- ex-employees;
- Crown employees; and
- police (although see the *Liversidge* and *McGlennon* cases on p **170** below).

Many of the exceptions to the legislation have been removed in recent years as a result of case law and the amendments to the *RRA 1976*. The main exceptions to the *SDA 1975* are:

- charities providing benefits to one sex only;
- sporting activities in which the average woman is at a disadvantage to the average man, due to physical strength or stamina; and
- insurance, where the discriminatory treatment relates to actuarial or other data.

The *RR(A)A 2000* prohibits discrimination in all public functions. This extends protection to a wide group of services, such as the police, customs and excise and the immigration service. As police officers are 'office holders', and not employees, they had previously escaped the remit of the *RRA 1976*. The *RR(A)A 2000* closed that gap in relation to race discrimination, but no similar amendment has yet been made to the *SDA 1975*.

Is intention necessary to prove discrimination?

Intention and motive have been discussed in a number of cases, and it is clear that the fact that an employer had no desire to discriminate, or did so for the best of motives, is irrelevant. The employment tribunal will look at *the effect* of the discriminatory act. A good example of this is the *James v Eastleigh Borough Council* case (see p **161** above) on direct discrimination, where the Council argued that its concessionary rates were for the benefit of members of the community who were less well off. The House of Lords found that, although the motive for the Council's policy was to be applauded, *the effect* achieved was discrimination and the motive was irrelevant.

The same principle also applies to indirect discrimination, as employers may apply employment policies which unwittingly have the effect of discriminating against a particular group. The law would be undermined if it was found in those cases that there was no discrimination simply because the employer had no intention to discriminate. This may seem harsh on employers, but the repercussions for the employer may be mitigated in the tribunal's decision as to the amount of compensation which the employer must pay the complainant. There is unlikely to an award for injury to feelings where the employer had no intention to discriminate. Indeed, in race discrimination cases no award for injury to feelings can be made where the discrimination is proved to be unintentional (*RRA 1976, s 57(3)*).

When is discrimination unlawful?

If a person establishes that he or she has been discriminated against, either directly or indirectly, he or she must then go on to show that the discrimination is 'unlawful'. This means showing that the employer's actions fall within the situations specified in *SDA 1975, s 6* and *RRA 1976, s 4*. These sections apply to discrimination before an employment relationship exists, that is, in the recruitment and selection process or in the terms offered, and include subjecting a person to *'any other detriment'*. Unlike most other employment legislation, the application of these statutes is wider and covers all aspects of the employment relationship, not just employees. The only difference between the *SDA 1975* and *RRA 1976* is that the *SDA 1975* does not apply to discrimination in pay (which is instead covered by the *EPA 1970*).

It is unlawful, therefore, for an employer to discriminate in a number of ways, including the following.

(*a*) In the recruitment process:

    (i)   in the arrangements made for the purposes of determining who should be offered employment;

    (ii)   in the terms on which an applicant is offered employment; and

    (iii) by refusing, or deliberately omitting, to offer an applicant employment.

(*b*) During employment:

    (i)   in the way an employee is afforded access to opportunities for promotion, transfer or training, or to any other benefits, facilities or services (note that any claims relating to contractual benefits are covered by the *EPA 1970* as they relate to pay); and

    (ii)   by refusing, or deliberately omitting, to afford an employee access to those opportunities, benefits, facilities or services.

(*c*) On termination of the contract:

    (i)   by dismissing an employee.

(*d*) Under the 'catch all' clause:

    (i)   by subjecting an employee to any other detriment (for example, sexual or racial harassment).

Protection from discrimination is, therefore, very broad and it extends across the whole recruitment, selection and employment process. It even extends to cover what may appear to be relatively trivial issues, such as dress codes (for example, not permitting women to wear trousers) and policies on hairstyle and jewellery (for example, penalising men with long hair or earrings). These policies may result in indirect discrimination on grounds of sex or race and, unless the employer can justify these policies on grounds other than sex or race, they will be held to be unlawful.

Key point: A diversity strategy must ensure that discrimination is avoided at all stages of the employment process.

Sexual and racial harassment

Neither the *SDA 1975* nor the *RRA 1976* refer to the term 'harassment', but the tribunals have recognised that such treatment could amount to direct discrimination. Detrimental treatment on grounds of sex or race, even if it is only on one occasion, includes sexual and racial harassment. 'Detriment', in accordance with *RRA 1976, s 4* and *SDA 1975, s 6*, has been interpreted by the tribunals as including words as well as physical conduct.

KEY CASE SUMMARY: Detrimental words

Reed and Bull Information Systems Ltd v Stedman [1999] IRLR 299

Mrs Stedman was subjected to suggestive remarks by her manager. She informed him that she was offended by the remarks and eventually resigned from her job. The company was aware of her situation even though Mrs Stedman had not made an official complaint. It was held that the test was a subjective one and if Mrs Stedman had found the remarks offensive, this constituted harassment.

Employers should take complaints of harassment seriously and adopt a clear policy statement condemning and punishing such behaviour, ensuring that employees are aware of the procedures for dealing with such complaints. Other relevant legislation includes the following.

- The *Employment Rights Act 1996 (ERA 1996)*: A claim for constructive dismissal may result if an employee with one year's service is forced to leave his or her job due to the employer's failure to act following a complaint of sexual or racial harassment.

- The *Protection from Harassment Act 1996 (PHA 1996)*: Criminal and civil action can be taken against a harasser within a six-year period.

- The *Health and Safety at Work etc. Act 1974 (HSWA 1974)*: Employers have a duty to protect the health, safety and welfare of their employees at work.

Guidance on eliminating discrimination can be found in the EOC's Code of Practice: Equal Opportunity Policies, Procedures and Practices in Employment (2000) and also the European Commission's Code of Practice: Protecting the Dignity of Women and Men at Work (1991).

'Even where a complaint is not upheld because, for example, the evidence is regarded as inconclusive, consideration should be given to transferring or rescheduling the work of one of the employees concerned rather than requiring them to continue to work together against the wishes of either party.'

A statutory definition of sexual harassment is to be included in UK law by 2005 in accordance with the revised Equal Treatment Directive (as indicated on p **190** below).

Other Unlawful Acts

Advertisements for posts are specifically covered by the legislation (*SDA 1975, s 38* and *RRA 1976, s 29*). An advert for a 'Head Waiter' without further reference to 'male or female' was held to have a sexual connotation, indicating an intention to recruit a man for the job. This was found to be unlawful (*EOC v (1) Masser and (2) Carriages Leisure Centre Recruitment [1991] IT, unreported*).

Informal methods of recruitment, for example by 'word of mouth', may be unlawful as this could result in some racial groups being excluded from the selection process because they would not hear of the vacancies. Where a member of such a group does hear about a vacancy, it could be found to be indirectly discriminatory. This raises a problem as far as the potential applicants are concerned, as they cannot claim they have been discriminated against if they have no knowledge of the vacancy in the first place.

Instructing or pressuring a person to discriminate, either by offering a benefit or subjecting that person to a detriment, is also unlawful.

When is Discrimination Lawful?

Justification of direct discrimination is not recognised by the legislation; however, the employer may avoid liability for indirect discrimination by demonstrating that a particular requirement or condition is objectively justifiable; for example, on economic or health and safety grounds.

Genuine occupational qualifications

Both the *SDA 1975* and the *RRA 1976* set out the circumstances when it is lawful to discriminate. These circumstances are termed *genuine occupational qualifications* (GOQs). They cover situations where the effective performance of a particular job requires a person of a particular sex or race.

On grounds of sex

It is lawful to discriminate on grounds of sex in the following instances.

- Where the essential nature of the job calls for a man for reasons of physiology (excluding physical strength or stamina) or in dramatic performances or other entertainment, for reasons of authenticity.

- Where the job needs to be held by a man to preserve decency and privacy because it is likely to involve physical contact with men in circumstances under which they might reasonably object to it being carried out by a woman, because they are in a state of undress or using sanitary facilities. For example, working in the changing rooms of a men's clothing store or in male toilets.

- Where the job involves living on an employer's premises which cater only for one sex and the employer could not reasonably be expected to provide separate facilities for the other sex.

- Where the job needs to be held by a particular sex because it is, or is part of, a single-sex hospital, prison or other establishment for persons requiring special care, supervision or attention.

- Where the holder of the job provides individuals with personal services promoting their education or welfare and those services can be provided most effectively by a particular sex.

- Where the job needs to be held by a man because it involves the performance of duties outside the UK in a country whose laws or customs are such that the duties could not effectively be performed by a woman.

- Where the job is one of two held by a married couple.

On grounds of race

It is lawful to discriminate on grounds of race in the following instances.

- Where the job involves participation in a dramatic performance or other entertainment and a member or a particular racial group is required for reasons of authenticity. For example, a film company requires a black actor for a multicultural production.

- Where the job involves participation as an artist's, or photographic, model and a member of a racial group is need for authenticity.

- Where the job involves serving members of the public with food and drink in a particular setting and a member of that particular racial group is needed for authenticity. For example, an employer could advertise for Indian waiters to work in an Indian restaurant.

- Where the holder of the job provides individuals with personal services promoting their education or welfare and these services can be provided best by a person of the same racial group. For example, a requirement for an Asian social worker to work for an adoption agency placing a high number of Asian children.

Where a GOQ applies, it is a complete defence to a complaint as the discrimination is rendered lawful (as in *Lasertop Ltd v Webster [1997] IRLR 498 (EAT)* where the EAT held that it was lawful for a ladies' health club to restrict employment to female staff).

Employers wishing to take advantage of the GOQs or other exceptions to *RRA 1976, s 29* and *SDA 1975, s 38* must state in their adverts the sections of the legislation which allow them to advertise for a particular sex or race. They must also give a clear indication as to why the exception is relevant to the job.

Special provision for training

It is lawful to take positive action to encourage people from a particular sex or racial group to apply for a job or training if they are under-represented in the organisation or at certain job levels (*RRA 1976, ss 37* and *38; SDA 1975 ss 47* and *48*). It is, therefore, possible to run a management-training programme restricted to female employees in order to address the gender balance of managers in an organisation, if the number of women carrying out such jobs in the preceding twelve months is comparatively small.

Positive discrimination

The law does not currently extend to positive discrimination at selection; for example, favouring female or ethnic minority candidates. The EU Treaty was amended in 1999 to allow some forms of positive discrimination, and this has been endorsed recently by the ECJ in *Lommers v Minister van Landbouw, Natuurbeheer en Visserij (Case C-476/99) [2002] ALL ER (D) 280 (Mar)*. Although the Government took advantage of the amendment to enact the *Sex Discrimination (Election Candidates) Act 2002* (which allows political parties to select women-only short lists), the Government has not indicated its intention to extend the provision further.

Who is Liable?

Employers are, of course, liable for their own acts of discrimination, and this can extend to both present and former employees as indicated above. Employers can also be liable for the discriminatory acts of their employees carried out during the course of employment, and for the acts of third parties.

KEY CASE SUMMARY: Employers' liability

Burton and Rhule v De Vere Hotels [1996] IRLR 596

The case was brought by two black waitresses who had worked at a hotel where the entertainment was provided by Bernard Manning. The comedian made several offensive remarks about black men's sexual abilities, referring to 'wogs', 'niggers' and 'sambos'. He also made insulting comments directed at the waitresses. The waitresses carried out their job under difficult circumstances but later made a complaint to the employment tribunal. The EAT subsequently held that the employer was liable for racial harassment as there was an element of control that existed over the situation. Managers should have been instructed to be on their guard and they could have allowed the waitresses to stop serving as soon as Bernard Manning became offensive.

Chief Constable of Bedfordshire Police v Liversidge [2002] ALL ER (D) 395 (May) and *Chief Constable of Cumbria v McGlennon [2002] ALL ER (D) 231 (Jul)*

In these cases a literal interpretation of the legislation was given when considering the liability of chief constables for the acts of other officers in their command. In both cases it was decided, somewhat controversially, that the chief constable of a police force is not liable for racial or sexual harassment of one officer by another. The EAT

---

in *McGlennon* did, however, agree that an administrative discriminatory act carried out on behalf of the chief constable could amount to vicarious liability. As was pointed out above, the *RRA 1976* has now been amended to close this gap, but the position still remains as it was under the *SDA 1975*.

Liability has been extended in cases such as *Coote v Granada Hospitality Ltd (Case C-185/97) [1998] ALL ER (D) 423* which widened the provisions of the *SDA 1975* to ex-employees. In this case an ex-employee who had complained of discrimination was held to have been victimised and discriminated against where the ex-employer failed to provide a reference. Although employment tribunals presently restrict this extension to ex-employees claiming victimisation, the revised Equal Treatment Directive, due to be implemented by 2005, extends the liability to all cases of discrimination.

Enforcement of the Legislation and the Costs to the Employer

Individual complainants

The *EA 2002* requires employees to exhaust the internal grievance procedure before taking their complaint to the employment tribunal. Since the *Employment Relations Act 1999* employees have had a statutory right to be accompanied at a grievance hearing where the complaint concerns a legal duty owed by the employer; this includes discrimination. Another alternative to the employment tribunal is conciliation through the Advisory, Conciliation and Arbitration Service (ACAS).

Individuals who wish to make a complaint of discrimination to the employment tribunal must do so within three months of the incident of discrimination. The EOC and CRE may offer assistance to individuals but, as the they do not have adequate finances to support all claims, or adequate powers to tackle the issue of discrimination at an institutional level, it is largely left to individual complainants. This means that the law requires an individual complainant to take his or her case through the tribunal system and the courts, by no means an easy option. Cases can take many months, if not years, to be settled. It requires a very determined applicant to see a case through to the end. Discrimination cases often last many days or weeks in the employment tribunal, which can be very trying for the complainant but also very expensive for the employer, as key personnel can be tied up in the tribunal, not to mention the time spent preparing for the hearing and the legal costs incurred (which cannot be recovered unless there are certain exceptional circumstances).

Questionnaire procedure

Both the *SDA 1975* and *RRA 1976* allow complainants to ask a number of questions of the employers/ex-employers. A job applicant who is not given an interview or not selected for the job can serve the employer with a questionnaire formulated by the CRE and EOC. Employers do not have to answer the questionnaire but failure to do so may be used against them. Replies to the questionnaire can assist a complainant in weighing up the evidence, ascertaining what is agreed or denied by the employer and then deciding whether or not to proceed with the case. It can also be used for cross-examination or comparison with evidence given at the tribunal hearing.

KEY CASE SUMMARY: Questionnaires

McCalla v Kerry Ingredients UK Ltd (17 January 2002) Case No 1402082/01

In this case inconsistent explanations, including misleading answers to the questionnaire, resulted in the employment tribunal drawing an inference of race discrimination by the employer.

The questionnaire and guidance notes included questions relating to the organisation's procedures for advertising, short-listing and appointment, and the breakdown of the workforce by sex and ethnic origin.

The Equal Opportunities Commission and the Commission for Racial Equality

The EOC and CRE play a crucial role in the development and enforcement of the law.

- They offer advice to potential complainants.

- They support cases which they believe will make some impact on discrimination law.

- They take legal action against discriminatory advertisements and against organisations attempting to pressurise others to discriminate.

- They also have an investigative role, with power to investigate discrimination in a particular field of employment or by a specific employer where there is evidence of possible discrimination.

Remedies

- Compensation. The main remedy for unlawful discrimination, as may be expected with a complaints-based system, is compensation for the victim of the discrimination. As far as the victim is concerned monetary compensation is the best he or she can hope for, although compensation is awarded in only a small minority of cases.

  There is no maximum amount of compensation which can be awarded. Recent years have seen record levels of awards; the most recent in 2002 being an award of £1.4 million for sex discrimination (*Bowers v Schroder Securities Ltd,*

EAT 678/01) and £815,000 for race discrimination (Chaudhary v BMA (19 June 2002) Case No 2401502/00).

- A declaration of the parties' rights in the matter, which simply provides vindication for the applicant.

- A recommendation that the employer take action to remove or reduce the discriminatory treatment of the complainant within a specified time.

Neither of the latter two remedies are particularly effective in preventing discrimination, as a declaration and recommendation cannot be enforced by the employment tribunal. In cases of non-compliance with a recommendation the tribunal is only able to award additional compensation.

Adopting good practice

In order to comply with the legal requirements and avoid high awards of compensation, employers need to adopt and implement employment policies and practices which promote and support diversity within their workforce. Historically, there has been no formal requirement to review and monitor employment practice. However, with the introduction of the *RR(A)A 2000* there is now a requirement for public authorities to monitor and review their workforce, and to put in place action plans for the promotion of racial equality.

In summary, employers should do the following.

- Introduce an effective equal opportunities/diversity and anti-harassment policy.

- Monitor and analyse equal opportunities policy and practice.

- Make sexual and racial harassment a disciplinary offence.

- Adopt objective criteria for recruitment and selection.

- Where possible, involve more than one person in recruitment and selection decisions.

- Avoid asking questions at an interview which could be interpreted as discriminatory.

- Avoid stereotypical assumptions based on sex or race.

- Train staff in equal opportunities issues.

Equal Pay

Scope of the law and definition of pay

The *EPA 1970* recognises the principle of equal pay for men and women in the following situations.

- Like work: Work of the same, or broadly similar, nature.

- Work rated as equivalent: Where a job evaluation scheme has been used.

- Work of equal value: Which can be assessed by an existing job evaluation scheme or by an independent expert.

In any claim, a comparable worker of the opposite sex to the applicant 'in the same employment' at the same time as the applicant has to be used. This has been subject to challenge recently in the case of *Lawrence and others v Regent Office Care Ltd and others [2000] IRLR 608* (see, however, the Advocate General's Opinion delivered on 14 March 2002, reported in *Equal Opportunities Review*, No 105, May 2002).

The definition of pay is broad and includes:

- pensions;

- redundancy pay;

- sick pay; and

- paid leave.

A great deal of controversy still surrounds the *EPA 1970*, and calls for changes to the legislation have been made in various quarters, including by the EOC. Although the Government recently rejected calls to extend the legislation, the *Kingsmill Report* on women, employment and pay encourages organisations to conduct employment and pay reviews (see **CHAPTER FIVE – IMPLEMENTING AND MANAGING DIVERSITY**, p **139**).

Presenting a claim

Employees presenting claims can do so at any time during employment and within six months of the last day of their employment. Claims have so far been brought by individuals rather than groups of workers, and some cases have taken years to resolve; for example, in *Enderby v Frenchay Health Authority and another (Case C-127/92) [1994] 1 ALL ER 495*, the speech therapist's claim took 14 years to complete. Cases generally, however, take an average of about 18 months to complete.

The *EA 2002* has introduced an equal pay questionnaire procedure to assist claimants in a similar way to the questionnaire procedure under the *SDA 1975* and *RRA 1976*.

Ensuring job evaluation schemes are free of sex bias

Guidance on avoiding claims of sex bias in job evaluation schemes has been provided by the employment tribunal in *Eaton Ltd v Nuttall [1977] 3 ALL ER 1131* where it was decided that schemes had to be:

'thorough in analysis and capable of impartial application. It should be possible to arrive at the position of a particular employee at a particular point in a particular salary grade without taking other matters into account except those unconnected with the nature of the work.'

An employer has a defence to an equal pay claim if he or she can prove that any difference in pay is due to a material factor other than sex. The employer must establish that a material factor exists; for example, the geographical location of the job or the need to pay market rates to attract particular skills or employees.

Payment systems must be open and accessible with objective criteria if employers are to demonstrate that their pay systems have been 'equality proofed'. The EOC recently launched a five-step Equal Pay Kit, which provides a step-by-step guide for employers on how to review their payment systems. It is hoped that the kit will raise awareness of unjustified pay differentials and that action plans will be drawn up to remove these inequalities.

Disability Discrimination

When considering disability discrimination, the common image conjured up is one of a wheelchair-bound applicant complaining that he or she could not get a job because the employer's premises were not accessible. Too often, an employer's initial response is to think about possible health and safety risks and the cost involved in making premises accessible by wheelchair. However, this reflects only a small part of the picture and the difficulties people with disabilities face, which are wide and varied.

Since 1995 legislation has been in place which prohibits discrimination on grounds of disability. Although this legislation goes some way towards promoting diversity (in requiring employers and service providers to make 'reasonable adjustments' to accommodate peoples' disabilities), there are still problems with the legislation. A contentious issue is the 'medical model' which is used in the definition of disability. An applicant has to establish that he or she has a disability within the strict requirements of the Act.

To promote diversity, a 'social model' of disability would be more helpful; ie, one which addresses the disadvantages faced by those with disabilities of whatever kind, rather than seeking to establish whether or not the disability has certain clinical effects. Employers who have embraced diversity need to go beyond the medical approach of the legislation and look at whether or not a disability, or perceived disability, has an impact upon an individual's ability to do the job.

The legislation, therefore, should provide employers with guidance to the minimum standards which should be applied. Promoting diversity will require a much greater appreciation of peoples' abilities rather than their disabilities.

The legislation

The main source of law in this area is the *DDA 1995*. This is supplemented by regulations, including the *Disability Discrimination (Employment) Regulations 1996 (SI 1996 No 1456)* (which provide clarification of the employer's defence of justifications) and the *Disability Discrimination (Meaning of Disability) Regulations 1996 (SI 1996 No 1455)* (which elaborate on the meaning of disability).

There are also Codes of Practice; in particular, the 1996 Code of Practice for the Elimination of Discrimination in the Field of Employment Against Disabled Persons or Persons who have a Disability. This sets out practical guidance on combating discrimination in employment. Although not legally binding in itself, it can be used in evidence in tribunal proceedings. In addition to the Code of Practice, the Secretary of State has issued guidance in the form of the *Disability and Discrimination (Guidance and Code of Practice) (Appointed Day) Order 1996 (SI 1996 No 1996)* which can help employers and employment tribunals in determining, amongst other things, whether or not a person's impairment has a substantial and long-term adverse effect on his or her ability to carry out normal day-to-day activities.

The importance of the Code of Practice and the guidance has been stressed by the EAT in *Goodwin v The Patent Office [1999] IRLR 4*, where it held that specific reference should always be made to any relevant provision of the guidance or Code of Practice which has been taken into account by a tribunal. It was also emphasised, however, that the guidance or Code of Practice should not be used as an extra hurdle over which an applicant must jump in order to prove his or her case.

The *DDA 1995* differs from the *SDA 1975* and *RRA 1976* in some important aspects.

- Whereas the *SDA 1975* and *RRA 1976* apply generally to everyone, the *DDA 1995* applies only to those who can prove that they have a disability as defined within the Act.

- The nature of discrimination against disabled people is different, therefore the definition of discrimination is different and it deals with discrimination for a *reason related to the person's disability*.

- There is no distinction between direct and indirect discrimination in the *DDA 1995*.

- The *DDA 1995* has a proactive element to it, in that employers and service providers are required to *make reasonable adjustments* to ensure people with disabilities are not disadvantaged.

Who does the law apply to?

The *DDA 1995* applies to the following.

- Job applicants and those already in employment.

- Employees with a contract of employment and self-employed who work under a contract 'personally to do any work' (*DDA 1995, s 68(1)*).

- Full-time, part-time or temporary workers.

- Contract workers, ie workers employed by the employer (usually an agency) but supplied under a contract to another 'employer'. This 'principal' is liable to the worker in the same way as he or she is to employees (*DDA 1995, s 12*).

- Trade unions, professional and employer organisations in relation to admission to membership, and employers (*DDA 1995, s 13*).

The *DDA 1995* does not apply to the following.

- Small businesses, ie employers with fewer than 15 employees at the date the alleged act of discrimination took place (*DDA 1995, s 7*), although this exemption will be removed by October 2004. In calculating the number of employees, all workers included in the definition in *DDA 1995, s 68* are included. However, there is no provision for the inclusion of workers employed by an 'associated employer'.

- Acts of discrimination after termination of the contract (see *Rhys-Harper v Relaxion Group plc [2001] ALL ER (D) 43 (May)*).

- Excluded categories, such as statutory office holders (including police officers), prison officers, fire fighters, and naval, military or air forces (*DDA 1995, s 64*). However, the Government has given a commitment to extend the provisions to certain groups by October 2004 (ie police officers, prison officers and fire fighters, but not the armed forces).

The meaning of disability

The *DDA 1995* applies only to a person who can establish that he or she has a disability as defined in the Act. This has given rise to a great deal of case law and much uncertainty. There are a number of elements to the statutory definition of disability, all of which must be satisfied by the applicant.

He or she must have had:

- a physical or mental impairment;
- which was substantial; and
- had a long-term adverse effect;

upon his or her ability to carry out normal day-to-day activities.

These elements to the statutory definition of disability will now be considered in detail.

Physical or mental impairment

This has proved to be difficult ground for an employment tribunal. Often faced with conflicting medical evidence, the tribunal has to decide whether or not the applicant does, in fact, have a medical complaint. The consideration of complex medical material is new to the tribunal and has given rise to some difficulties, not least in relation to mental conditions.

There is no statutory definition of 'physical or mental impairment'. Examples of common ailments which have been held to be physical impairments include:

- epilepsy;
- back injury;
- cerebral palsy;
- diabetes;
- migraines;
- dyslexia;
- visual impairment; and
- ME or chronic fatigue syndrome.

Mental impairment is expanded upon in *DDA 1995, Sch 1, para 1(1)*. It states that a mental impairment includes one which results from, or consists of, a mental illness only if that mental illness is a 'clinically well-recognised' illness. This means, according to the guidance, an illness which is recognised by 'a respected body of medical opinion', such as illnesses specifically mentioned in publications including the World Health Organization's (WHO) *International Statistical Classification of Diseases and Related Health Problems (ICD-10) in Occupational Health*.

Guidelines for establishing the existence of a mental impairment were set out in *Morgan v Staffordshire University [2002] IRLR 190*.

- Proof of a mental illness specifically mentioned as such in the WHO's *International Statistical Classification of Diseases and Related Health Problems (ICD-10) in Occupational Health*.

- Proof of a mental illness specifically mentioned as such in a publication 'such as' that classification, presumably therefore referring to some other classification of very wide professional acceptance.

- Proof by other means of a medical illness recognised by a respected body of medical opinion.

- Proof by substantial and specific medical evidence of a mental impairment which neither results from nor consists of a mental illness.

Substantial adverse effect

Even if an applicant can establish that he or she has a physical or mental impairment, the applicant must then go on to show that the impairment has a substantial adverse effect.

'Substantial' has been interpreted as meaning 'more than minor or trivial', rather than 'very large' (*Goodwin v The Patent Office [1999] IRLR 4*).

The employment tribunal must decide whether or not an impairment is substantial, taking account of the observations in the medical report (*Abadeh v British Telecommunications plc [2001] IRLR 23*).

Long-term effects

In order to fall within the definition of disability in the *DDA 1995*, the substantial adverse effect has to be a 'long-term effect'. It can relate to a current or past disability. The effect of an impairment is long term if it has lasted, or is likely to last, at least twelve months, or is likely to last for the rest of the applicant's life (*DDA 1995, Sch 1, para 2(1)*).

The long-term effect is determined at the date of the tribunal hearing and not at the date of the discriminatory act (*Greenwood v British Airways plc [1999] IRLR 600*).

Normal day-to-day activities

The impairment (which is substantial and long term) must also affect a person's ability to carry out 'normal day-to-day activities'.

The guidance provides that 'normal' does not include activities which are normal only for a particular person or group of people; the activity must be one which is normal for most people.

According to the *DDA 1995, Sch 1, para 4(1)*, an impairment is to be treated as affecting a person's normal day-to-day activities only if it affects one of the following:

- mobility;
- manual dexterity;

- physical co-ordination;

- continence;

- the ability to lift, carry or otherwise move everyday objects;

- speech, hearing or eyesight;

- memory or the ability to concentrate, learn or understand; or

- perception of the risk of physical danger.

The meaning of discrimination

Direct discrimination

Similar to the *SDA 1975* and *RRA 1976*, the *DDA 1995* prohibits 'less favourable treatment' (*DDA 1995, s 5(1)*) for a reason which relates to the disabled person's disability. The issue of an appropriate comparator has arisen in a number of cases and the 1996 Code of Practice (see p **176** above) states that:

> 'a disabled person may not be able to point to other people who were actually treated more favourably. However, it is still less favourable treatment if the employer would give better treatment to someone else to whom the reason for treatment of the disabled person did not apply. This comparison can also be made with other disabled people not just non-disabled people. For example, an employer might be discriminating by treating a person with a mental illness less favourably than he treats or would treat a physically disabled person.'

Duty to make reasonable adjustments

Unlike the *SDA 1975* and *RRA 1976*, the *DDA 1995* does not specifically refer to indirect discrimination. However, the definition of discrimination in the *DDA 1995* also places employers under a duty to make adjustments. *Section 6* of the Act refers to 'arrangements' or 'any physical feature or premises' which place a disabled person at a 'substantial disadvantage'. In such a case, there is a duty on an employer to 'take such steps as is reasonable, in all the circumstances of the case,' in order to prevent the arrangements or feature from having that effect. The *DDA 1995* was, therefore, the first piece of British legislation to impose a positive obligation on employers to take measures to prevent the discriminatory effect. (As noted above, the recent *RR(A)A 2000* has also adopted this stance in certain cases.) The employer has a duty to do what is reasonable; the employment tribunal decides what is reasonable in all the circumstances.

DDA 1995, s 6(3) gives examples of steps which an employer may have to take. These include:

- making adjustments to premises;

- allocating some of the disabled person's duties to another person;

- transferring the disabled person to fill an existing vacancy;

- altering the disabled person's working hours;

- allowing time off for rehabilitation or treatment;

- arranging training;

- acquiring or modifying equipment;

- modifying instructions or reference manuals;

- providing a reader or interpreter; and

- providing supervision.

In determining whether a step is reasonable, *DDA 1995, s 6(4)* requires a number of issues to be taken into account, including how effective the relevant step would be, the financial costs and the employer's financial and other resources.

The EAT has taken a fairly wide view of the extent of this duty.

KEY CASE SUMMARY: Duty to make adjustments

London Borough of Hillingdon v Morgan (1999) EAT 1493/98

The EAT made it clear that the Code of Practice (see p **176** above) had to be referred to when deciding what is reasonable. In this case, it was decided that the employer had failed to comply with the duty to make adjustments when an employee who had become disabled was not allowed to work from home temporarily in order to assist her transition back into full-time employment.

Wearing v John Miller (11 February 2002) Case No S/401464/2000

A maintenance engineer had worked for his employer for three months when it was discovered that he had epilepsy and he was dismissed. The employment tribunal held that the employer did not carry out a proper risk assessment and failed to make reasonable adjustments to the arrangements and physical features, including the requirements that he work at heights and on moving machinery.

Employment rights for the disabled are set to improve even further in 2004 when the requirement that those providing goods and services also make reasonable adjustments to remove barriers to disabled people is due to be implemented. The Government has also expressed its intention to impose a duty on the public sector to promote equality of opportunity for the disabled in line with that recently introduced for race. These changes have the potential to enhance employment prospects for the disabled.

When is discrimination lawful?

Although the *DDA 1995* contains a similar definition of direct discrimination to that found in the *SDA 1975* and the *RRA 1976*, there are crucial differences. The *DDA*

1995 allows the employer the defence of justification, which is not a valid defence to direct discrimination under the *SDA 1975* and the *RRA 1976*. Under the *DDA 1995, s 5(3)*, discriminatory treatment is justified 'if, but only if, the reason for it is both material to the circumstances of the particular case and substantial'.

KEY CASE SUMMARY: Justification

Baynton v Saurus General Engineers Ltd [1999] IRLR 604

In this case, the EAT stated that it is necessary to consider the circumstances of the disabled employee as well as the employer's conduct when deciding on justification. Baynton became disabled when his thumb was crushed in an accident at work and he was dismissed following an absence of twelve months. The employer argued that his dismissal was justified as he was unable to perform his job and had long-term absence. Any other employee, he said, would have been dismissed in those circumstances. However, the employee argued that he had been dismissed without prior warning and a few days before he was due to see his specialist when he hoped to be declared fit to return to work. The EAT accepted the employee's argument that the tribunal should take into account his position, as well as the employer's conduct.

Who does the law apply to?

The *DDA 1995* mirrors the provisions of the *SDA 1975* and *RRA 1976* regarding liability for the employer's acts and acts carried out by his or her employees in the course of employment. It states:

> 'Anything done by a person in the course of his employment shall be treated for the purposes of this Act as also done by his employer, whether or not it was done with the employer's knowledge or approval.' (*DDA 1995, s 58(1)*)

The cost to the employer

Enforcement and remedies under the *DDA 1995* are similar to those under the *SDA 1975* and the *RRA 1976*. The biggest remedy is compensation, and claims have soared recently. A record amount of £278,800 plus interest was recently awarded in *Newsome v The Council of the City of Sunderland (26 November 2001) Case No 6403592/99*. The DRC has recently argued that tribunals should be empowered to order reinstatement under the *DDA 1995* due to the difficulties disabled people have in securing employment. The Government is yet to respond.

Adopting Good Practice

An organisation's diversity policy needs to take account of the special requirements that people with disabilities might need. This means adopting similar good employment practices highlighted in relation to sex and race discrimination, but requires additional considerations in order to ensure compliance with the law. The

DDA 1996 goes further than the *SDA 1975/RRA 1975* in that it requires employers 'to make reasonable adjustments'. The minimum legal requirement is to make such adjustments where there is an individual employee (or candidate) who requires such an adjustment to be made. A diversity approach would mean an employer making adjustments in order to attract potential candidates, and not simply reacting to current needs of his or her employees.

Religion

Legislation covering discrimination on grounds of religion is presently restricted to Northern Ireland under the *Fair Employment and Treatment (Northern Ireland) Order 1998 (SI 1998 No 3162 (NI 21))*, originally contained in the *Fair Employment Act 1989 (FEA 1989)*. The legislation was the first UK legislation to impose positive duties and aims to reduce differences in employment levels between Catholics and Protestants in Northern Ireland. Employers are responsible for promoting fair participation, and they are expected to monitor the composition of the workforce and undertake periodic reviews of employment practices. If fair participation is not evident in the organisation, the employer must engage in affirmative action (not discrimination) to redress the balance. The legislation encourages contract compliance by public authorities. It is worth noting that the legislation has resulted in increased Catholic participation in the workforce.

Work-life Balance

The Labour Government has made clear its commitment to encouraging employers to recognise the benefits of ensuring workers can balance their work with other aspects of their life. However, the policy and legislation of the Government revolves around working life and childcare commitments.

This chapter cannot cover the detail of the legislation in this area. An outline of the various rights relating to work–life balance is shown in *Table 1* below. However, this provides the minimum rights to allow working parents to balance their work time with their parenting. A diversity approach would be much wider than this. Diversity recognises the needs of different groups, not just working mothers. Work–life balance applies to all working people, not just mothers. For example, older people may want to reduce their working hours as they approach retirement, workers may have caring responsibilities for elderly relatives or workers may want to spend some time taking up training/educational opportunities; it's not just about childcare.

However, as pointed out above, the law concerns itself with the rights of working parents, and the table below highlights the following areas:

- maternity rights;
- paternity rights;

- parental leave;

- flexible working; and

- adoption leave.

Table 1: Current and future rights relating to work-life balance

Legislation	Current law	Forthcoming changes
Maternity rights:		
The right to time off for antenatal care (*ERA 1996, s 55*).	1. No qualifying service. 2. Right not to be *unreasonably refused* paid time off to attend antenatal appointments. 3. Evidence of the appointment to be produced at the request of the employer.	None
The right to receive Statutory Maternity Pay (SMP) (*Social Security Contributions and Benefits Act 1992*).	1. Qualifying period: 26 weeks' continuous employment by the 15th week before the expected week of childbirth. 2. Period of pay: 18 weeks. 3. Amount of pay: six weeks at 90% of usual pay; twelve weeks at a rate equivalent to Statutory Sick Pay (SSP).	1. The rate of SMP is to be increased from £75 to £100 per week from April 2003. 2. A woman will be entitled to maternity pay for 26 weeks; six weeks still at 90% of the salary, and 20 weeks at the rate of SMP.
The right to maternity leave (*ERA 1996, ss 71 and 73*).	*Ordinary maternity leave (OML)* 1. No qualifying service. 2. Period of leave: 18 weeks. 3. Employee has to give the employer 21 days' notice of the start of maternity leave. 4. If the birth occurs before notice has been given, the leave starts from the date of the birth and the employee has a duty is to give notice as soon as it is reasonably practicable. 5. If an employee is absent for a pregnancy-related reason any time in the six weeks before the birth is due, her maternity leave will start automatically. 6. The contract of employment continues during the period of OML, therefore, all terms and conditions continue as if the employee were not absent, except for provisions relating to remuneration (as pay during maternity leave is dealt with under the SMP provisions).	From April 2003 the following improvements will be made to the maternity leave provisions. 1. The length of OML will be increased and pregnant employees will be entitled to 26 weeks' OML, regardless of how long they have worked for their employer. **2. Women who have completed 26 weeks' continuous service with their employer by the 15th week before their expected week of childbirth will be able to take AML. AML will start immediately after OML and continue for a further 26 weeks.** 3. Maternity leave will be automatically triggered if

	Additional maternity leave (AML) 1. Qualifying period: one year's service by the eleventh week before the birth is due.the	employee is absent due to sickness within *four weeks* prior to the expected birth date.
	2. Employee is entitled to take up to 29 weeks' leave, from the date of the birth (plus up to eleven weeks prior to the birth: 40 weeks' leave in total). 3. Notice requirements set out above for OML also apply for AML.	due to sickness within *four weeks* prior to the expected birth date.
	4. Certain contractual terms continue to apply during AML (such as implied terms of trust and confidence, disciplinary and grievance procedures, notice of dismissal/redundancy, notice periods); other terms of the contract are suspended. 5. AML does not affect continuity of employment but does not count for the accrual of rights such as annual leave.	
Automatic unfair dismissal where the principal reason for the dismissal is connected with pregnancy, childbirth, maternity leave, parental leave or time off for antenatal care (*ERA 1996, s 99*). The right not to suffer a detriment on grounds connected with pregnancy, childbirth, maternity leave, parental leave or time off for antenatal care (*ERA 1996 ,s 47C*).	1. No qualifying period. 2. Dismissal is automatically unfair. 3. Redundancy: a woman on maternity leave must be offered a suitable alternative vacancy if there is one, otherwise dismissal will be automatically unfair. 4. If a woman becomes incapable of work due to pregnancy, dismissal would be automatically unfair; she is entitled to take sick leave or maternity leave. 5. If it would be unlawful for a woman to continue in her employment (for health and safety reasons, perhaps), it will be automatically unfair to dismiss her; she has the right to be offered alternative employment or suspended on maternity grounds (*ERA 1996, s 66*).	None
The right not to be discriminated against on grounds of sex (*SDA 1975*).	1. Details of the *SDA 1975* are dealt with above (see p **160** *et seq*).	None

Parental leave:		
Parents of children under five years of age have the right to take parental leave (*Maternity and Parental Leave etc Regulations 1999 (SI 1999 No 3312)*).	1. Qualifying period: one year's continuous service. 2. Period of leave: up to 13 weeks' unpaid leave per child under the age of five. 3. The scheme for taking leave is to be agreed between employer and employee, either individually, collectively or by workforce agreement. 4. The 'default scheme', where there is no such agreement, provides that the leave must be taken in periods of a minimum of one week at any time, and a maximum of four weeks in any one year.	None
Time off for dependant care:		
Employees have the right to take 'reasonable' time off to care for dependants (*ERA 1996, s 57A*).	1. No qualifying period. 2. No right to paid time off. 3. Right to reasonable time off when a dependant is ill, giving birth or has been injured or assaulted. 4. Right to reasonable time off to arrange care for an ill or injured dependant. 5. Right to reasonable time off on the death of a dependant. 6. Right to reasonable time off because of unexpected disruption to care arrangements for a dependant. 7. Right to reasonable time off to deal with an unexpected incident concerning the employee's child during school hours. 8. 'Dependant' is defined as a spouse, child or parent of the employee, or someone who lives in the same household who is not an employee, lodger, tenant or boarder (therefore, a dependant would include unmarried partners and same-sex partners).	None

Flexible working:

The right for parents to request a change to flexible working hours.	None	1. Due to come into force in April 2003. 2. Detailed guidance to be issued nearer the time. 3. The right is *to request* a change in the number of hours worked, a change in the hours worked or to work from home. 4. Employers must consider the request seriously, and give reasons for a refusal. 5. In order to make a request under the new right an individual will:
		(a) be an employee; (b) have a child under six, or under 18 in the case of a disabled child; (c) have worked with his or her employer continuously for 26 weeks at the date the application is made; (d) make the application no later than two weeks before the child's sixth birthday, or 18th birthday in the case of a disabled child; (e) have, or expect to have, responsibility for the child's upbringing; (f) be making the application to enable him or her to care for the child; (g) not be an agency worker; (h) not be a member of the armed forces; and (j) not have made another application to work flexibly under the right during the past twelve months.

Paternity leave:

The right to two weeks' paternity leave.	None	1. From April 2003, predominantly, fathers will have the right to take two weeks' paid paternity leave. 2. Qualifying period: 26 weeks' continuous service 15 weeks before the expected week of the birth. 3. In order to qualify, employees must also show: (a) that they have or expect to have responsibility for the child's upbringing; and (b) that they are the biological father of the child or the child's mother's husband or partner. 4. Leave can start on any day of the week on, or following, the child's birth but must be completed: (a) within 56 days of the actual date of birth of the child; or (b) if the child is born early, within the period from the actual date of birth up to 56 days after the expected week of birth. 5. Statutory Paternity Pay (SPP) will be at the same rate as SMP: £100 per week from 6 April 2003.

Adoptive leave:

The right to adoption leave.	None	1. From April 2003 adoption leave and pay will be available to: (a) individuals who adopt; and

		(b) one member of a couple where a couple adopt jointly (the couple may choose which partner takes adoption leave). 2. The partner of an individual who adopts, or the other member of a couple who are adopting jointly, may be entitled to paternity leave and pay.

FUTURE DEVELOPMENTS

Positive Duty to Promote Equality

Despite the *SDA 1975*, the *RRA 1976* and the *DDA 1995*, the number of incidences of discrimination in Britain remains high. Means of addressing inequality has been vigorously debated in a number of circles and there has been a noticeable move towards positive duties, which are proactive rather than reactive.

The EU Race Directive (Directive 2000/43/EC implementing the principle of equal treatment between persons irrespective of racial or ethnic origin) requires Member States to designate a body to 'promote' race equality but the Equal Treatment in Employment Framework Directive (Directive 2000/78/EC establishing a general framework for equal treatment in employment and occupation), which covers age, sexual orientation, religion and disability, does not contain a similar provision. The recently revised Equal Treatment Directive for men and women does not require Member States to *promote* equal treatment but does *encourage* employers to 'promote equal treatment for men and women in the workplace in a planned and systematic way'.

As highlighted above, the British Government has already embarked on a route of positive measures with the new *RRA 1976* which places a duty on public authorities to promote race equality. Also, the *DDA 1995* places a duty on employers 'to make reasonable adjustments', again requiring positive action from the employer.

There have been a number of calls to extend the requirement to take positive action further. For example, in its response to the Government's consultation document, *Towards Equality and Diversity: Implementing the Employment and Race Directives 2001*, the TUC argues:

> 'If we really wish to promote equality at work, we shall have to go beyond negative prohibitions and incorporate positive duties to promote equality of opportunity.'

This approach is certainly welcomed by a number of groups (including the CRE, the EOC and the DRC) and is likely to correct future discrimination law.

Sexual Discrimination and Sexual Harassment

The EU Council and Parliament recently agreed a number of amendments to the Equal Treatment Directive which will result in substantial changes to equality legislation, in particular sexual harassment. Member States will be required to implement the Directive by 2005. Included in the Directive are new definitions of direct and indirect discrimination, which will bring sex discrimination in line with the definition in the Race Directive (Directive 2000/43/EC implementing the principle of equal treatment between persons irrespective of racial or ethnic origin) and Equal Treatment in Employment Framework Directive. The Government has already announced its intention to ensure that the new legislation on sexual orientation, religion and age use the definitions set out in the Directive. Sexual harassment is also defined.

- Direct discrimination: 'Where one person is treated less favourably on grounds of sex than another is, has been, or would be treated in a comparable situation.'

- Indirect discrimination: 'Where an apparently neutral provision, criterion or practice would put persons of one sex at a particular disadvantage compared with persons of the other sex, unless that provision, criterion or practice is objectively justified by a legitimate aim, and the means of achieving that aim are appropriate and necessary.'

- Sexual and sex-based harassment: 'Where any form of unwanted verbal, non-verbal or physical conduct of a sexual nature occurs, with the purpose or effect of violating the dignity of a person, in particular when creating an intimidating, hostile, degrading, humiliating or offensive environment'. Sex-based harassment allows the inclusion of bullying, physical or verbal abuse based on sex but not sexual conduct.

Sexual Orientation

Discrimination in employment on grounds of sexuality is not presently covered in any statutes. Attempts to include sexuality in the *SDA 1975* on the basis of the *HRA 1998* have failed (see *Pearce v Governing Body of Mayfield School [2001] IRLR 669*) alongside those cases argued at the ECJ. Despite the fact that the ECHR in *Lustig-Prean and Beckett v United Kingdom (1999) 29 EHRR 548* and *Smith and Grady v United Kingdom [1999] IRLR 734* set the scene for changes in the law, its impact was fairly limited and restricted to the armed services. This is set to change, however, as the EU Equal Treatment in Employment Framework Directive places an obligation on all Member States to introduce legislation relating to discrimination on grounds of sexual orientation in employment and training (but not access to goods, facilities and services) by December 2003.

The Directive does not contain a definition of sexual orientation, this is left open to Member States. It is envisaged that one of the practical benefits of the legislation will be in providing protection against discrimination for same-sex partners in pensions and other fringe benefits. However, where the rules of the scheme restrict benefits to surviving spouses, this is permitted under the Directive. A draft consultation document published by the Government suggests that discrimination should be defined on grounds of 'heterosexual, homosexual or bisexual orientation'. Stonewall (a campaign organisation for gay and lesbian rights) prefer the definition 'on grounds of sexual orientation' to be used as it believes that the word 'homosexual' has negative connotations.

Stonewall has also expressed concern regarding the definition of harassment which is apparently more stringent in the EU Equal Treatment in Employment Framework Directive than existing British case law on race and sex. It seems likely that the Government will apply the existing case law definition to the new forms of discrimination.

Religion

In line with the proposals for sexual orientation, and in accordance with the EU Equal Treatment in Employment Framework Directive, legislation on grounds of religious discrimination must also be in place by December 2003. The Government's consultation document, *Towards Equality and Diversity: Implementing the Employment and Race Directives*, proposes to allow the courts to define what constitutes religion or belief (but not political belief). This has been welcomed in some quarters, for example by the EOC, but attacked in others as being too vague and problematic. Some concern has been expressed about the Government's proposals to allow organisations with an ethos based on religion or belief to introduce employment policies which support that ethos, as long as it is justified. The EOC claims that this could lead to conflict with other aspects of equality law and cites examples such as a Roman Catholic school which might decide to dismiss a teacher who becomes pregnant outside marriage and other religious organisations which might adopt a policy of not employing any gay or lesbian staff.

The Government's consultation document points to a number of practical issues for employers. The legislation will not require employers to automatically agree to all requests for leave for religious observance, nor require employers to make special arrangements for diet, dress and religion observance. However, employers must take care not to:

- directly discriminate by refusing leave just because of the employee's religion or belief; or

- indirectly discriminate by applying rules on leave which disadvantage some groups over others.

Specific guidance on such matters will be published by the Government in due course.

Age Discrimination

There is presently no legislation on age discrimination, although the Government introduced a voluntary Code of Practice for age diversity in employment in 1998. The purpose of this Code of Practice, according to the draft published in December 1998, is to:

'help employers, employees and applicants alike by setting a standard. The Code will show how businesses and employers can take steps to ensure they choose, retain and develop the best person for the job by eliminating the use of age as an employment criterion.'

This Code of Practice is not, of course, legally enforceable. The Government has attempted to use it to urge employers to ensure that age is not a barrier to jobs and opportunities. In launching the Code of Practice in the House of Commons, the Employment Minister, Andrew Smith, pointed out that by the year 2000 more than one third of the workforce would be aged over 45. Thus, it does not make commercial sense for employers to exclude such a large part of the workforce.

In accordance with the EU Equal Treatment in Employment Framework Directive, age discrimination legislation is required by 2006. This longer time period recognises the complex issues involved and the fact that there may be differences of treatment which can be justified on grounds of age. The Directive includes a list illustrating the different types of treatment which may be justified, including:

- special conditions on access to employment and vocational training for particular categories of people in order to promote their vocational integration or to ensure their protection;

- minimum conditions of age, experience or seniority for particular advantages; and

- a maximum recruitment age based on the training requirements of the post.

The Government's consultation document is attempting to establish which types of treatment would be acceptable and which would not. A particularly controversial issue relates to retirement ages. Presently, employers can fix the retirement age, usually between 60 and 65. The consultation document also seeks views as to whether there should be any legal limits placed on retirement age.

CONCLUSION

Although the UK legislation on equal opportunities does not directly address the issue of diversity, it is clearly a driving force behind many diversity strategies already adopted. The law provides a basic framework to work to when drawing up a strategy but, clearly, if diversity is to be successfully implemented an organisation's policies need to go further than the law requires.

The future developments in the law demonstrate that the legal system is catching up with the move towards diversity, and that organisations which are able to demonstrate a workable diversity policy will be better placed to meet the growing demands of the law.

CHECKLIST

✔ Have you 'equality proofed' your organisation's employment policies?

✔ Does your organisation meet the requirements of the sex and race discrimination legislation, in relation to both direct and indirect discrimination?

✔ Have you conducted an equal pay review?

✔ Has consideration been given to the requirements of employees (and potential employees) with disabilities? Have all reasonable adjustments been made?

✔ Is there sufficient flexibility to allow for work-life balance options to be implemented?

✔ Have future developments in the law been considered? Are managers aware of the forthcoming legislative requirements?

Chapter Seven
Case Studies on Diversity

OVERVIEW

This chapter includes the following.

- Case studies from organisations at the leading edge of diversity strategy.

- Detailed discussion of why and how organisations implemented diversity policies.

- The overall philosophy and the motivating factors of the organisations implementing the policies

- Details of organisations' policies relating to specific aspects of diversity strategy, ie disability, culture and ethnicity.

B&Q

Introduction

B&Q, the DIY (do-it-yourself) retailer, has been at the forefront of developments on diversity policy and practice. It began looking at recruiting a diverse workforce in 1998, and started with age diversity. It conducted an 'experiment' on employing older people by staffing a newly opened B&Q Supercentre in Macclesfield entirely by people over 50. Within six months this showed clear advantages over other stores.

- Profits were higher by 18%.

- Staff turnover was six times lower.

- Absenteeism was down by 39%.

- Customer perception of service improved.

- The skill base amongst staff increased.

B&Q now has a strategy on disability and, more recently, cultural diversity (see **CHAPTER EIGHT – MODEL POLICIES**). This has been a success story from the start and is an appropriate starting point in this chapter.

Following is the B&Q diversity vision statement.

'We want to be a great company that can be trusted to respect the quality of life of all the people and communities we touch.'

Mike Cutt, B&Q's personnel director, explains the company's approach to diversity.

'At B&Q we want to attract a balanced workforce which reflects the local community and encompasses a range of skills to enrich the business. We are constantly working on our diversity strategy, which covers issues such as age, disability, race, gender and sexual orientation, to ensure that all people are treated fairly and equally, both as customers and employees.'

To fully integrate these values throughout the organisation, B&Q began implementing a diversity policy and programme in 1998.

This commitment to diversity and the action taken by B&Q to support disabled people and encourage cultural diversity within the company is considered below. This is followed by a step-by-step guide to B&Q's implementation of its disability diversity strategy.

B&Q: Delivering a Winning Disability Programme

Organisation profile

B&Q has been in the DIY business for more than 30 years (originally as Block and Quayle) and is the UK's most successful home improvement retailer. Attracting three million customers each week and employing over 26,000 staff, the company has a presence in virtually every major town. There are more than 300 B&Q stores throughout England, Wales, Scotland and Northern Ireland, including 240 Supercentres and around 60 warehouses. An ambitious store-opening programme aims to have 125 B&Q warehouses in the UK by the end of 2003.

B&Q's philosophy

Corporate reputation

B&Q believes that its corporate reputation depends as much on social as it does on commercial imperatives. It is the most successful DIY company in the market based on all measurable criteria; it has the biggest turnover, profit, investment plans and number of staff.

Like all market leaders, B&Q is concerned with commercial success but, as the number one brand, the company also emphasises that it has a responsibility to consider all its stakeholders, whether that includes the city, customers, staff, suppliers, Government or local communities. In particular, B&Q recognises that it has a wide influence in the community and, as such, takes its responsibility to be a better neighbour seriously. Tackling disability issues at a local level is one way of achieving this.

Valuing the individual

B&Q's aims in relation to disabled people sit well with the company's purposes and values regarding people, which include treating people with respect, honesty and fairness. In particular, valuing an individual's contribution and not their position is believed to be an important part of the company's success.

Social responsibility

The company argues that retailers have a responsibility to effect real change in the lives of disabled people, given the pressure they can exert as major employers in raising the understanding of disability issues, and the practical differences they can make to improving accessibility for disabled people.

The company has, therefore, committed itself to a vision where disabled and elderly people can shop with confidence in its stores, secure in the knowledge that they will be able to access goods and services easily, find solutions to meet their needs and be treated with respect by staff.

Proactive response to legislation

B&Q was determined to respond proactively to the *Disability Discrimination Act 1995* (*DDA 1995*), as well as comply with all aspects of the legislation in terms of providing both positive work opportunities for disabled people and accessible shopping. In response to the new legal requirements (see p **196** below), the company set itself the challenge of finding creative solutions to the problems faced by disabled people, to exceed their expectations and set the standard for other organisations to follow.

Reasons for the policy

Compliance with legislation

The company's work on a disability policy and programme was prompted primarily by the scheduled introduction of the goods and services provisions of the *DDA 1995* in October 1999. While it had been unlawful for service providers to treat disabled people less favourably for a disability-related reason since December 1996, from October 1999 service providers were given new duties to make reasonable adjustments for disabled people in the way they provide their services. The duty will be extended in 2004 when service providers must take reasonable steps to alter physical features which make it impossible, or unreasonably difficult, for a disabled person to access their services.

Business benefits

The company is also very much aware of the commercial benefits of adopting a disability policy (see CASE STUDY: B&Q'S DISABILITY BUSINESS CASE, p **206**). B&Q asserts that any company implementing an effective disability programme for all staff who deal with customers, will be likely to gain a larger share of a relatively untapped market. If a business can get it right for a disabled customer, it will get it right for all customers.

Improvement in customer service

Disabled people who work for the company are seen as making a valuable contribution to the organisation, as well as enhancing the quality of services offered to the public. For instance, deaf employees who use sign language can easily communicate with deaf customers. While existing staff can be trained to learn sign language, B&Q argues that having people in store who already have these skills increases the organisation's ability to meet customer needs.

Key aspects of the strategy

Leadership

From the outset, senior-level commitment was seen as vital for success, and B&Q's managing director is the champion of the disability initiative. His personal commitment encourages others to get involved, and leadership at this level ensures that the disability agenda is mainstreamed within the business.

Mainstreaming

The disability strategy is implemented by a small, dedicated team reporting directly to the managing director. The board receives regular updates on the disability programme and is keen to integrate it into all areas of the business. This top-level commitment is absolutely critical when driving the disability strategy through the business, and it ensures that disability is in the hearts and minds of the board of directors.

Performance indicators

The disability strategy was designed to be measurable at every stage and has been built into the annual *store standards competition*, which measures stores against a number of key performance indicators. Store standards are taken very seriously by the business and disability awareness is now a key part of the measures.

Inclusive and holistic approach

From the start, the company strongly believed in taking an inclusive and holistic approach to disability. The disability programme sits firmly within its diversity policy and programme, and covers both customer service and employment issues.

Sue O'Neill, diversity co-ordinator at B&Q, argues that disabled people are not 'different' or 'special'.

> 'Our approach has been to encourage the employment of a diverse range of people who happen to have different employment requirements. We do not believe in positive discrimination, but we do believe in ensuring that we offer equality of opportunity to everyone.'

Disability-friendly initiatives

Consultation

The company began its disability programme by consulting with disabled customers and employees. It believed that the best way to learn about how its stores could be made easier to shop and work in was to listen to disabled people. In August 1998 a series of customer focus groups, mystery shopping and telephone surveys were conducted to help establish the difficulties encountered by disabled people. Disabled B&Q employees also took part in the focus groups. Local organisations were contacted to ensure no type of disability was missed.

The consultation exercise revealed that physical accessibility, staff behaviour and product range all fell short of acceptable levels of service for customers. Problems for disabled people working at B&Q were also highlighted, even though those problems were not always overt. The problems mainly revolved around reasonable adjustment issues and the lack of procedures and guidance on dealing with them. Without a disability policy in place, some disabled employees may have felt uncomfortable about raising issues and managers were unsure about what support they could provide.

Utilising external expertise

Following the consultation exercise, the company developed a new approach to the whole issue of disability, in conjunction with disability experts and voluntary groups. The aim was to deliver a sustainable disability policy which embraced employment, employee awareness, customer service, community partnerships, access design, product design and supplier involvement.

Customer support

On the customer service side, an intensive action plan was introduced. B&Q redesigned a warehouse store to incorporate new access features. These included motorised wheelchairs, accessible parking, lower counters and check-out desks for wheelchair users, clearer signs, portable induction loops designed for people with hearing impairments, and sign language and sub-text on all in-store videos.

Work also began on expanding the company's '*daily living made easier*' range of goods, which appeal to all customers but particularly those who are disabled and elderly. There is now a rolling programme to ensure that all stores become fully accessible. B&Q has already completed 300 'store access' audits and has appointed a dedicated 2004 compliance manager.

O'Neill points out that these measures, primarily aimed at improving customer service, have also raised B&Q's public profile as a disability-friendly employer.

> 'We believe the high-profile installation in stores of additional features to aid accessibility and easier-to-use products not only assist disabled staff working in our stores as well as our customers, but makes it clear that B&Q is an employer who welcomes disabled employees.'

Disability awareness training

A disability awareness training package was developed with the help of specialist consultants, Churchill and Friend. The package offers customer awareness training with a focus on disability, as opposed to just disability awareness. The emphasis is an important one for the company, as O'Neill explains.

> 'The board believes that if we get customer service right for a disabled person then we get it right for everyone.'

Senior-level training

The new training package was provided first for senior store teams and store disability champions (see p **201** below). A disabled trainer delivered the training in three-hour sessions. Designed to be very interactive, the training proved highly successful.

Disability awareness distance training

Rolling out similar training, however, to 23,000 employees in a cost–effective way that did not take people out of the stores, and which was delivered in a measurable way, required some innovative thinking. The answer was a disability awareness distance training package which facilitates the training of large numbers of people and incorporates a measurable pass rate.

The rollout of staff training began in July 1999 when the company's disability policy, *Is this what we see?*, was formally launched. The disability policy booklet and training workbook were issued to every member of staff at store level by managers at team briefings.

The workbook contains sections on the following:

- B&Q's disability policy;
- why disabled people are important to the business;
- an explanation of disability and the law;
- how to respond to disabled customers' individual requirements; and
- ways to improve communication skills.

Stressing that the course is just a starting point and not an end in itself, the workbook emphasises that the best way to learn about disability is by talking to disabled people directly and by recognising that no two individuals are alike.

The members of staff are invited to study the book at their own pace and, as soon as they feel familiar with its contents, take part in a telephone quiz. Badges are awarded to all participants who successfully complete the final interactive test. B&Q also donates 25 pence to the Leonard Cheshire charity for every badge awarded.

Success tables

To ensure that the training remained a priority for each store, 'league tables' of successful passes were produced. This gave the pass rate a boost as stores competed to achieve the standards. Some 70% of staff participated within six months of the launch, and over 85% of staff have passed disability awareness training to date. This surpasses the company-wide pass rate target of 80%. A 100% target was considered unattainable because of the turnover of starters and leavers.

Induction training

The B&Q induction training programme for all new staff includes disability awareness as a core module, and the disability champion (see p **201** below) ensures that all new members of staff undertake the disability awareness training package. O'Neill emphasises that:

> 'Although the training is aimed at improving customer service, it is also equally beneficial in positively heightening manager and staff awareness about the issues involved in working productively with disabled colleagues.'

Disability policy booklet

The interactive training was supported by the launch of the company's disability policy booklet, *Is this what we see?*. The booklet explains in detail B&Q's commitment to improving its facilities for disabled people and its disabled employment policy (see **CHAPTER EIGHT**). A major feature of the booklet is a confidential, tear-off questionnaire for disabled employees, requesting details of their impairment and how the company can improve their working environment.

Awareness dissemination

The programme launch was supported by a poster campaign from the diversity team and the creation in each store of a diversity information board. A company newsletter was also launched to help maintain the momentum.

Supporting line management

Line managers were crucial in helping to plan the training rollout and giving their support to the disability programme. Regional managers and store managers received additional training to cover the business case for implementing the disability policy, the benefits of the diversity policy linked to the company values of respect for people, and a detailed explanation of the *DDA 1995* and the company disability programme. This training was rolled out to over 300 stores and involved approximately 350 people.

Line managers also have access to a legal briefing on the *DDA 1995*, primarily in relation to customer service. The company is now in the process of producing an information pack for line managers in relation to employment provision. Further support is provided by the disability champion (see p **201** below).

Disability champions

Each store is expected to take ownership of the disability initiative in order to make real changes at a local level, and a major feature of the disability programme has been the appointment of a dedicated 'disability champion' for each store. The disability champion provides appropriate support to ensure that the programme is moved forward in the right way by promoting the project, motivating the local team and assisting the store manager.

The champions are encouraged to participate by the store manager. Many of the champions either have a disability or know someone who is disabled. 'Many of them saw this as their chance for recognition and to make a difference,' comments O'Neill.

The champions also offer an extra informal contact for disabled employees. For example, some disabled members of staff who experience problems at work, or who have 'hidden' impairments, may lack the confidence to approach their line manager direct for information about making reasonable adjustments. In these instances, the disability champions become a vital channel between staff, the head office diversity team and line managers to resolve any problems to the benefit of both the individual and the business.

Champions' training includes sign language and disability awareness training. Two 'away days' have been held for the champions in order to motivate them to take the programme forward and to find their community partner (see p **202** below).

Community partners

An important part of the disability champion's role involves taking the initiative into the heart of the local community by working with a group or organisation which represents disability in some form. The partnership scheme is unique in that there are no predetermined objectives, other than each store building a friendship with a community partner. The partner is asked to help the store improve its learning on disability issues and in return the store helps the partner.

The objective is to make answering questions on disability a straightforward process for the store. In return, the partner can seek help from the store for a range of issues, including employment, shopping experience or a small donation. Donations can also take the form of time and support if requested.

O'Neill has the following to say with regard to the community partner scheme.

'This two-way flow of information between the store and its partner has a real effect on changing attitudes and the understanding of disability. The friendship encourages personal involvement, which helps to give the disability programme a life of its own leading to sustainability and genuine enthusiasm.'

Monitoring

Feedback from the B&Q booklet questionnaire (see p **201** above) enabled the organisation to establish baseline data about its disabled employees for monitoring purposes and also to receive advice from employees themselves about the disability issues they wanted tackled.

In the same way that a company already conducts regular business audits in relation to financial reporting, stock control and store productivity, B&Q argues that diversity monitoring should take place with the long-term aim of measuring the success of its diversity strategy. Tasks were identified based on the key diversity issues which are observable and measurable. From these a set of key performance indicators were compiled.

One of the key indicators is the number of disabled people employed by the company. A target has been set of increasing the number of disabled employees in B&Q's workforce to reflect the national population of disabled people (currently 14%) by 2004. The company's latest monitoring figures (June 2001) show that it employs over 1,300 disabled people, representing 5.3% of the workforce. This represents an increase of 300% in 18 months.

The company undertook a follow-up employee questionnaire in November 2000 to continue the learning process in relation to understanding disability issues regarding employment, accessibility and customer service. The questionnaire was sent to all store managers and to 1,228 employees identified as disabled.

The overall purpose of the questionnaire was to gain an insight into:

- how disabled employees view working for the company;
- how B&Q can assist in providing reasonable adjustments; and
- store managers' understanding of the disability strategy.

The diversity team is in the process of updating the employment strategy for disability, based on the results of the survey.

Recruitment procedures

Candidates applying for mainstream job opportunities are required to apply to B&Q through the company's national recruitment response centre (RRC), where they are asked to complete an automated telephone screening interview (ATSI). Some disabled people may experience disproportionate difficulty in applying to work for B&Q in this way. The company has, therefore, consulted with the Royal National Institute for the Deaf (RNID) and other organisations to ensure ease of access.

Reasonable adjustment is provided where appropriate. For example, a candidate with a hearing impairment can use the text-phone to complete the ATSI. The answering time has also been extended. The ATSI begins with a brief introduction and includes a reference to the availability of reasonable adjustments.

When a store manager has vacancies, an employment match is sought from the RRC computer. These files contain the work experience only of candidates and give no personal information at all, such as age, address or disability. The need for a reasonable adjustment at the interview stage remains confidential until the person is actually selected for interview. Once the store manager commits to receiving the candidate's details from the computer, a central check is made to ensure that an interview takes place. Feedback is required from all interviews.

It is believed that the system has removed bias from the recruitment and short–listing stages and that the recruitment procedure is now very robust in relation to encouraging diversity, which also benefits disabled applicants. A member of the central recruitment team has a specific responsibility for ensuring that reasonable adjustments, if requested, are made when interviews take place. He or she must also be available to attend sites throughout the UK to help provide these adjustments.

Reasonable adjustments guidance

Line managers have been issued with guidelines on the *Access to work Scheme*; a government-funded programme to assist employers with reasonable adjustment for disabled employees. The guidelines explain the law in relation to making reasonable adjustments for disabled employees and give detailed information on how managers can use the scheme to provide the necessary changes in order to assist both existing and new employees.

Supported employment

While seeking to employ disabled people in mainstream employment, B&Q is also keen to take advantage of the *Workstep Scheme*, the *Job Introduction Scheme* and work experience. Managers and HR (human resources) specialists have received detailed guidelines about how to make the most of the schemes in relation to offering employment opportunities to disabled people and implementing best employment practice.

Positive publicity

As part of its drive to recruit more disabled people, disabled members of staff have fronted B&Q's TV advertising campaign. The impetus for getting a wide range of B&Q staff to feature in the commercials, says O'Neill, came from the Leonard Cheshire *VisABLE Campaign*. The campaign, which was backed by, what was then, the Department for Education and Employment (DfEE) (now part of the

Department for Education and Skills (DfES)), helps to encourage more companies to use disabled people in their advertising and to tackle discrimination against disabled people at every level of society.

'The campaign spurred us to find some employees who would like to be featured,' O'Neill said, 'so we asked our store disability champions if they would, or knew of others who would like to star. The aim was not to single out anyone with a disability but to make sure everyone had an equal opportunity.' O'Neill points out that the policy is not only good for promoting B&Q as a diverse employer, but is also good for raising the profile of all disabled people.

The success of B&Q's disability initiatives has also meant that the company is reaching a much wider recruitment pool in terms of disability. For example, a B&Q disabled employee is featured on the posters and fliers promoting the Government's *New Deal for Disabled People Scheme*, aimed at helping disabled people find fulfilling work. A new RNID information video has been filmed in a B&Q warehouse with an employee making use of her sign language skills. And a BBC *See Hear* programme was filmed in another B&Q warehouse, featuring a store disability champion and local community partner.

> 'This kind of publicity,' asserts O'Neill, 'not only helps create a more positive image of disabled people generally, but is invaluable for establishing our credentials as a genuinely diverse employer, thereby promoting B&Q as the employer of choice to the widest possible pool of talented people. Along with the business awards we have won for our disability initiatives, this kind of external endorsement packs a powerful business punch.'

External recognition and awards

B&Q's positive approach to employing disabled people and meeting the needs of its disabled customers has resulted in the company winning a clutch of business awards. In 2000 the company won the *Business in the Community Award for Innovation*, and it won the national *Queen Elizabeth Foundation's EASE Award* (ease of access, service and employment for disabled people) two years running (in 2000 and 2001).

B&Q's efforts to encourage a diverse workforce, particularly its proactive response to disability, also helped the company win the *Retail Week Employer of the Year Award* in 2001. The company's work in relation to disability was also recognised with the appointment of Kay Allen, then B&Q's diversity manager, as a commissioner to the new Disability Rights Commission (DRC) at the beginning of 2000. B&Q's advertising campaign was also reported on BBC national news programmes because it included disabled employees.

Tips from the employer

- *Adopt an integrated approach:* O'Neill is convinced of the importance of the inclusive and holistic approach which the company has taken. 'The three-fold increase we have seen in disabled staff numbers is in no small way due to the proactive approach that we have taken to diversity as a whole, and because people have noticed the changes we have made in our stores in relation to making them more accessible for disabled people.'

- *Stress the business case:* Building on its integrated approach to tackling disability issues, O'Neill argues that the company is now in a strong position to maximise the commercial return from what is perhaps the last substantial untapped customer base in the UK. For B&Q, there is a clear strategic fit between existing business goals, company values and the commercial desire to capture a larger market share of available DIY customer base.

- *Get expert guidance:* According to O'Neill, 'meeting the needs of disabled employees and customers is not difficult, it just requires utilising the appropriate expertise for guidance. Once this has been acquired, the rest is down to good practice and common sense.'

- *Measure to improve:* Cutt explains the importance of monitoring to the company. 'Measurable data are essential if we are to prove the business case for diversity. By gauging employment patterns, we will be able to locate areas for improvement. It is important that we constantly strive to be better. B&Q has achieved much, but we appreciate that this is just the beginning of the journey. There is much still to do.'

- *Reinforce the positive message:* B&Q has proactively sought positive publicity about its disability initiatives in order to raise awareness of the company's disability-friendly credentials with customers, employees and potential recruits.

CASE STUDY: B&Q's disability business case

It is estimated there are around 8.6 million disabled people in the UK who have an impairment leading to difficulties with daily living. This means that the number of disabled people in the UK is greater than the combined populations of Scotland and Wales, There is, therefore, a substantial number of potential customers who have disabilities.

In addition, there is also a major indirect market, as seven million people act as personal assistants and carers to a disabled person. This means that one in four people either have a disability or know someone who is disabled. Consequently, it is not just disabled people who are a potential source of sales, but their families and friends as well. Someone shopping with a disabled person is far more likely to choose to shop somewhere that is easily accessible.

Some 90% of disabled people live in their own homes, which means they require access to the same range of goods, facilities and services as anybody else who lives locally. Many businesses fail to recognise that disabled people want to use the same services as everyone else, not just specialist ones for 'the disabled'.

Only 8% of disabled people are born with their disability. Disabilities can be present at birth but, more often, they arise during a person's life. While people tend to lose some of their abilities as they get older, it is estimated that about 100,000 people become disabled each year as a result of accidents or other traumas in their lives.

B&Q estimates that it will be targeting approximately five million adults of working age who receive the national average income and are either disabled or act as carers. The aim of the disability strategy is to capture a far higher proportion of the available market.

In addition, simply growing old is relevant to disability. With 18 million people in the UK today over the age of 50, the age band where disabilities become more frequent, greater attention to the needs of disabled customers will pay commercial dividends.

B&Q: Cultural Diversity

Reasons for the policy

Following are the areas which B&Q decided to cover in its policy when considering cultural diversity, and the reasons for their inclusion.

Proactive not reactive

The original decision to look at cultural diversity at B&Q was made because the company had in the past been reactive rather than proactive in the area of race. Sue O'Neill is a member of B&Q's social responsibility team and manages the company's diversity programme.

> 'We have focussed on disability over the past two years and have continued to maintain our policy on achieving a balanced workforce, together with a strong older workers policy. We wanted to progress our agenda in an area where we could make a significant impact.'

Ethnicity, culture and religion

B&Q decided to look at issues relating to ethnic minorities from the broader perspective of cultural diversity, in particular to include religion.

'Managers need to understand the way in which culture, religion and ethnicity can interact and be able to support staff appropriately,' says O'Neill.

> 'The types of issues we have come across have involved, for example, female managers from Asian backgrounds who have had difficulties with

men from Asian backgrounds who find it hard to work for female Asian managers. This is because in some cultures women are seen as inferior.

We have also witnessed tension between, for example, Muslim managers and Hindu staff based on historical differences. In both cases there was a realisation that we needed to support managers and ensure that they have an understanding of different cultures and are able to deal with situations in an appropriate way.'

Legislation

Future legislation was also a consideration. Under the EU Equal Treatment in Employment Framework Directive (Directive 2000/78/EC establishing a general framework for equal treatment in employment and occupation), the UK must introduce measures to protect employees from religious discrimination by December 2003. O'Neill's view is that 'it doesn't make sense to introduce policies that you will then have to change in two years' time.'

Recruitment and retention

Although B&Q had a fairly high proportion of ethnic minority employees across its stores as a whole (5.6%), they were not necessarily based in stores where there were similar ethnic minority communities, nor were they well represented at a management level. O'Neill said:

'We also knew that ethnic minorities were leaving in larger proportions to white Europeans. One of the reasons for this was because a lot of ethnic minority employees work part time; many are students. They often work at weekends to fit in with their studies. In selected areas such as London and Birmingham, universities have higher proportions of ethnic minority students and we will, therefore, also have a higher proportion. In one area we ran an ethnic minority recruitment fair and found that students simply did not see retail as a choice of career or a culture that they fit into. We have done a lot of research on this area, and it is not just about ethnic minorities. Feedback from graduates in general revealed that they saw B&Q as a place for shelf fillers and did not identify it as a place where they could further their career. Many graduates felt overqualified and it became clear that we were not doing enough to advertise jobs in head office, where we employ around 14,000 staff, or in our offices internationally.'

Increasing the customer base

As an employer, B&Q wanted its employees to reflect the community in which its stores were based. But more than this, B&Q recognised that encouraging cultural diversity in the workplace would help to increase the ethnic minority customer base. According to figures compiled by B&Q, ethnic minority groups have an estimated spending power of £15 million, they make up 7% of the population, 47% of them were born in the UK and the Asian business community alone own over 50% of independent retail outlets. It was a source to be tapped.

Key aspects of strategy

B&Q's cultural diversity strategy has been in operation since September 2001 but it was only launched to the business in February 2002.

Starting at the grass roots

Because race and religion were seen as sensitive issues, it was decided to seek views at a grass roots level before moving forward. To ensure that people felt comfortable to freely express their views, an independent consultant was brought in to run focus groups with staff and customers. One of the main findings of the consultation exercise was the need for effective communication, especially in terms of providing managers with the necessary information to enable them to understand the diverse mix of their employees.

There was a feeling amongst some ethnic minority employees that they had no voice, and that their views were not always listened to because managers didn't understand their religion and culture, and only dealt with issues if they had to. Comments arising from the consultation included, 'managers are likely to promote people they can relate to', 'no flexibility in shift patterns when we are fasting', 'want more support from managers in terms of flexibility due to religious circumstances'.

In relation to religion, managers tended to take one of two approaches, says O'Neill.

'They either assumed they were discriminating against the employees so they agreed without question, or because they didn't understand they said "no" to the request and didn't bother to find out the reasons behind it. Managers knew this was a sensitive area but they didn't understand the impact it had on staff morale and so they just buried their heads in the sand.

What we aim to do is to create a culture where people are treated with respect, feel comfortable to talk freely and know they will be treated positively. We want a culture where it is ok to be different and people don't feel they have to conform.'

Steering group

Once the initial consultation was complete, the diversity team set up a steering group to decide what issues to take forward. It was driven by the HR director and key people from across the business, including staff from human resources, recruitment, marketing and public relations, and from the retail stores.

Constant communication

At the heart of the new strategy was a commitment to communicate the new policy across the company at all levels and on a regular basis, so that the issues were constantly reiterated and no one was allowed to forget about them.

'In particular we wanted to ensure it was a policy managers would buy into,' says O'Neill.

Internal staff consultation

B&Q did not stop at the initial staff consultation, however. It continued to keep up two-way communication between the head office and staff in stores, and it was very much individuals on the ground who helped to make the policy the success it is.

When O'Neill made a formal presentation to the board on cultural diversity she brought with her two colleagues from different stores. Both felt passionately about the new strategy and had been actively involved in the diversity team's work on developing policy in the area.

'We send round something on cultural diversity once a month and we always receive new ideas from staff in response,' says O'Neill.

Kav Patel, team leader from B&Q's Wednesbury store says: '*Respect for people* is probably one of the most important values and underpins the B&Q Cultural Diversity Policy and strategy. As a team leader, the information I receive about different cultural and religious festival dates is fantastic. It provides me with knowledge and helps me to understand my staff and what is important to them. This adds value both to my staff and to me. It is like learning a new skill that helps us all become better people and colleagues. The calendar of religious festivals is a much-welcomed tool to both staff and managers. Colleagues are now better informed of important dates amongst their teams, and managers can also plan rotas etc more effectively. Instead of assuming no one wants to work the Christmas period, we are now aware that we can offer a better service to our staff who would prefer different times off, but also to our customers in ensuring good service cover is available for them when they shop in our stores.'

Business sense

Internal two-way communication has been important in informing staff of policy, but also in understanding the customer base and marketing products more effectively.

As a result of information collected from employees, the buying team is now looking at promotional and product opportunities. 'We had never been big on candles, for example, and we have started looking at introducing them, in particular bringing them in around the time of festivals such as Eid and Diwali,' says O'Neill.

Cultural diversity initiatives

Calendar of religious festivals

The team began by sending out a calendar of religious festivals to managers. 'We realised that this on its own was not enough because it did not explain the link between people's culture and their religion,' says O'Neill, 'so it was accompanied by a briefing paper, explaining the relevance of the different festivals and how requests for holidays should be treated, as well as a reminder of their duties under the *Race Relations Act* and future legislation.' Managers were asked to display the posters on staff notice boards and to use information to generate discussion with staff.

> 'Every month we send round a reminder about festivals coming up asking managers to be aware that some employees in their stores may wish to take some time to celebrate those festivals. We keep reiterating it.
>
> Next year we are incorporating the religious calendars into desk diaries with all the business dates as well. That will be the only calendar to go out to the business. We felt that this would raise awareness more effectively because it would be something that people are constantly using. It's too easy to forget about the wall calendars, they just become part of the furniture.'

Support line

There is a support line number for any queries or suggestions so that people know where to go if issues arise. 'One caller asked for the inclusion of pagan dates and these are now included on the monthly bulletin,' says O'Neill. 'We have also been asked for a brief explanation of particular festivals and how they are celebrated, which we also now include.'

In-house booklet

As a result of the focus groups, the diversity team realised it needed more information about the cultural identities of employees. It set up a staff group from diverse backgrounds. 'They each wrote a piece for an in–house booklet on faiths and cultures, but more specifically on how their cultures transferred to the UK,' explains O'Neill.

What began as a relatively small project grew into a much more comprehensive resource. The booklet begins with an overview of the different cultures which exist in the UK today. There are sections on the history of the UK's diverse culture, statistics on when different groups arrived, background and history of different countries and regions, and a section on each religion with more detailed information on festivals.

SAMPLE DOCUMENT: Extract from B&Q's in-house booklet on different cultures and religions

Sikh culture

All Sikh men take the religious name Singh (meaning lion) and all Sikh women have Kaur (meaning princess) as their second name. However, the name Singh does not necessarily mean that a person is a Sikh and, in the UK, some Sikh wives attach the name Singh to their own.

Turbans are worn, mainly by Sikh men, to keep their long hair tidy. Cutting hair is seen as interfering with nature. The traditional dress of Sikh women consists of salwar (trousers) and kamiz (long over-shirt), with a chumi (chiffon scarf). White, rather than black, is worn during a period of mourning.

The extended family plays an important part in the Sikh community, and several generations may live together. Elders are regarded with great respect.

Diet

Many Sikhs are vegetarian and any meat must be jhatka, where the animal is killed instantaneously, with one stroke. Sikhs will avoid eating meat prepared according to the rituals of other religions. Traditionally alcohol and other intoxicants are not allowed.

Jasvinder: employment legal specialist

'My full name is Jasvinder Kaur Sohal but I am generally known as "Jas". I am a non-practising Sikh and consider myself to be a British Asian. I am married with twin boys and part of a strong extended family. My parents-in-law are both Khalsa (practising) Sikhs and, through them, I have learned a lot about my religion. I am a solicitor who specialises in employment law and joined B&Q in July 2001 to work as an employment legal specialist.

My parents emigrated from India and were married in the UK where I was born. I was brought up in Hampshire amongst a predominantly white, English population. As a child I sometimes found it was difficult for my peers to understand my religious and cultural differences, such as keeping long, uncut hair, wearing trousers rather than skirts and knowing I would have an arranged marriage.

Nowadays, I find people in the UK from different cultural backgrounds are more accepting and genuinely interested in my religion and culture. I feel this is because there is a greater emphasis and exposure on diversity in the fields of education, the media and employment. I am proud to be a Sikh and enjoy the cultural differences it involves, such as being able to speak another language (Punjabi), wearing the traditional dress, attending Sikh weddings and enjoying its music and dance, known as Bhangra.'

Countries where there are many Sikhs

North-west India – the Punjab

Canada

USA

Languages spoken by Sikhs

Punjabi

English

Largest Sikh communities in the UK

Birmingham

Bradford

Cardiff

Coventry

Glasgow

Leeds

Leicester

Greater London (especially Southall)

Slough

Wolverhampton

Etiquette

- It is important to accommodate a Sikh's need to observe essential prayer times. Older Sikh people may feel awkward speaking to, or meeting the eyes of, members of the opposite sex.

- Sikhs born in India are likely to describe themselves as Indian, but those raised in Britain may describe themselves as British Asian.

- Because, historically, Muslim leaders tried to convert Sikhs into Muslims, sensitivities may still exist between these two communities.

As well as consulting with its own staff, the diversity team used resource materials from organisations such as the Interfaith Network and the Multi-Faith Centre[1] at the University of Derby, and the Shap Working Party on World Religions in Education.[2]

Training

The social responsibility team has developed an e-learning programme for all employees on diversity generally, including information on legislation as well as existing policies on gender, sexual orientation, age and religion. 'We see it as a starting point, building on our work around disability and inspiring our employees to learn more. The next stage will be to run diversity and equal opportunities workshops for managers. These will focus on real life case studies and be highly participative,' says O'Neill.

There is still some debate around whether there should be separate workshops, or whether the issues should be incorporated into existing training sessions. Diversity is already included in all management training from customer service to employee relations. O'Neill hopes that feedback from e-learning sessions will give the team a clearer vision of the most effective approach.

Flexibility

B&Q is also looking at various initiatives in relation to flexibility, says O'Neill.

> 'We are going to look at people's shift patterns and rotas. As a business, we are open long hours and we have to be flexible about adapting to the needs of different faiths. This already happens to a certain extent. For example some of our Jewish staff leave early on a Friday but work Sunday instead. This is agreed at a local level. We want to ensure that managers have the right information so that they feel comfortable and confident about handling this type of request.'

The HR team is working on a work-life policy. It is running trials for annualised hours, core hours, job-sharing, and term-time contracts. Feedback from focus groups has revealed many ad hoc arrangements and no formalised guidelines on how to handle requests from, for example, women returning from maternity leave who want to work part-time, or someone who wants to go back to India for six weeks. 'Clearly there needs to be a more standardised approach,' says O'Neill.

Quiet room

Quiet rooms, set aside where employees can pray, are gradually being introduced although rooms are not exclusively for this purpose. 'When I worked as a store manager at B&Q in Beckton,' says O'Neill, 'staff would use a training room or office to pray. We want to offer our staff somewhere more appropriate.' But she stresses, 'Our approach in all aspects of diversity is about being inclusive and treating people with respect, not about segregation.

> 'Guidelines now specify that quiet rooms are to be incorporated in all new stores. At head office we are trialing quiet rooms to see how successful they are and to check they are not used and abused. Guidelines for old stores

direct managers to talk to employees and find out what is most appropriate for them. What is important is that there is a culture where employees feel comfortable to ask and managers feel confident about responding to requests.'

Dress

The question of dress, a common source of discrimination for faith groups, has never arisen at B&Q, according to O'Neill. A visit to B&Q head office reveals why. Not a suit or a shoulder pad in sight! The company has an informal dress code and everyone, including senior managers, wears casual clothes. There is a pervading atmosphere of openness and informality unusual for a head office of a major corporation. Many offices are open plan and meetings often take place outside the office setting. The specially-designed building has large landings and communal areas with room for tables and chairs where staff frequently gather for brainstorming and planning meetings.

Language badges

One example of how B&Q sought to use the benefits of cultural diversity amongst its staff in order to generate more business from ethnic minority customers was through the use of language badges. O'Neill says:

> 'We had found that non-English speakers were coming to stores and only being able to communicate through their children. Often misunderstandings would arise because the children didn't understand exactly what it was their parents were after, and perhaps more importantly weren't interested.'

A survey of all B&Q staff in July 2001 found that over 1,200 staff spoke more than 60 different languages, with many staff being multi-lingual. Languages spoken include Afrikaans, Punjabi, Gujarati, Zulu, British Sign Language (BSL) and Welsh. O'Neill says:

> 'We introduced language badges for staff who wanted to wear them, indicating which languages they spoke so that customers could approach them directly without needing an interpreter. We have held 'how to' demonstrations in Gujarati to give people confidence to tackle DIY jobs on their own. And, in one of our stores in Birmingham, we advertised interpreters in different languages for some of our demonstrations.'

Managers were instructed to put up a language poster and spread sheet on diversity notice boards so that staff were aware of the languages spoken at their store.

Community initiatives

Alongside more specific policies on cultural diversity, B&Q has also targeted ethnic minority communities as part of its policy on corporate social responsibility. Stores are encouraged to work with local community organisations through the *B&Q Better Neighbourhood Programme*. In Wednesbury, the store arranged a 'better neighbour grant' for the local mosque, as well as providing materials for a housing association for people from ethnic minorities.

In addition to running ethnic minority recruitment fairs to encourage graduates to look at the organisation as a serious career option, B&Q is involved in the ethnic minority mentoring programme at Southampton Institute. 'We have had three of their students working at our head office learning about the different departments, and they have been very positive about B&Q as a place to work' says O'Neill.

When a new store opened in Bolton the HR manager recognised that they were not getting many applications from ethnic minorities. The manager contacted the Bolton ethnic minority business centre and organised a day when people could come in to the centre and discuss job opportunities with representatives from B&Q. The store has been open for a year now and a long-term relationship has developed which is mutually supportive, according to O'Neill.

O'Neill has also held briefings with resourcing managers and given them information on regional demographics so they can identify whether or not they have an issue with recruiting. She also gives them details of local groups who might be able to help.

> 'We have new store opening in Redditch for which we have produced information in other languages and given details to ethnic minority press to advertise the new store and to aid recruitment.'

Tips from the employer

Business benefits

The business case for cultural diversity is an integral part of B&Q's core values, says O'Neill.

> 'Within B&Q, our values talk about treating people with dignity and respect; the business case for being inclusive with regard to different cultures and faiths reinforces those values and helps us to better fulfil our visions of being a "great place to work and shop" for everyone. Some of the ways in which this is demonstrated is through: improved retention; increased employee satisfaction and loyalty; creating better team work,

understanding, pride and belonging; wider recruitment pool; and increased perception of career opportunities.'

Achieving cultural change

Mike Cutt, personnel director at B&Q, has the following to say about cultural diversity in B&Q.

'We have positioned cultural diversity in B&Q as a business opportunity first, and a moral imperative second. That is not to belittle the moral dimension – we have a very distinctive culture in B&Q that is firmly based on company values that are inherently supportive of diversity. The problem is our employees' awareness and understanding of minority cultures. I believe the best way to progress that is to *pull* it by harnessing their strong commercial instincts, rather than to *push* it by confronting prejudices born out of ignorance. We have already found that store staff are keen to learn about other cultures and religions so as to appeal to their business needs and this immediately helps their appreciation of diversity in employment'.

Implementing a Diversity Strategy: Using a Step-By-Step Approach

The following case study looks at how B&Q implemented its strategic plan and business plan for diversity by using a step-by-step approach.

CASE STUDY: How B&Q developed its strategic plan and business plan for disability

Step One: Diversity research

A series of research initiatives was launched which were designed to gather information on customer and employee issues and disability.

Key factors of the research initiatives:

- they were customer driven; and

- all those taking part were disabled people.

Warrington was chosen as the research area. With a representative group assembled, disabled volunteers then embarked on a programme of customer focus groups, mystery shopping and telephone surveys to help establish the difficulties encountered by disabled people when shopping. After a number of feedback sessions, B&Q were able to build up a picture of the access and customer service problems encountered by disabled and elderly people when shopping at B&Q. The stores already had a policy on older people and it made sense to link the two.

The research from Warrington showed that stores had several access and customer care issues, which resulted in people with impairments finding shopping in stores difficult. Access and navigation were major issues, as was choosing the products. The feedback sessions also showed that disabled people had, in the past, either been excluded from shopping altogether or received a poor level of service. Difficulties included:

- getting around the store;
- choosing the right product;
- communication with staff;
- access to the store;
- reading the signs and the Point of Sale information;
- lack of rest points;
- counters being to high;
- poor car parking;
- attitudes;
- lack of auxiliary aids;
- lack of awareness regarding the *DDA 1995*; and
- potential negative public relations (PR).

Step Two

The Board at B&Q recognised and accepted the findings and agreed that its vision should be to offer an inclusive shopping experience for disabled people. The lessons learnt in Warrington led to Norwich B&Q warehouse being opened as the first fully accessible store proving that B&Q was able to include disabled people into the main customer base.

Key factors include the following.

- Expert advice in the development of the store from a design point of view and in developing the awareness training.

- Every department in the development of the new store from property design to marketing was involved.

- The vision was communicated to all departments to see how they could impact on accessibility.

Step Three: Developing the action plan

Lack of awareness of disability was the single biggest issue of concern from the Warrington feedback. Most disabled people understood issues on physical barriers and were realistic about what could be changed. However, poor customer service and lack of understanding was simply unacceptable. It became clear that staff awareness training was going to be a crucial issue if B&Q was to achieve a cultural change that went right across the business. This led to an understanding of the needs of disabled employees and the recognition that B&Q was weak in this area.

The action plan led to a decision that all new stores would be inclusively designed, whilst existing stores would all start to receive training and auxiliary aids. A full range of services became available for disabled people in the stores.

- Wider, accessible car parking spaces with footpath access to the store.
- Electronic 'Spacehogs' for monitoring the use of accessible spaces.
- Level kerb areas.
- Reflective strips on all bollards.
- Improved signs in store using black on white and use of icons where appropriate.
- Lowered counters.
- Wider doors with full vision panels.
- Switches re-set at wheelchair accessible height.
- Installation of a stair lift.
- Recessed non-slip mats.
- Accessible toilet facilities.
- Sign language interpretation and sub-text on all customer facing videos and staff training videos.
- The provision of both electric and manual wheel chairs.
- Portable induction loops to assist hearing impaired shoppers.
- Wider aisles.
- Braille on all door signs.

Training

The board believed that if B&Q could get customer service right for a disabled person, it could get it right for everyone. However, this would only work if B&Q could train every member of staff. A distance learning workbook was created in partnership with the Grass Roots Group (GRG) and supplied to every member of staff. The members of staff were invited to study the book at their own pace. As soon as each person felt familiar with its contents he or she took part in a special automated telephone test which asked random questions based on the workbook. The test was private and required a pin number for identification. A 'pass' was recorded

if the person achieved ten correct answers; those who failed could take the test again as soon as they were ready. To ensure the training remained a priority for each store, 'league tables' of successful store passes were produced, resulting in 70% of staff having participated within six months of the launch. Aside from meeting B&Q's own objectives, this measurable training may prove important in meeting the requirements of the *DDA 1995*.

Disability champions

Employees at all levels were engaged in order to sustain the initiative. 'Disability champions' were appointed for each store. The champions were all taken on an 'away day' in Blackpool where they received a day's briefing from Philip Friend, B&Q's specialist consultant. In order to support the champions a reference manual was launched containing information on disability. Following the champions away day, a series of team briefs were launched to support the training workbook. In addition, B&Q realised that it need to support the stores on a day-to-day basis with local issues. The disability organisations in the community were to play an important role in the sustainability strategy. The relationship in Norwich with the Vauxhall centre had been so successful in generating innovation through partnership that a nation wide search for community partners on disability was launched. This partnership scheme is unique in that there are no predetermined objectives other than for each store to build a friendship with a local organisation which represents disability in some form. The partner is asked to help the store improve it's learning and the store can, in return, help the partner. This friendship encourages personal involvement, which is helping to give the disability project a life of its own leading to sustainability.

Key factors in B&Q's success

- There was top-level understanding and participation from the beginning.

- The disability strategy was informed and driven by the business objectives.

- Employee engagement was achieved to drive change throughout the business.

- Management commitment was achieved through performance recognition as the project was built into store standards.

- There was clear communication with regular newsletters and notice boards.

- Awareness and knowledge went across the whole organisation.

- Measurement and reporting was high profile appearing in the annual report.

- The community involvement ensured sustainability.

- Most importantly, this was a holistic approach carried through to completion. It was not a set of ad hoc initiatives pulled together.

In summary, B&Q was able to design a holistic approach to disability which resulted in a change of attitude to marketing, building design, training, product development and staff recruitment. Business benefits which could be measured included good PR, customer satisfaction, product sales, recruitment and retention. It achieved recognition by working in partnership with local communities and experts and, above all, it was able to demonstrate its achievement. B&Q was proud to receive the *EASE Award* in 1999 and 2000, and the *Business in the Community Award* for innovation through partnership. Diversity was seen as a business issue, with accountability lying directly with the managing director who personally ensured the strategy was driven throughout the company.

How the business case was argued

The business case was argued using the following research data.[3]

Disabled people as a customer base

- There are 8.6 million disabled people in the UK.

- 93% of disabled people become disabled after the age of 21.

- Conservative estimates suggest that over 70% of disabled adults live in their own home or with family.

- One in four people either are disabled or know someone who is.

- Seven million people act as carers to a disabled person.

Of the 8.6 million disabled people:

- 5.8 million are deaf and hard of hearing (5.2 million are hard of hearing);

- 2.5 million have mobility problems (350,000 wheelchair users); and

- 1.7 million are blind and partially sighted (1.5 million are partially sighted).

(Note that some people have more than one impairment usually as a result of the onset of age, hence the total of ten million in the breakdown.)

Of the 8.6 million disabled people, 1.5 million are severely disabled, live in residential care or fall below the national income average. 5.3 million disabled people are of working age

Additional business benefits

All the initiatives, which are recommended to make shopping easier for disabled people clearly have benefits to all customers.

- Access issues for wheelchairs users and people with mobility impairments, such as level kerbs and wider aisles make it easy for trolleys and parents with children.

- Clearer signs, using black on white lettering, and icons for people with dyslexia, help people where English is not the first language. Navigation of the store is difficult for people with mental health problems or learning difficulties; clearer maps and directional signs are extremely helpful.

- Disability awareness training is delivered in a unique and powerful way incorporating customer care training. 'If business can get service right for disabled people, then it can get it right for most people,' should be the philosophy.

- PR benefit to the brand is likely to be significant as diversity and ethical issues are beginning to influence corporate reputation.

- Employee satisfaction benefits as people become engaged with a new aspect of their job.

YORKSHIRE ELECTRICITY

Yorkshire Electricity: Supporting Deaf and Hard-Of-Hearing People

Organisation profile

Yorkshire Electricity was one of the key energy providers in the country before being acquired by the Innogy Group in April 2001. The company is now part of 'npower'. Employing about 2,000 people, Yorkshire Electricity was a major supplier of electricity and gas in the Yorkshire region and beyond. The company operated in an area from the Pennines in the west to the coastline and the Humber estuary in the east.

Yorkshire Electricity made a major commitment to improving its facilities for disabled people, both customers and employees. In particular, it worked closely with the RNID to develop amenities and opportunities for deaf and hard-of-hearing people.

As result, in September 1999, the RNID awarded Yorkshire Electricity the Institute's prestigious *Louder than Words Charter* for the company's support of customers and staff who are deaf or hard-of-hearing. The RNID commended Yorkshire Electricity for its 'genuine commitment to understanding the problems faced by deaf and hard-of-hearing people and to providing practical solutions'.

Yorkshire Electricity's philosophy

Ethical concerns

'Yorkshire Electricity's commitment to excellent service is integral to everything the company does for all its stakeholders; employees and shareholders, as well as customers,' declares Tally Singh, contracts and projects manager at Yorkshire Electricity.

> 'It is our policy to ensure that all those dealing with the company are treated fairly and in a polite and professional way. In particular, where a disability could be a barrier, the company is working to adopt measures that help remove such obstacles, thereby providing equal access to services and employment opportunities.'

Business benefits

The drive to improve access for deaf and hard-of-hearing people is considered to be very much a business issue by Yorkshire Electricity, tying in with the company's key business imperative of providing the best customer service available. Yorkshire

Electricity has identified significant business benefits from proactively introducing measures that support disabled people in relation to widening its customer base, enhancing Yorkshire Electricity's public reputation, and improving employee performance (see p **231** below).

Respond proactively to the DDA 1995

'In addition,' says Singh, 'Yorkshire Electricity was eager to comply with the *Disability Discrimination Act 1995*. However, we wanted to do more than be merely *re*-active to the requirements of the Act. The company was keen to be *pro*-active in planning ahead to meet the needs of current and potential disabled customers and employees.'

Reasons for the policy

To comply with the DDA 1995

'The initial impetus stemmed from the need to comply with the *Disability Discrimination Act 1995*,' explains Singh. *Part III* of the *DDA 1995* provides that 'disabled people should not be treated less favourably by those who provide goods, facilities or services to the public'. All service providers, and particularly public utilities, are required to:

- make 'reasonable adjustments' for disabled people, such as providing them with auxiliary aids and services;

- change practices, policies or procedures which make it impossible or unreasonably difficult for disabled people to make use of services; and

- provide a reasonable alternative method of making services available to disabled people, where a physical feature makes it impossible or unreasonably difficult for disabled people to make use of them.

Regulatory pressure

'Within the utilities industry,' Singh continues, 'the *DDA 1995* is reinforced by the Utilities Act 2000, and Ofgem (the regulatory body for the gas and electricity industry) also wholeheartedly supports the legislation. They are pushing utilities, such as Yorkshire Electricity, to comply with the Act to the greatest extent possible.'

Improve company performance

While priding itself on the high level of customer service it already offers, Yorkshire Electricity acknowledges that to maintain and improve on this standard depends upon a well-trained and motivated workforce. The company contends that the measures it is implementing to support people with hearing difficulties make an enormous contribution to achieving these business goals.

By improving and expanding its service to disabled customers, Yorkshire Electricity expects to retain and attract new customers. In addition, making services accessible and attractive to disabled customers will also appeal to a much wider range of customer, such as senior citizens.

Key aspects of the strategy

Utilising external expertise

Recognising that the company did not have the in-house expertise to comply with the *DDA 1995* to the high standards it wanted, Singh looked outside the company to discover what assistance was available. 'We came across the RNID's *Louder than Words Charter*,' he explains. 'This was comprehensive enough to ensure that by achieving its standards we would also deliver best practice in relation to other types of disability.'

Mainstreaming

Yorkshire Electricity's approach to meeting the RNID's requirements reflects the company's view that improving access for disabled people is a mainstream business issue. 'Ensuring compliance with the *DDA 1995* was viewed as a routine business performance project,' Singh declares, 'therefore, responsibility for implementing the RNID recommendations fell under the aegis of the policy and projects team.'

While working closely with the HR department, it was recognised that the policy and projects team had the expertise and resources to roll out the initiative throughout the company. According to Singh, ensuring that disability awareness was embedded into company thinking throughout the organisation was essential.

Ensuring long-term change

Singh stresses the importance of on-going action to bring about long-term behavioural change: 'The whole company was very proud to achieve the RNID's charter and it recognised the hard work everyone had put in. But we always saw the award of the charter as a starting point rather than an end in itself.

'The charter was just the launchpad. We know that we still have a long way to go and that we have not actually got there yet in terms of where we want to be. Yorkshire Electricity is committed to long-term change and that is not something that happens overnight. We are trying to tackle people's behaviour and attitude, rather than just changing symbols, etc. Changing behaviour takes longer.'

Disability-friendly initiatives

The Louder than Words Charter

The process of achieving the *Louder than Words Charter* began with the RNID conducting a disability audit within the company. Yorkshire Electricity was then given a list of action points to implement. Yorkshire Electricity spent more than a year introducing deaf awareness initiatives to achieve the quality standards required by the charter. However, Singh stresses that this was regarded as just the beginning: 'The award of the charter was always seen as a starting point, rather than an end in itself, and we have continued to work with the RNID to improve our service to both deaf and hard-of-hearing customers and employees.'

Equal opportunities policy

To raise awareness of disability issues within the company, Yorkshire Electricity introduced a new equal opportunities policy which included disability matters (see **CHAPTER EIGHT – MODEL POLICIES**). Introducing a new policy specifically dealing with issues faced by staff and customers with disabilities was pivotal to complying with the RNID's initial action points. The new policy was designed to ensure that customers and employees who are disabled in any way are able to take advantage of Yorkshire Electricity's services and job opportunities.

Disability awareness raising training

The introduction of the new policy was consolidated with a two-week rolling programme of disability awareness training encompassing all employees. The training was conducted off-site and lasted half a day. This was designed to get employees interested in the policy and to deliver long-term commitment throughout the company to fairness and equal access.

All training was conducted by the RNID and covered the new equal opportunities policy and disability awareness raising. As well as seminars and workshops, the training included hands-on sessions, such as testing hearing aids and wearing blinker type glasses. The positive business case was also fully explained.

Getting senior management endorsement

Training began with the executive team (comprising the chief executive, the managing directors of supply and distribution respectively, the retail director and the energy trading director). It was considered crucial to get the team's endorsement for the new policy and its backing for the programme of work to be undertaken. The senior management team (comprising 13 branch heads) also attended a full day's off-site training.

Other training initiatives

Supervisors received a full day's on-site training and then passed on the training to their teams. Singh, who arranged the disability awareness training, says: 'I took a holistic approach and involved all sections of the business; domestic and business units and the support services. The training was well received and very successful. The executive team became committed to it and everyone pulled together to try and improve services for deaf and hard-of-hearing customers and staff.'

For example, the company agreed to sponsor 54 staff who wanted to take British Sign Language (BSL) classes in their own time. Some 85% passed the course and over half of these have gone on to the next stage.

In addition to the initial roll-out of training across the company, the corporate induction training has been changed to include disability awareness raising for all new starters.

Disseminating information

Yorkshire Electricity implemented other measures to raise awareness of disability issues within the company. For example, a leaflet detailing the *Louder than Words Charter* and, in particular, the obligations of staff to comply with it, was sent to all 2,000 Yorkshire Electricity employees. A *Message of the Day* email about disability issues was also sent to all staff, and the disability policies were placed on the company intranet where they are accessible to all employees.

Updates relating to disability are regularly featured in employee magazines, and RNID information leaflets have been made available to staff and customers in the company's reception areas. Yorkshire Electricity also contributes to the RNID members' magazine, *One in Seven*.

Customer support training

Disability awareness training has been reinforced where appropriate with practical, job-related training. In particular, Yorkshire Electricity has introduced a number of measures to assist employees communicate with deaf and hard-of-hearing customers. These include the following.

- All staff who deal with customers, such as meter readers, customer liaison officers and receptionists, now receive training in deaf awareness and in communications tactics. This is done by the Yorkshire Electricity training team as part of the routine training programme.

- Staff who have extensive dialogue with customers off site, such as the twelve customer liaison officers, now carry a personal listening device that amplifies sound to aid conversation. Appropriate communication support is identified for deaf or hard-of-hearing customers before an appointment takes place and assistance is offered for customers who are hard of hearing.

- All call centre staff now receive, as part of their normal job training, training in the difficulties faced by hard-of-hearing customers and how to communicate effectively with them. They are also made aware of the textphone and typetalk facilities available (see '*Technological improvements*' on p **229** below).

- The company is registered with BT's Typetalk service which enables deaf or hard-of-hearing customers to communicate. All supervisors and team managers are aware of the account details and how to use the service.

- All letters to customers are now in 11 point font size in compliance with the Royal National Institute for the Blind's (RNIB) clear print guidelines and it is intended to adopt this font size for all literature published for the public. The textphone number is advertised with the main telephone number. All television advertising has closed caption subtitles and cinema advertising is subtitled. A separate textphone number is included on subtitles for customers to ring.

- Whenever a public meeting is held, a portable room loop or mini-loop is made available to assist hearing aid users. Also, if deaf people are present, it is established whether or not they require an interpreter.

Improving employment practices

To ensure that disabled people have the opportunity to get a job and to compete equally in the workplace, Yorkshire Electricity also changed its employment practices to be more inclusive of the needs of people with disabilities. For example, on the advice of the RNID, the company's equal opportunities statement in recruitment advertisements was amended to read, '*We are an equal opportunities employer including people with disabilities*'. The textphone number is printed on all internal and external recruitment advertisements (see '*Technological improvements*' on p **229** below).

The recruitment procedure was also altered so that the health questionnaire which requests disability information is no longer required at the application stage. This information is only requested should a candidate make it to the second stage; applicants are then asked if they have any special requirements.

On recruitment of a deaf or hard-of-hearing employee, the section manager or supervisor is required to identify if any specialised assistive devices may be needed to help the employee in his or her job. It is recommended that deaf or hard-of-hearing employees be tested by the company nurse to help identify the type of assistive devices which may be needed.

However, Mary Reid and Louise Nelson of Yorkshire Electricity's HR team, stress that: 'We always try to make sure that a disabled worker is not put in an awkward position. The onus is on us to find out what the job entails and what adjustments we can make to ensure that the individual can really do the job. We then put those adjustments in place.'

Employee communication support

The need to provide additional communication support for deaf and hard-of-hearing employees is also being addressed. A deaf person needs communication support whenever important information is to be relayed, such as at job interviews, appraisals and disciplinary hearings. Lack of complete understanding in such cases may have serious consequences for employees, and for employers who later may face employment tribunal proceedings.

A system was introduced by Yorkshire Electricity to identify the type of support required by employees with hearing loss on an individual basis. Three types of support are now provided:

- a BSL-user to a high level of competency for deaf sign language users;

- lipspeakers for people who became deaf after acquiring language; and

- assistive listening devices, such as induction loops (see '*Technological improvements*' on p **229** below), for hearing aid users.

Attention is also now paid to environmental matters, such as reducing background noise and not standing in front of a window when addressing a deaf or hard-of-hearing employee. Similarly, when staff with hearing problems attend a meeting or team brief, the person holding the meeting/briefing is expected to ensure that assistive listening devices are available. When communication support cannot be provided, as much information as possible is given in writing.

'Often the adjustments needed to help a disabled employee are really simple,' says Nelson. 'For example, a location change to cut down on background noise or issuing a headset with two earpieces rather than one. These are little things that can make a big difference to that individual getting to grips with the job.'

Technological improvements

Yorkshire Electricity also introduced a number of practical technological improvements to help overcome physical barriers for people with hearing difficulties. For example, textphones enable deaf or hard-of-hearing people to get in touch with the company direct without the need to go through a third party. As such, textphones with freephone numbers have been installed into key areas of the business, including the customer contact centre in Bradford, the HR department in Scarcroft and the business call centre in Hull.

These moves have proved popular with employees working in these departments. Chris Watson, team leader at Hull says:

> 'We had at least one business customer who regularly had to use a third party to contact us. When we got our own textphone, we were able to advise her that she could contact us direct. As the word spreads we expect more people to use this facility.'

On the employment side, Jamie Stuart and Debbie Sheldon, HR recruitment consultants at Yorkshire Electricity, believe that: 'The textphone will increase the opportunities we already offer to all people with disabilities, making us even more approachable and straightforward to contact.'

In addition, a number of mini-loops have been purchased and are kept at reception desks in each supply office to assist deaf or hard-of-hearing people. The loops cut down background noise and make it easier for people with hearing aids to hear what is being said. Receptionists are being trained in the use of mini-loops and members of staff or customers who may benefit from the use of a mini-loop can ask for one at reception.

Supporting the RNID

As well as introducing internal improvements to company practices and facilities, Yorkshire Electricity continues to actively support and participate in the RNID's campaign, *Working for Change*. The campaign aims to get the business and the voluntary sectors to work together to improve employment opportunities for deaf and hard-of-hearing people.

In particular, the company has taken a leading role in the RNID's latest employment project, *Head Start*. Intended to boost work opportunities for deaf and hard-of-hearing graduates, the initiative will team up university students with companies for careers' advice, work experience and mentoring.

'We see the *Head Start* project as a natural continuation of the work that we have done to date,' says Singh. 'We want to ensure students develop the skills that are needed in today's workplace so that they can successfully apply for jobs and enter the workforce.'

Yorkshire Electricity will be fully supporting the project by offering work placements, face-to-face mentoring, work shadowing, peer mentoring, e-mentoring, CV writing workshops, and help with mock interviews.

Tips from the employer

Update training regularly

Singh stresses the importance of updating the disability awareness training at regular intervals so that it remains a live issue within the company.

> 'We are aiming to change behaviour and that cannot be done on a one-off basis. It is intended to reinforce the initial roll out of training with quarterly awareness raising sessions to ensure that disability awareness becomes firmly rooted in company procedures and practices. We do not want the initiative to become nothing more than a tick-box exercise.'

Maintain momentum

A programme of action has been instigated to maintain momentum. This will regularly assess how to improve policies and practices and implement practical adjustments to expand access for disabled people. Yorkshire Electricity is determined that it will continue to work hard to make sure that disability awareness is spread throughout the organisation, both in terms of making company procedures and practices more inclusive and in making practical adjustments to accommodate disabled people.

Keep the message simple

Neil emphasises the need to keep the message simple:

> 'We try to raise people's awareness that being disabled does not mean being different and that making adjustments is not about making a fuss or spending vast amounts of money. Most of our disabled employees do not want a fuss. We do, however, urge them to come and talk to us if they require support. Often the adjustments needed to help a disabled employee are really straightforward and inexpensive.'

Business Benefits of Developing Support for Disabled People

Yorkshire Electricity has identified key business benefits in relation to developing support for disabled people. These include increasing its customer base, enhancing Yorkshire Electricity's public reputation and improving company performance.

External motivators

- Disabled people and their carers form one of the most under-represented and under-used economic markets. There are an estimated 8.6 million disabled people in Great Britain (14% of the population), representing a combined annual spending power of £33 billion. Providing services which meet the needs of this group will also win the support of their families and carers, increasing the combined annual spending potential to £68 billion.

- Improving and expanding its service to disabled customers will allow Yorkshire Electricity to retain and attract new customers, as well as appeal to a wider range of customers, such as senior citizens. Over half a million disabled people live in the Yorkshire region (approximately 14.3% of the Yorkshire population), yet Yorkshire Electricity only has 4,300 customers on its Priority Services Register (a database of elderly and vulnerable customers with special power supply needs). This indicates that there is a large market in the region for the company's services and products for disabled people.

- In particular, one in seven of the company's customers is likely to be deaf or hard of hearing; therefore, making appropriate adjustments in this area will benefit existing customers and staff, and provide excellent opportunities for enhancing Yorkshire Electricity's public reputation, making it the company of choice for customers, investors and employees.

- Being the first utility company in the market place promoting these services will put Yorkshire Electricity ahead of its competitors; the company will be seen as the innovator and others as imitators.

- Yorkshire Electricity will be able to maintain market share. More and more companies are developing services to meet the needs of older and disabled customers. As people come to expect these services, Yorkshire Electricity argues that those companies failing to provide them will suffer a significant loss of market share.

Internal motivators

Implementing measures to support people with hearing difficulties will help deliver a well-trained and motivated workforce, which will contribute to the company's key commercial goal of offering customers the highest possible standard of service.

Singh cites some of the benefits to company performance as:

- giving access to a pool of 3.3 million people of working age in the UK who are deaf or hard-of-hearing;

- enabling managers and staff to better understand the problems facing deaf or hard-of-hearing staff and customers, thereby improving customer services generally;

- breaking down barriers between hearing and deaf or hard-of-hearing colleagues;

- improving communication skills across the business;

- helping to create a multi-skilled, enlightened workforce;

- increasing staff morale;

- ensuring that the company complies with the *DDA 1995*;

- introducing new ideas and fresh ways of doing things; and

- providing the company with a sharper edge in an extremely competitive market place.

BRADFORD & BINGLEY PLC

Bradford & Bingley plc: Encouraging Ethnic Diversity

Organisation profile

After 149 years as a mutual building society, Bradford & Bingley converted to plc status in December 2000. Having expanded rapidly in recent years through organic growth, acquisition and partnership, the company has transformed itself from a traditional building society into a plc offering a broad range of financial and property services through a variety of channels, including online facilities.

Bradford & Bingley is now the UK's fourth largest estate agency, one of the biggest high street independent financial advisory businesses, and a leading mortgage broker. Based in West Yorkshire, the company has a national distribution network comprising over 500 branches, over 800 financial advisors and a number of third party distributors. Employing approximately 7,600 employees, Bradford & Bingley has over four million customers. Profit for the year ended 31 December 2000 was £231.4 million before tax.

The appointment of Christopher Rodrigues as chief executive in June 1996 gave stimulus to the development of Bradford & Bingley's ethnic diversity strategy. He made it clear that his long-term vision for the organisation was to create a more diverse workforce, especially in relation to increasing the number of women and Asian staff in management positions.

Bradford & Bingley's philosophy

Moral principle

Bradford & Bingley's values support respect for the rights of others, honesty, commitment to diversity and involvement in the local community. Reflecting the communities it serves is regarded as an important moral principle for the company.

Valuing the individual

Bradford & Bingley recognises the importance and benefits of welcoming and respecting individual differences and perspectives of people from all backgrounds. By valuing and developing the potential of each individual, the company aims to establish a highly-skilled and flexible workforce, which is able to provide the highest standard of service.

Reflecting the customer base

'We recognised that the local labour market is extremely diverse, and therefore it was essential for us to draw our employees from a wider range of backgrounds to improve and strengthen the business,' explains Candida McKay, one of Bradford & Bingley's job-sharing diversity managers. 'Our overriding aim is to ensure that our workforce reflects the community in which we do business.'

Reasons for the policy

Reflecting the customer base

'In an extremely competitive, customer-driven industry, it is vital to have a workforce that matches the diversity of our customers,' says McKay. 'Only by ensuring that the demographics of the organisation represent the communities it serves will the company gain access to all potential sources of talent, and deliver the best possible customer service.'

Encouraging Asian job applicants

Rodrigues' particular emphasis on raising the proportion of Asian employees in the organisation reflects the importance of the large Asian communities living in, and around, the Bradford and Keighley areas. For example, the organisation found that the highest concentration of Pakistanis in the country is in the Bradford area, representing 14.6% of the Bradford district population and 60% of the ethnic minority labour force in the district.

As one of the biggest employers in the locality, employing over 1,000 people in its head office alone, Bradford & Bingley was particularly concerned at the under-representation of ethnic minority groups within the organisation. The current figure for minority employees in its head office workforce is approximately 8.7%.

Encouraging Asian women

Ethnic minority groups as a whole are under-represented in Bradford district's labour force, forming one fifth of the working-age population, but just one sixth of the labour force. This discrepancy is mainly due to the particularly low levels of economic activity experienced by Pakistani and Bangladeshi women.

Key aspects of the strategy

A dedicated diversity manager post

Bradford & Bingley's commitment to achieving a more diverse workforce was formally recognised in 1998 with the creation of a dedicated diversity manager post. This was filled at the beginning of 1999 on a job-share basis.

Mainstreaming

The prime purpose of the new post was to develop a diversity strategy for the company which encompassed ethnic minority issues, disability, gender and age. The overarching intention is to work towards mainstreaming diversity as an essential consideration for the business, so that it is automatically incorporated into strategic decision-making within the company.

Senior-level commitment

Eileen Millman, Bradford & Bingley's other job-sharing diversity manager, is quick to point out the importance of Rodrigues' role to the success of the diversity strategy:

> 'Senior-level commitment and involvement has been essential to the development and implementation of the diversity strategy. The chief executive, in particular, has given his personal support to the strategy and wants to see it developed as an integral part of the business.'

Rodrigues signified his personal commitment to the racial agenda by signing up to the Commission for Racial Equality's (CRE) *Leadership Challenge* in 1997, and is providing ongoing leadership by participating in the development of the CRE's new *Leadership Challenge Framework*.

In addition, Rodrigues hosted the first of the Influencers' visits and encouraged the ongoing dialogue with the Influencers (see p **238** and p **238** below). This included focus groups to develop positive action initiatives, which were then agreed by the chief executive.

Getting line management support

The importance of getting line management commitment is also emphasised by Millman: 'Line managers must be made aware of diversity issues and own the strategy, so that it lives in the culture of the organisation, not merely in policy statements.'

As such, the diversity managers have clarified and highlighted the business case for diversity (see p **242** below), emphasising its importance for Bradford & Bingley's business strategy. In addition, there is an equal opportunities policy published on the company intranet to reinforce Bradford & Bingley's commitment to diversity (see **CHAPTER EIGHT**).

Utilising external expertise

Prior to the creation of the diversity post, Bradford & Bingley had undertaken a number of ad hoc projects with the Bradford-based charity, 'Quest for Economic Development' (QED), to raise the profile of the company as a diversity-friendly employer among the local Asian communities. McKay confirms:

> 'We believed it was imperative to learn from, and get the support of, local ethnic communities when devising our ethnic strategy. QED has been an invaluable source of expertise in this process.'

In developing its ethnic diversity strategy, the diversity managers built on the work already undertaken with QED to reinforce its diversity-friendly status.

Ethnic diversity initiatives

The diversity managers worked closely with QED in developing the ethnic diversity strategy, which consists of the following three areas:

- internal training;
- community awareness training; and

- a discrimination training programme.

These initiatives are discussed in detail below.

Internal training

The company has implemented two major pilot training programmes for its personnel. One programme is designed to raise awareness of the beliefs and values of Asian minority communities in the UK generally, while the second provides an explanation of discrimination law and related equal opportunities issues for line managers.

Community awareness training

The *Community Awareness* programme was developed in conjunction with QED and was initially piloted with Bradford & Bingley's HR community, involving about 25 people. The three half-day, QED-led training sessions concentrated on the Asian culture in recognition of its multi-faceted nature. The specific objectives of the course were to:

- gain an overview of the nature of the UK's, and, in particular, Bradford district's, diverse communities, including their history, composition and demographic trends;

- increase participants' understanding of the cultural values and norms, including religious beliefs and practices inherent to the various ethnic minority communities residing in the UK;

- gain an appreciation of the changing nature of educational, employment, enterprise and community development issues affecting ethnic minority communities; and

- inform participants of current anti-discrimination legislation, including examples of indirect discrimination and of positive action measures.

'The training programme was extremely well received and the next step is to extend this type of training to line managers in areas where there is a high Asian population, and then to all line managers,' comments McKay. The diversity managers also aim to make the training accessible to all Bradford & Bingley employees.

'The intention is to roll out the training to everyone,' McKay continues. 'The ongoing cultural awareness programme will help to develop an understanding amongst all our employees of the cultural values and norms of the various ethnic minority communities in the UK.'

Given the size of the workforce, however, it is unlikely that Bradford & Bingley will be able to resource face-to-face training for everyone. Options being considered for ongoing training, therefore, include commissioning a video based on the training or publishing a booklet for dissemination to all employees.

Discrimination training programme

The community awareness training has been reinforced by a discrimination training programme. Devised by the diversity managers in conjunction with the Race Relations Advisory Service (RRAS), the discrimination training programme has been put in place to enable Bradford & Bingley's HR community to provide training for line managers.

Delivered over a two-day period, the initial training was undertaken by the RRAS. Three sessions were held involving approximately 25 people from the HR department. The aim of the course was to give the company's trainers the knowledge, skills and confidence to deliver discrimination law and equal opportunities policy training to operational managers.

The specific objective of the training was to enable trainers to:

- state and explain the definitions of unlawful discrimination, including direct and indirect forms, genuine occupational qualifications (GOQs), positive action, victimisation and institutional racism;

- gain an understanding of the grounds covered/not covered by the main pieces of legislation, including the features of an ethnic or racial group;

- describe the broad facts and significance of the major leading cases;

- advocate the business and moral reasons for Bradford & Bingley's values and policy;

- understand the basic psychology of prejudice and discrimination;

- generate their own scripts/materials for independent delivery;

- handle questions and objections from trainees, either directly or with further research/support; and

- motivate and enable managers to monitor their own, and their team's, performance, and effect change where necessary.

The second-tier training of operational managers is now being rolled out throughout the company.

External consultation

Bradford & Bingley has also embarked on a consultation exercise with ethnic minority groups to raise awareness in the local community of the its positive approach to ethnic diversity. These consultations have also provided invaluable feedback in terms of suggesting positive action measures which it can adopt to encourage a diverse workforce.

Influencers' visits

The consultation initiative has taken the form of annual visits to the company by 'Influencers' from the local Asian community. Set up by QED, the visits are designed to raise awareness within ethnic minority communities of the career opportunities with Bradford & Bingley.

Influencers are well-respected people from the Asian community (such as youth training workers) who provide wide-ranging advice on topics such as education and careers,' explains Millman. 'The purpose of their visits is to make them aware of job opportunities at Bradford & Bingley and to provide informal interaction with line management and HR representatives.'

The first visit was held in July 2000 and involved about 40 people, including Bradford & Bingley's HR director and chief executive, Rodrigues, who hosted the first event. Rodrigues outlined what the company wanted to achieve by the meeting and he took the opportunity to stress the company's commitment to widen its recruitment pool and increase the ethnic minority representation within the organisation.

The visit featured a company video describing the types of careers available at Bradford & Bingley. This was based on the experiences of six ethnic minority employees and focused on their personal achievement within the company. In addition, the Influencers were given an information pack, containing summaries of available jobs and person specifications, details of the recruitment process, including where vacancies are advertised, and examples of aptitude tests and typical interview questions.

Influencers' workshops

'The initial meeting was considered a success, with extremely useful feedback being obtained on working more closely with the local community,' McKay emphasises. However, it was acknowledged that the visits formed just the beginning of what should be an ongoing dialogue. It was decided, therefore, to follow up the first visits with three workshops to explore more fully the recommendations which came out of the initial meetings.

The follow-up workshops involved QED representatives and influencers involved in youth training, employment and communications. Participants from Bradford & Bingley included the HR director, diversity managers, and the managers of the local Bingley estate agency and Bradford branch.

The overall objective of the workshops was to increase the number of Asian employees working for Bradford & Bingley and other organisations in Yorkshire by working with local ethnic communities. As such, the workshops examined various ways in which the participants could work together to achieve a greater representation of Asian employees from the local community.

Positive action

Recommendations for various positive action measures came out of the workshops, which were then agreed for implementation by Bradford & Bingley.

- *Perception survey:* Recognising the need to acquire accurate baseline data at the commencement of any diversity programme, Bradford & Bingley is to commission a survey to obtain information about the local ethnic minority community's perception of the company as an employer. QED is working with Bradford & Bingley to finalise the questions for the survey questionnaire.

- *Placement programme:* Given that the unemployment rates amongst the Pakistani and Bangladeshi communities are four times that of the white population, Bradford & Bingley has undertaken to develop contacts with local colleges, universities and schools which have a large Asian population to offer placements for students.
  The aim is to provide ethnic minority students with valuable experience in overcoming barriers to employment. The placement programme will be supported by successful Asian role models in order to motivate others from similar backgrounds.

- *Impact programme:* The company is also actively involved in the *Impact* programme run by the universities of Bradford, Huddersfield and Leeds Metropolitan. *Impact* is a positive action project designed to enhance employment skills and increase employment opportunities, primarily among UK minority ethnic students.
  Bradford & Bingley's personnel provided training to ethnic minority students to give them an insight into the company's recruitment process and to encourage job applications. In particular, sessions were run on 'Demystifying interviews', 'Applications, all you need to know', and 'Competency-based interviews'. These were completed earlier this the year and were very positively received.

- *Recruitment procedures:* Bradford & Bingley has also introduced positive action measures within its recruitment process to attract more applications from individuals from different cultures. 'By doing this, Bradford & Bingley wants to send out a message that the company is actively seeking applications from Asian people,' Millman asserts.

The traditional methods of advertising job vacancies has been extended to encourage applications from ethnic minorities, this includes advertising vacancies in local community centres, enabling a wider advertising of jobs in the Bradford and Keighley area.

In addition, work will be done to amend careers and advertising literature to reflect a diverse community with the intention of sending out a message of inclusion to ethnic minority communities. Nationally, in areas where there are large Asian communities, QED has played a key role in translating posters advertising branch vacancies into five Asian languages.

It is seen as particularly important to use the local community centres to raise awareness among ethnic minority communities of the company's commitment to developing a diverse workforce. This approach will be pursued throughout the UK where there the proportion of ethnic minorities in the population is high.

- *Diversity network:* Bradford & Bingley is also involved in a diversity network facilitated by QED. Participating organisations in the network share best practice in promoting positive action in order to increase ethnic minorities' representation in the workforce. According to McKay, 'The network is an invaluable mechanism for local organisations to learn from one another about what works on the ground.' Three network meetings have already been held, with representation from local retail and finance sector organisations.

Policies and procedures

Recruitment policy guidance

Positive action measures in recruitment have been underpinned with the incorporation of policy guidance for managers on diversity issues into recruitment documentation, procedures and training. For example, a section on discrimination law has been expanded to clarify how the legislation specifically applies to the recruitment process.

Steering group

A steering group comprising QED, Bradford & Bingley's HR director and the diversity managers has been set up to meet on a regular basis to monitor progress and identify issues. This group, for instance, considered and supported the positive action recommendations which came out of the workshops with Influencers.

Monitoring

Work is currently being undertaken to ensure that the company's HR systems comply with the CRE's Code of Practice on Monitoring. Agreement was obtained to introduce a system for recording all job applicants' ethnic origin by location, with a record of reasons for non-selection, where applicable, at each stage of the recruitment process.

Whereas the original application form enabled the company to record and monitor the ethnic origins of successful applicants only, a new form has been devised incorporating a tear-off slip for use by all applicants to record their ethnic details and return to the company.

This information will be held on the HR system and regular analyses will be carried out to identify where particular groups are under-represented. 'These analyses will serve to evaluate the success of any measures put in place to increase under-representation and achieve equal opportunities. This is essential to ensure that positive action is properly targeted and results monitored,' affirms McKay.

However, the new system has not provided the quality information envisaged and there has been under-reporting of ethnic minority details on the application forms. The application form is, therefore, being amended again to reinforce the importance of completing and returning the tear-off slips. It is hoped that this will encourage a more representative response.

Tips from the employer

Demonstrate top-level commitment

'Christopher Rodrigues' appointment gave visible senior-level support to the process of culture change within the organisation which is ongoing,' stresses McKay. 'The chief executive's strong backing for diversity ensures that Bradford & Bingley is on course to develop into an organisation that truly reflects the communities it serves.'

Engage with the local ethnic community

Bradford & Bingley' believes that its proactive approach of engaging face-to-face with local ethnic groups gives it the best possible chance of ensuring that any measures it introduces will meet the needs of both the organisation and of the ethnic minorities it wishes to attract. McKay asserts: 'We believe we have laid firm foundations in the past 18 months, especially as a result of our ongoing dialogue with local Asian groups.'

Provide comprehensive training

Training has an important role to play in achieving cultural change and people at all levels and in all parts of the organisation need to be involved. In particular, a programme of diversity awareness training for senior managers is seen as essential and plans for delivery of this training are currently being formulated.

Resources have been put into pilot training programmes within the company which not only support a greater appreciation of the cultural norms and values of the ethnic communities they wish to employ, but also explain the employment provisions of discrimination legislation. The intention is to make this type of training available to all employees.

The need has also been identified to mainstream diversity into routine management training and team building programmes, as well as to include the organisation's policy and values around diversity in an induction programme. This will ensure that all new employees are made aware of the importance that Bradford & Bingley gives to diversity issues.

Monitor progress

Emphasis has also been given to putting in place monitoring systems to assess the success of the positive action measures the company has introduced. In addition, the diversity managers plan to implement more positive action initiatives to ensure Bradford & Bingley's goals in relation to ethnic diversity are achieved.

Do not underestimate the task

The diversity managers are the first to acknowledge that they have just started on the journey to achieving a more ethnically diverse workforce at Bradford & Bingley. Millman admits: 'We recognise that we are just at the very start of the process, and as an organisation, there is a long way to go before we achieve true diversity in everything we do.'

Bradford & Bingley's Business Case for Diversity

The benefits of promoting diversity within Bradford & Bingley include the following.

- Gaining a competitive edge by improving customer service to all sections of the community, resulting in increased market share.
- Cost savings on recruitment and training by retaining employees.
- Reaching a larger pool of talented people.
- Creating a committed and flexible workforce.
- Meeting employee expectations and aspirations.

- Responding to social change and demographic factors, such as the growth of ethnic minority groups, which impact on the labour market.

- Establishing a strong set of organisational ethics and values.

NATIONWIDE BUILDING SOCIETY

Nationwide Building Society: Creating an Age-Diverse Workforce

Organisation profile

Nationwide is the world's largest building society and is firmly committed to keeping its mutual status. Nationwide is the UK's fourth largest mortgage lender and ninth biggest retail banking, saving and lending organisation. It offers a broad range of retail financial services, including mortgages, savings, current accounts, life assurance and investment products, personal loans and household insurance.

Nationwide has assets in excess of £74 billion. Profit before tax for the year to 4 April 2001 increased by 9.9% to £465.7 million. Nationwide employs 14,500 people, with almost one fifth based at the Swindon head office and 12% at the Northampton administration centre. Over half (53%) work in nearly 700 retail branches and the rest in technology and printing support functions.

Nationwide's main business objective is: 'To provide a full range of top value, quality financial services that are widely available and delivered with speed, courtesy and reliability – backed by policies of fairness, honesty, employee importance and corporate responsibility.'

Age discrimination was included in Nationwide's equal opportunities policy in 1991. 'Since then,' says Denise Walker, head of corporate personnel, 'the promotion of age diversity has become a core component of Nationwide's equal opportunities and diversity strategy. Nationwide is committed to an inclusive employment environment that aims to attract and retain employees across the age spectrum, and has developed an age strategy that is based on promoting the business benefits of an age-diverse workforce.' (See p **245** below for information on key aspects of Nationwide's strategy.)

Nationwide's philosophy

Happy employees means happy customers

Nationwide sees itself as an employer of choice, valuing the contribution of all its employees. 'The bottom line is that if you keep your employees happy, you keep your customers happy and that is good for business,' asserts Walker.

A holistic approach

Nationwide takes a holistic approach to diversity. Policies and practices focus on appreciating the contribution of every employee. 'By striving to meet employees' individual needs, we enable them to give their best at work,' says Walker.

Reflecting the customer base

One of Nationwide's corporate objectives is to employ a workforce which reflects its customer base, and promoting age diversity in the workplace is seen as a key component of achieving that objective.

Reasons for the policy

Reflecting all age groups

According to Walker, the key driver in Nationwide's quest for age diversity is simple: 'The Society is selling products to a broad spectrum of ages and therefore needs employees who reflect all age groups. How can you possibly have an organisation which relies on 25-year-olds when your customer base includes 75 to 80-year-olds?'

Countering corporate memory loss

Following Nationwide's merger with the Anglia Building Society in 1987, many older employees left the business as the newly-formed society shed staff. This resulted in a huge loss of corporate memory, which had a detrimental affect both on the business and composition of the workforce. 'We let too many over-50s go when we merged with Anglia and we were still suffering the consequences of that loss of experience in the early 1990s,' explains Walker.

Promoting mixed-age teams

Whilst Nationwide was losing its older workers, it was increasing its intake of younger employees. The success of Nationwide's FlexAccount launched in 1987 meant that it had to expand its workforce quickly. Specifically, a large number of school leavers were recruited to the Swindon head office. Within a few years, however, there followed a high turnover of staff – up to 45% in some areas of the business.

In response, Nationwide pursued a number of initiatives to improve the age balance in its workforce with the aim of creating more stability in the workforce by encouraging mixed-age teams. Walker contends:

'An age-diverse workforce can benefit team working. It creates a balance of skills and nurtures confidence, leading to improved performance. While younger employees may have the ability to grasp new technology quickly, they do not have the years of experience that an older employee can offer.'

Key aspects of the strategy

Gaining senior commitment

As head of corporate personnel, Walker has been the advocate for age diversity in Nationwide and the driving force behind the development of the age strategy. She has raised the profile of the importance of an age-diverse workforce by selling the commercial benefits to the board, senior managers, across the business and to other personnel managers (see p **246** and p **249**).

'Top level support,' Walker argues, 'is essential to achieving any organisational change, and Nationwide's board and chief executive's committee have expressed their commitment to the Society's diversity strategy. They have pledged their support for specific diversity initiatives and are closely involved in all aspects of diversity policy development.' Progress reports are regularly sent to the board on equal opportunities issues.

Monitoring at a senior level

The diversity agenda is overseen by the Promoting Equality of Opportunity Group (PEOG), which is chaired by the personnel and development divisional director, with membership comprising heads of business areas. To ensure that age diversity remains a priority, the group formally monitors the effectiveness of employment policies in relation to all aspects of equal opportunities, including regularly reviewing workforce composition and monitoring external benchmarking data. This high-level business forum also makes recommendations for improvement. A recent example is the work-life balance initiative (see p **247** below), which was also supported by the chief executive.

Setting key performance indicators

The personnel and development division has agreed to age diversity as a key performance indicator. This ensures that real progress can be monitored at a senior level. Targets on age profile were set for the division for the first time in 2000. The aim was for 9% of the workforce to be aged 50 and over. This was met and a 10% target was set for the next financial year. Given that Nationwide employs 14,500 people in total, this is seen as a more challenging goal.

Mainstreaming

While the corporate personnel department is responsible for developing and implementing positive and inclusive strategies for managing an ageing workforce, Walker emphasises that the responsibility for promoting age diversity is spread across the organisation:

> 'There is no specific budget for equal opportunities and any costs arising from implementing the age diversity agenda are absorbed into other project work. This is part of Nationwide's overall approach of integrating equal opportunities into all business areas, rather than it being seen as a "marginal activity".'

As a result, age awareness has been built into all aspects of the business, with Nationwide adopting policies and practices which are conducive to an inclusive working environment. This includes, for example, allowing greater employee choice in how and when to work, and for how long. In particular, practices are monitored to ensure that age discrimination does not feature in recruitment, selection, training and development, promotion, retirement and redundancy procedures.

Promoting the business case

Walker has aimed to change behaviour within Nationwide by demonstrating the positive aspects of diversity and showing how it can benefit the business as well as individual employees. 'The business benefits are obvious,' Walker argues, 'with our statistics showing that older workers perform better. In our appraisal system, 40% of people aged over 50 received a score of "excellent" or "exceptional", compared with just under 9% of people under 20.'

Nationwide's sickness records confirm that employees aged over 50 do not have more periods of sickness absence than younger staff, and with a mixed-age workforce, the Society's staff turnover is below half the industry average. 'This translates into a saving of £10 million in recruitment costs in 2000,' asserts Walker.

These demonstrable benefits, along with features and positive case studies, are used to signal Nationwide's commitment to age diversity through such channels as the employees' news magazine, *Nationwide Live*, the audio-news programme and the intranet. These all provide employees with the opportunity to give feedback on age diversity at work.

Age diversity initiatives

Nationwide has pursued a number of initiatives to improve the age balance in its workforce, including the following.

Telephone interviewing

One of the first and most radical initiatives taken by Nationwide was to develop a new recruitment procedure. In 1993 Nationwide experienced high employee turnover in the sales force and Nationwide was determined to improve its recruitment procedure for this area of the business.

In conjunction with The Gallup Organization, Nationwide developed a telephone interviewing process to initially recruit customer advisers in the retail branch network. This initiative was based on objective skills criteria from existing best performing sales people.

The preliminary assessments of candidates is made through telephone discussions, which lowers the risk of assumptions being made based on appearance and qualifications. The candidate is then contacted at an agreed time and date by an interviewer trained in equal opportunities selection procedures. If the candidate's skills profile matches the specified criteria, a face-to-face interview is arranged with a line manager.

According to Walker, telephone interviewing has helped broaden the age range of new employees, with a number of people in their 50s being recruited who traditionally might have been rejected at the short-listing stage. The telephone short-listing process has been expanded to a wide range of appointments, including senior customer advisors, senior branch managers, financial consultants and retail management trainees.

Recruitment advertising

Other recruitment measures were the removal of age bars from all recruitment advertisements, and designing and targeting job advertisements to attract a wider age range of applicants. For example, Nationwide has recently targeted people from both ends of the age spectrum in its recruitment campaign for its IT department by featuring employees from the relevant age groups in recruitment literature.

Work-life balance

Under the umbrella of work-life balance, Nationwide has developed a range of policies which recognise the need for working arrangements to suit employees at different stages in life, rather than just meeting the needs of older workers. These include part-time working, job share, compressed working week, working from home, employment breaks (which includes time off for carers) and term-time working. There are also a number of paid, and unpaid, leave policies.

These flexible working arrangements are supported by Nationwide's flexible benefits scheme, *Choices*, to enable employees to choose benefits which suit individual circumstances. In the long term, these policies are expected to result in higher workforce satisfaction as employees work in an environment where managers support flexible working, enabling individuals to continue working without compromising their career or personal responsibilities.

Nationwide's corporate plan includes a critical success factor based on employee satisfaction; age awareness issues have been included age in the annual employee satisfaction survey. In the 2001 employee satisfaction survey, 80% of respondents felt that management supported equality of opportunity regardless of age. Some 60% of employees aged over 50 thought that Nationwide was a better organisation to work for than a year ago.

Long service awards

A new long service recognition scheme was launched in July 2000 to highlight that Nationwide values all its employees and is keen to retain their skills. Awards are given to employees with 10, 20, 30 and 40 years' service. Analysis shows that the average length of service for employees over the age of 50 is 19 years, so the policy favours older employees.

Working beyond retirement age

Other initiatives in the pipeline to support older workers include a review of the age at which an employee is recruited and the development of a policy to retain employees beyond the standard retirement age. Currently, all contracts of employment automatically terminate at age 60 and a fixed-term contract for a period of up to two years is offered to employees wishing to continue working for Nationwide after taking normal retirement.

However, Nationwide is in discussions with the staff union to develop arrangements for recruiting and retaining employees up to age 70. Walker comments: 'Existing staff will be able to continue to work on the same basis, and the Society is in discussions with the staff union to agree issues relating to benefits.'

Flexible retirement

In addition, Nationwide's pension fund is also reviewing the guidelines for flexible retirement and investigating the possibility of extending the early retirement age from 50 to 55, as proposed by the Government. The pension fund trust deed and rules have been improved to enable employees to continue in the fund beyond age 60.

External initiatives

Nationwide does not limit its promotion of age diversity to internal action; it has been an enthusiastic and committed campaigner for the cause outside the organisation. For example, Walker works closely with the Employers' Forum on Age and is chair of the Forum members' advisory group. She was also involved in the development of the Government's Code of Practice for Age Diversity and continues to contribute to various government departments' work on age diversity issues.

Nationwide is keen to share its expertise with other employers and often participates in external conferences and seminars. Its external involvement with campaigning to promote age diversity has raised its profile as a caring and progressive employer.

Nationwide is regarded as an expert on good age diversity practices and, as a result, has received much positive media coverage in both the national press and professional magazines. This enhances Nationwide's reputation as an employer of choice.

In November 2000 Nationwide won the then DfEE-sponsored *Personnel Today* Award for promoting age diversity in the workplace. Its approach to managing age diversity was also accredited in the *Sunday Times*' '50 best places to work for' survey, when Nationwide was rated 30th.

Tips from the employer

Demonstrate business benefits

The outcome of Nationwide's commitment to promoting age diversity in the workplace is that both the corporate objectives and those of the personnel and development division are met. From recruitment through to retirement, Nationwide has demonstrated that real business benefits can be achieved by embedding age diversity into all employment practices.

According to Walker: 'Developing robust procedures and policies that demonstrate our commitment to promoting an age diverse workplace has truly added value to the business. Nationwide's age-diverse workforce now reflects the diversity of its customer base.'

She continues: 'This has enabled the Society to retain the loyalty of existing customers by having a better understanding of their needs, and also to access new markets through meeting the requirements of customers who previously have been largely ignored. This can obviously lead to increased sales and greater customer satisfaction.'

Recent employment conditions have also confirmed the commercial sense of Nationwide's commitment to age diversity. With full employment in Swindon,

Nationwide has experienced difficulties in recruiting for specific job roles. In this business environment, Nationwide's commitment to promoting a diverse workforce allows it to recruit from the widest pool and ensures that the best people for the job are recruited and retained regardless of age, enabling Nationwide to achieve competitive advantage.

Mainstream commitment

In discussing the best way to bring about the culture change necessary to achieve the competitive advantage of an age-diverse workforce, Walker says: The first step is to educate senior and line managers of the business benefits of an age strategy. Once top-level commitment has been gained, new policies and procedures can be introduced to deliver the strategy.'

In the same way, she stresses the importance of gaining commitment from all business areas and not just the personnel department. The inclusion of age diversity as a key performance indicator means that progress can be monitored at the highest level.

Regularly reviewing the effectiveness of policies and benchmarking them against external best practice criteria ensures age diversity is kept high on the corporate agenda. 'We are determined not to be complacent,' concludes Walker, 'Nationwide intends to keep at the forefront of good practice and to continue reaping the financial rewards gained from employing a mixed age workforce.'

Nationwide's Business Rationale of an Age-Diverse Workforce

Nationwide believes age diversity benefits three key areas.

Employees

- Valuing the contribution of all employees improves motivation, morale and productivity, which results in better employee satisfaction.

- Employees see a more stable environment where Nationwide is keen to retain their skills.

- Promoting the benefits of a diverse workforce recognises that a broad range of employees with different insights and backgrounds widens the breadth of knowledge and experience within the organisation, leading to greater creativity.

Members

- An age-diverse workforce, which reflects the diversity of Nationwide's customer base, enables it to understand customer needs and to develop business solutions which meet market needs.

- It helps to retain the loyalty of existing customers by having a better understanding of their needs and to deliver access to new markets through customers whose needs previously have been largely ignored or excluded. This results in increased sales and improved customer satisfaction.

- Nationwide's external statisticians calculate that for every 3% increase in employee satisfaction, there is a 1% increase in customer satisfaction.

Organisation

- Recruiting older workers gives Nationwide access to a wider recruitment pool from which to select the best person for the job.

- By developing a policy for the retention of employees beyond retirement age, Nationwide benefits from retaining corporate memory.

- There are substantial cost savings as a result of reduced employee turnover, recruitment and training costs. Nationwide estimates that it costs between £5,000 and £8,000 to recruit and train a new employee.

CASE STUDY: Nationwide's workforce profile (June 2001)

- 22% of employees are aged under 25.

- One in ten employees are aged 50 and over (compared with only 0.3% in the late 1980s).

- 8% of employees recruited over the past five years (from March 1996 to March 2001) are now aged 50 and over.

- In the retail network, the youngest branch manager is 19 and the oldest is 60.

- Senior branch managers range in age from 27 to 50.

- Financial consultants range in age from 21 to 61.

- In the technology division, 22% of employees are under 30, 41% are aged between 30 and 39, 25% are aged between 40 and 49, and 12% are over 50 years of age.

- Turnover for employees aged 16 to 24 was only 2% and for employees aged over 55 it was 0.3%, compared with Nationwide's average turnover of 9.8%.

References

1. The Multi-Faith Centre (www.multi-faithnet.org) and the Interfaith Network (www.inter-faith.org.uk) together publish a *Directory of Religions in the UK*. The directory (priced £25) is available from the Multi-Faith Centre at the University of Derby, Kedlestone Road, Derby, DE22 1GB. Tel: 01332 591285.
2. Shap produces a calendar of religious festivals every year. Available from the National Society's RE Centre, 36 Causton Street, London SW1P 4AU. Tel: 020 7932 1190.
3. Labour Force survey (1998).

Chapter Eight

Model Policies

OVERVIEW

This chapter contains the following model policies.

B&Q's Diversity Strategy

'B&Q's diversity strategy aims to set standards of behaviour based on treating people with dignity and respect both at work and in the community. By promoting the company values of "respect for people" and "being a good neighbour", B&Q hopes to:

- make customers feel welcome and respected in its stores;

- ensure fair and equal employment policies and practices;

- recognise that a diverse workforce brings a range of skills which can enrich the business and reflect the local community where B&Q stores operate;

- recruit the best people who will exceed customers' expectations; and

- avoid the adverse costs of discrimination cases.'

B&Q's Cultural Diversity Policy

Cultural diversity and B&Q

At B&Q, we already serve a diverse customer base and include amongst our colleagues many ethnic minorities. But the evidence shows that we do not fully reflect the local population around our stores amongst our employees and we are not as receptive to the needs of our customers as we should be.

Our values talk about treating people with dignity and respect. We are developing initiatives that will improve our understanding of peoples' cultures, beliefs and values and better fulfil our vision of being a 'Great Place to Work and Shop' for everyone. The aim for each of our stores is to have a workforce which reflects the local population and is receptive to the needs of its customers, from our Welsh speaking customers in Bangor, to our Punjabi speaking customers in Birmingham.

B&Q's performance on this is only as good as the combination of what each and every one of our employees does every day at work. Please play your part in this by understanding this policy and using the materials and training available at work to help build a B&Q that values difference and is welcoming to employees and customers from minority groups.

Mike Cutt
Personnel Director, B&Q

If you require this booklet in alternative media format please contact the Diversity Team at B&Q on 02380 257338 or email Diversity@b-and-q.co.uk.

Being a better neighbour

B&Q is a multinational multicultural company with around 30,000 employees working in over 300 stores in the UK and we source 40,000 products from over 60 countries. This means that we have a significant impact on local communities across the world.

In a world of increasingly competitive retail markets, the trust and goodwill of the local community is becoming a vital ingredient in attracting customers and retaining employees.

We believe that the best way to be a better neighbour is to learn about the people we work with and the communities in which we trade, by building good relationships.

Here are some examples of how B&Q is striving to be a better neighbour.

Stores that communities welcome

Each of our stores is encouraged to establish a community partnership with local organisations. The partner can help the store to learn about and engage with the local community and the store can support the community partner in many ways, such as the donating of certain waste materials, or using the B&Q Better Neighbour Grant Scheme

For further information on the Better Neighbour Grant Scheme please visit our website www.diy.com.

B&Q's Better Neighbour vision:

'By being a better neighbour we will improve the quality of life of all the people our business touches.'

Respect for people

We are a multicultural business, the more we understand cultural diversity, the more we understand our employees, customers and suppliers. Empathy with people's cultures, beliefs and values makes our company a more attractive place to work and shop at all levels. Working in and with the local community provides a great opportunity to create a real sense of teamwork and belonging.

All of our stores have been issued with a calendar of significant religious and cultural festivals to help our people understand and respect different cultural beliefs, this information is also useful with staff scheduling.

Our people have assisted us with a cultural diversity information pack to help our stores understand the needs of our culturally diverse employees and customers. Staff are encouraged to use their language skills to improve how we are able to communicate with customers where English is not their first language. Look out for language badges in store. Where there is local demand, some stores hold 'How to' Demonstrations in other languages.

Suppliers

Our buyers source products from all over the world, working across geographical and cultural boundaries. Our buyers will receive training to help them understand how different cultures do business. We believe that our business should improve the quality of life of all the people involved in it, from our suppliers in China to our customers in the UK. To achieve this we need to be sensitive to different cultural beliefs and ways of doing business.

If you would like more information about our ethical trading policy for supply chains please visit our web-site www.diy.com and look under 'About B&Q'.

B&Q International

B&Q and our parent company Kingfisher have stores in eleven countries, including France, Germany, Turkey, Poland, China and Taiwan. Our employees have been sharing their experiences of working in different countries to increase cultural awareness within our business.

The Race Relations Act 1976

The *Race Relations Act 1976 (RRA 1976)* makes it unlawful for B&Q to treat a person less favourably on the grounds of their race, colour, nationality and national or ethnic origin. Under the European Framework Directive this will be extended to include religion. The act covers the provision of goods and services, and therefore applies to our customers, as well as every aspect of employment, including recruitment, promotion, training, pay and benefits and terms and conditions of work.

The RRA 1976 is concerned with people's actions and the effect of their actions on the individual (ie did the action actually cause offence), and not their intentions or beliefs (ie did they mean to cause offence).

Direct discrimination

This occurs when the individual is able to show that they have been treated less favourably on racial grounds than people from a different racial group in similar circumstances.

Indirect discrimination

This occurs when an employer applies a condition or requirement to everyone, but the individual or people from that particular racial group areless likely to be able to comply, and that this cannot be justified. For example a requirement that employees must not wear headgear could exclude Sikh men and boys who wear a turban, or Pakistani women and girls who wear a hijaab, in accordance with practice within their racial group.

Our commitment to the Race Relations Act

B&Q is committed to meeting all the provisions of the Act and to creating a culture in which diversity is genuinely valued. Regular monitoring does take place to ensure that everyone within our business understands the Kingfisher Code of Conduct and the B&Q Diversity and Equal Opportunities Policy and adheres to it.

For example the collection of diversity monitoring information is used to ensure that our recruitment policies and procedures are operating fairly. All employees receive diversity training as part of the B&Q induction programme.

B&Q is committed to the full use of talent and resource and to having an environment that encourages good and productive relationships and promotes business innovation. Our aim is to eliminate all forms of discrimination and ensure equality of opportunity in employment.

If you would like further information about the RRA 1976, you can contact the Diversity Department on 023 8025 7338, the HR Service Centre on 023 8025 7000 or the Commission for Racial Equality on 0207 828 7022.

Everyone is not the same

At B&Q, we do believe in treating people with equality and respect, that means treating people as individuals and not treating everyone the same.

B&Q is committed to:

- consultation with employees and customers to better understand the diverse needs of all the people we work with;

- cultural diversity awareness training for everyone;

- robust employment policies and procedures which do not discriminate on racial, religious or cultural grounds;

- community involvement;

- monitoring performance and management accountability;

- B&Q is a member of Race for Opportunity.

Learning from you

Customers and employees

We welcome your feedback, you can help us to continue to learn how to be a better neighbour to all of the people and communities we touch. If you are an employee or a customer of B&Q the Diversity Team would like to hear from you.

Any information provided by you on this form will be treated confidentially.

Ray Baker
Social Responsibility Controller, B&Q

Please complete the form.

Tear-off.

Fold along the crease.

Seal.

Send FREEPOST (no stamp required).

Or email: Diversity@b-and-q.co.uk.

Thank you! Your comments can make a difference.

How would you describe your ethnic origin?

....

....

Have you been treated less favourably while working or shopping in B&Q, please provide details?

....

....

What can we do to improve the services we are able to offer to our diverse customers?

....

....

What can we do to be a better employer to our diverse workforce?

....

....

Self declaration (optional)

Name.

....

Address.

....

....

Contact number.

....

Store (if a B&Q employee).

....

Position (if a B&Q employee).

....

Would you like the Diversity Team to contact you to discuss your feedback?

....

B&Q's Disabled Employment Policy

'It is unlawful for B&Q to treat a disabled person less favourably than someone else because of their disability and to refuse them an interview, employment, promotion or training. B&Q has a duty to look at what changes or reasonable adjustments we can make to the workplace or to the way the work is done, which would help overcome the effects of the disability. All recruitment in B&Q will be carried out against a skill profile which will ensure that the best person for the job is recruited – a person's disability will not prevent them from being considered for a position in B&Q.'

Disability and B&Q

'We have been learning about the needs of disabled customers and employees in B&Q.'

There are 8.6 million disabled people living and working in the UK, with an additional 7 million people working as carers. This means that one in four people have a vested interest in the need to improve accessibility. In 1998 B&Q started to learn about the needs of disabled customers and employees and to understand the barriers to employment and shopping which disabled people often face on a daily basis.

This led the board at B&Q to commission a thorough review of our business and embark on an ambitious plan to improve customer service and access to our stores. The business is now starting to see the benefits of our disability policy, as more disabled people come to shop and work in our stores.

Mike Cutt
Personnel Director, B&Q UK

Purpose and values

B&Q has agreed its values around people to include respect, honesty and fairness. Valuing individual contribution and not position is an important part of our success.

The vision for B&Q is that we want disabled and older people to shop with confidence in our stores. Secure in the knowledge that they will be able to access our goods and services easily, find solutions to meet their needs and be treated with respect by our staff.

B&Q can do better and we are seeking to make working and shopping at B&Q easier for all disabled people.

If you have any comments or suggestions why not give us a ring or you can use the FREEPOST form at the back of this booklet.

If you require this booklet in alternative media format please contact the Diversity Team at B&Q on 02380 257338 or email Diversity@b-and-q.co.uk.

Sharing our learning

What B&Q can do in the future.

Parking

- Improve and move the car parking for disabled people as close to the entrance as possible.

- Advise people not to abuse the car parking facilities for disabled people.

Communicating

- Provide induction loops at customer service points.

- Train staff in British Sign language.

- Improve the signage in store.

- Ensure all videos carry sign language interpretation and/or sub-titles.

- Provide written material in alternative media format including audio tape, Braille, large print and CD-Rom.

Getting around our larger stores

- Provide electric wheelchairs for the larger stores and manual wheelchairs for all stores.

- Widen the aisles and keep them free for wheelchair access.

- Lower checkouts and service desk areas.

Staff awareness

- Provide all staff with disability awareness training.

Independent living

- Sell products with accessible design features.

Employment

- Ensure all employment policies and procedures are accessible.

Disability Discrimination Act 1995

What it means for B&Q

This Act gives disabled people new rights in the areas of employment and in the areas of getting goods and services

For Employment: This means it is unlawful for B&Q to treat a disabled person less favourably than someone else because of their disability and refuse them an interview, employment, promotion or training. B&Q will have a duty to look at what changes or reasonable adjustments we could make to the workplace or to the way the work is done, which would help overcome the effects of the disability. All recruitment in B&Q will be carried out against a skill profile which will ensure that the best person for the job is recruited – a persons disability will not prevent them from being considered for a position in B&Q.

For Customers: B&Q have a duty to provide reasonable adjustments to overcome the effects of disability where our practices, policies or procedures would make it impossible or unreasonably difficult for disabled people to access our services. B&Q wish to work within the spirit of the legislation, and we are working hard to learn about the needs of disabled people and improve customer service and access to our stores.

From 2004 we will have to take reasonable steps to alter our stores in order to avoid physical features which make it impossible or unreasonably difficult for a disabled person to access our stores. For example doors which are too narrow for wheelchair access.

Call the Disability Rights Commission Help Line for further information on the *Disability Discrimination Act 1995 (DDA 1995)*:

08457 622 633 – Telephone

08457 622 644 – Textphone

Our commitment to the Disability Discrimination Act 1995

B&Q will be fully committed to meet all the provisions of the *DDA 1995* by the year 2004. We will provide the best environment possible for disabled customers and employees, staying ahead of the rest by constantly improving.

What is B&Q doing?

Top-level commitment is essential for success, and the board at B&Q, will ensure that this agenda is integrated into all aspects of the business.

B&Q is committed to:

- market research to understand disabled people's preferences and requirements;
- independent living products which are easier to use;
- designing accessibility into our buildings;
- awareness training for everyone involved with B&Q;
- improved communication with customers;
- encouraging major suppliers, contractors and third party organisations to adopt our policy;
- community involvement;
- monitoring performance.

B&Q is a Gold Card member of the Employers' Forum on Disability.

B&Q is always striving to be better.

Customers and employees

We welcome your feedback, you can help us to continue to learn and look for new ideas and solutions. If you are an employee or a customer of B&Q and you have a disability we would like to hear from you. If you are unsure of the implications of the *DDA 1995*, contact the Diversity Team on 02380 257338.

Ray Baker
Diversity Controller, B&Q

The following information will be treated in confidence and will only be used as an example of the type of problem experienced and for a means of finding a solution to any difficulties you have encountered.

A disability can be any kind of impairment which has an effect upon your daily life.

This does not have to be a physical disability. For example, dyslexia, diabetes, mental health illness, learning disabilities and facial disfigurement are all covered under the *DDA 1995*.

Your comments will give us a real chance to influence B&Q s future actions in support of disabled customers and employees.

Please complete the form.

Tear-off.

Fold along the crease.

Seal.

Send FREEPOST (no stamp required).

Or email: Diversity@b-and-q.co.uk.

Thank you! Your comments can make a difference.

How would you describe your disability?

....

....

How long have you been disabled?

....

What is your job?

....

....

Have you experienced any problems (or are you likely to experience problems in the future?)

....

....

Can B&Q make it easier?

....

Self declaration (optional)

Name.

....

Age.

....

Address.

....

....

Contact number.

....

Store (if a B&Q employee).

....

Would you like the Diversity Team to contact you to discuss how B&Q can help?

....

British Telecommunications plc's Equal Opportunity Policy

BT is an equal opportunity employer and it is the aim of this policy that all persons, wherever they are in the world, should have equal opportunity for employment and advancement on the basis of their ability, qualifications and suitability for the work.

It is BT's policy that no job applicant or employee receive less favourable treatment in any aspect of employment on racial grounds, or on grounds of gender, religion, disability, marital status, age or sexual orientation, gender status or caring responsibilities, or be disadvantaged by conditions or requirements which cannot be shown to be justifiable. To this end our policies will become the global benchmark, reflecting sensitively the particular circumstances and local cultures of each country and community in which we operate.

There must be no unlawful discrimination, direct, indirect or institutional, against any person whether in recruitment, selection, training, promotion or in any aspect of employment. Harassment of any form at work is also a form of discrimination and will be treated as such under the terms of this policy. No form of harassment or bullying, including derogatory remarks at work, will be tolerated. Cases will be dealt with under the BT Harassment and Bullying Policy.

The intention of BT's policy is to build upon the statutory position, so that we reflect the diversity of our people, partners and the global cultures in which we operate and to pursue an effective policy of promoting equal opportunity throughout the business. The statutory position is set out in the *Sex Discrimination Act 1975*, the *Equal Pay Act 1970*, the *Race Relations Act 1976*, the *Disability Discrimination Act 1995*, the *Employment Relations Act 1999* and the *Human Rights Act 1998*.

All procedures will be monitored to ensure that the aims of the policy are a reality for all BT people and to ensure that individuals are recruited, selected, trained and treated in all other respects on the basis of their relevant merits and abilities. All employees shall be given equality of opportunity and encouragement to progress within the organisation, in line with their skills and potential.

Positive measures will be taken to encourage the recruitment and employment of any under-represented minority group. Our goal is to reflect the diversity of all the communities within which we operate and to carefully monitor our progression toward this goal.

All BT people have an obligation to uphold this policy and disciplinary action will be considered where a breach takes place. This could also be unlawful.

It follows that all employees must:

- uphold the BT values and respect each other;

- uphold BT's business principles and treat all individuals fairly and impartially, without prejudice, and never tolerate harassment in any form;

- uphold the wealth of BT's personal capabilities and value differences.

Leadership

BT's equality and diversity champion is Pierre Danon, Chief Executive BT Retail, who chairs the BT Global Equality and Diversity Forum.

The forum's membership is made up of 'diversity champions' who are senior managers representing each of our business units. Specific groups, including race, gender, age and disability, are also championed by senior managers on the forum. Sexual orientation will also be represented during 2002.

The forum's role is:

- to create, sustain and deliver the global equality and diversity strategy for the BT group;

- to provide highly visible and inspirational leadership of the equality and diversity agenda;

- to promote processes, practices and behaviours that actively drive equality and diversity in the BT group, relentlessly opposing inequality, prejudice and unethical behaviour;

- to protect BT's reputation for being at the heart of the equality and diversity agenda, to ensure that this reputation is deserved, is credible within the organisation and is understood across BT's operations around the world;

- to agree and implement equality and diversity initiatives across the BT group and within individual lines of business;

- to be spontaneous, open, honest, challenging, forward-looking, change-embracing role models for equality and diversity in business;

- through equality and diversity action, to increase market value of the BT group.

Ethnic minorities

We believe that diversity is the lifeblood of our business. In this section we look at our current representation and measures we are taking to improve on it.

Profile

7.7% of BT people have declared themselves to be of ethnic origin, including 7.6% of non-managers and 7.9% of managers. These figures do not include those people who work in our subsidiaries; around 10,000 of our overall workforce of around 108,600.

Initiatives

- Higher education – our customer and supplier bases are encouraging students from inner city schools and ethnic minorities to seek university entrance, particularly in science subjects, through initiatives such as the Oxford Access Summer Science School [see www.oxford-access.org/].

- Ethnic Minority Network for BT employees – this active network runs development courses, holds an annual conference and contributes to the national debate on diversity. At the 6th annual conference in October 2001 'Make it Happen – Keys to Success', Sir Christopher Bland, BT Chairman, said 'It is vital that we enable people to reach their full potential irrespective of their gender, background or ethnic origin.'

- Supplier Diversity Programme – this programme is at the leading edge of supply chain diversity and is designed to encourage minority businesses to participate in BT's procurement process. A website for our Supplier Diversity Programme is currently under construction.

People with disabilities

A significant number of people in our society have disabilities. As part of our diversity policy to ensure we meet the needs of all our customers, BT encourages applications from, and supports the professional development of, people with disabilities.

As a 'two ticks' employer, BT guarantees job interviews for all suitably-qualified disabled applicants.

Profile

Currently 2% of our workforce have declared a disability, including 2.4% of non-managers and 1.1% of managers. These figures do not include those people who work in our subsidiaries; around 10,000 of our overall workforce of 108,600.

Initiatives

- Employers' Forum on Disability [see www.employers-forum.co.uk/index.htm] – we are a founder member of this group and sponsored its report, Unlocking the Evidence – The New Disability Business Case.

- Able2 – an active employee network for BT people with disabilities, Able2 supports individuals by providing impartial and confidential advice, and runs a series of roadshows to enable people to discuss their needs with senior BT managers.

- Accessibility – we are committed to making our workplace as accessible as possible. In particular BT supports AbilityNet [see www.abilitynet.co.uk/], which is based in one of our central London buildings. AbilityNet is a charity that brings the benefits of computer technology to adults and children with disabilities, both within BT and the communities in which we operate.

  New BT people benefit from pre-recruitment assessments designed to ensure they have the most productive and comfortable equipment available as soon as they join the company.

  Existing BT people benefit from easier access to expert assessment and advice, and earlier provision of appropriate reasonable adjustments to their working environment. People in the community also have access to expert assessments and advice.

- Age and Disability Team – this team looks after the interests of our elderly and disabled customers. Their mission is 'To drive consideration of disability issues deep into the operations of BT so that we enable equality of access to BT's portfolio; and to communicate that effectively to our target audiences, so as to improve the quality of life of disabled people, and enhance shareholder value.'

The Age and Disability Team [see www.bt.com/aged_disabled/index.jsp] aims to achieve this by:

- consultation with disabled people and their representatives;

- understanding and influencing legislation and regulation;

- improving BT's product and service portfolio;

- research and development;

- providing practical, day-to-day assistance for disabled people;

- raising awareness of disability;

- enhancing BT's reputation in the disability arena.

Networks

Four employee networks are actively supported by BT's most senior management and use BT technology to reach members across the globe. These are:

- Able2 for employees with disabilities;

- BT Ethnic Minority Network;

- BT Women's Network;

- Kaleidoscope – for our gay, lesbian and bisexual employees.

Kaleidoscope, launched in March 2002 by John Steele, BT's Director of Human Resources, is the most recent addition to our network portfolio.

BT joined StoneWall as a Diversity Champion and attended its launch event. Angela Mason, Director of StoneWall, commented at the Kaleidoscope launch that 'BT's business case for diversity is the most eloquent I have heard'.

Our established networks support employees in a wide variety of ways, providing:

- support and advice;

- mentoring programmes;

- development programmes;

- annual conferences;

- information websites;

- regular roadshows;

- a conduit to senior managers;

- contributions to the national and international debate.

We're also pleased to be a supporter of the Government-backed People into Management Network [see www.pmn.org.uk/] which offers work placement and senior mentoring opportunities in the public and private sector to young people from ethnic minorities.

External contacts and benchmarking

Equality and diversity issues are not, of course, exclusive to BT. We are working with a range of not-for-profit organisations, the Government and

other employers in both the public and private sectors to share ideas and best practice.

We are members of the following organisations:

- Business in the Community;

- Employers' Forum on Disability;

- Opportunity Now;

- Race for Opportunity;

- Employers for Work-Life Balance;

- Employers' Forum on Age;

- Stonewall;

- Parents at Work.

BT has taken part in the external benchmarking of our policies and results regarding gender and ethnic minorities by Opportunity Now (gender) and Race for Opportunity (ethnic minorities).

Benchmarking was against other large and medium-sized employers in the public and private sectors.

Opportunity Now benchmarking 2002 (gender) – BT results

216 organisations from the public and private sector took part in the Opportunity Now benchmarking exercise. BT's sector classification was Information and Communication.

Sector	Norm	BT score	Standard
Motivate	78	100	Platinum
Act	83	99	Platinum
Impact	69	94	Gold
Overall	77	98	Platinum

Platinum standard indicates a score of 95–100, Gold indicates a score of 80–94, Silver 50–79 and Bronze 20–49.

Race for Opportunity benchmarking 2001 (ethnic minorities) – BT results

93 organisations from the public and private sector took part in the RFO benchmarking exercise. BT's sector classification was Information and Communication. We are pleased to report that as well as achieving the top performance in this sector, BT also achieved the top performance of all private sector organisations taking part in the exercise.

Sector	Average total	Benchmark	Average BT score
Leadership	64	57	86
Making the investment	67	51	89
Planning and policy	61	58	91
Communication	61	52	75
Marketing	73	55	93
Sharing ownership	37	42	77
Employment	68	61	99
Community involvement	66	56	93
Supplier development	50	25	100
Results/impact	54	50	94
Overall	60	51	90

BT received a Gold Standard for our overall average score.

Platinum standard indicates a score of 95–100, Gold indicates a score of 80–94, Silver 70–80 and Bronze 60–70.

Diversity

The following figures show the percentage of our people who are women, have declared themselves from an ethnic minority, or have declared a disability. These figures do not include those people who work in our subsidiaries – around 10,000 of our overall workforce of around 108,600.

	Management	*Non-management*	*All BT*
Women	22.9%	24.3%	23.9%
Ethnic	7.9%	7.6%	7.7%
Disability	1.1%	2.4%	2.0%

Data as at 31st March 2002.

In March 2001 these were:

	Management	*Non-management*	*All BT*
Women	24%	27.3%	26.4%
Ethnic	7.3%	7.5%	7.5%
Disability	1.0%	2.4%	2.0%

Discrimination-related litigation 2001/02

There were a total of 30 discrimination related litigation cases involving BT in the 2002 financial year. Eleven were withdrawn, none judged against BT, 15 settled and four judged in favour of BT. This is a reduction on the 43 cases involving BT in the 2001 financial year.

Data relating to discrimination related litigation going back to 1999 is available in the 'Data' section of this site.

London Borough of Camden: Valuing Diversity Policy

The background history

The 1970s were a landmark decade in Britain. The enactment of the *Sex Discrimination Act 1975 (SDA 1975)* was soon followed by the *Race Relations Act 1976 (RRA 1976)* in terms of legislation to curb discrimination. The purpose of both measures was to ensure a new degree of equality for specific sections of British society. These pieces of legislation embodied a clear recognition that various forms of sexual and racial discrimination were part of day-to-day reality in our society. This led to the introduction of specific forms of legal protection for those members of the community who are directly affected by such discrimination. This new consciousness and the changed legislative landscape that related to it have come to serve as the bedrock for the ongoing evolution in the theory and practice of 'equal opportunities'.

The London Borough of Camden was to the fore in responding to the challenges posed by this new legal framework. In 1977, the Council began to develop relevant policies and by the early 1980s specialist Units and Committees were established which used the legal framework to curb discrimination and raise the consciousness of the issues amongst its staff and residents.

However, a real concern had emerged by the start of the 1990s that it had taken far too long to take tiny steps towards achieving the agenda for equal opportunities. To many, the gains that had been achieved were too limited in scope.

Among those actually working in the equal opportunities field there was a widely held view that, despite the development of anti-discrimination legislation, many major problems that confronted the most vulnerable sections of society had still not been adequately addressed. For example, the big differentials between ethnic groups in terms of unemployment rates and economic status still persisted.

The demand for new forms of thinking and action grew ever more pressing.

In 1992, Camden created a single Equalities Unit from the four separate equalities-related units that existed. The appointment of a new Head of Equalities in 1993 provided an opportunity to develop a new approach in Camden. In order to push the agenda forward, Camden had to look beyond the simple prevention of discrimination and towards a far more proactive approach.

The failure of existing anti-discrimination legislation to cover issues other than gender and race was further evidence of the inadequacy of the previous framework. This was evident seeing as Camden and many other local authorities had recognised that age, disability and sexuality were also grounds for discrimination and vulnerability and therefore also required protective legislation.

To advance the agenda, Camden recognised the need to adopt a fresh frame of mind that was far more inclusive. Key to such a rethink were:

(*a*) a recognition of the real advantages to be gained from living in a diverse community; and

(*b*) the development of new methods to go forward from such a recognition.

So in 1994/95 the London Borough of Camden pioneered a new approach to equal opportunities. This new approach was entitled '*Valuing Diversity*'.

The current background

At the start of the 21st century, Valuing Diversity is very much at the heart of our social and political priorities. Indeed, this is easily seen when one considers the clear parallels between the social policies adopted by the member states in the European Union to enhance 'social inclusion' and the 'Valuing Diversity' approach that Camden has pioneered. The key European definition of social exclusion, which encapsulates the relationship between poverty, inequality, social membership and democracy, underpins this view. Hence, the European Council defines social exclusion as:

> '[A] broader concept than poverty, encompassing not only low material means, but the ability to participate effectively in economic, social, political and cultural life. And in some characterisations, alienation and distance from mainstream society.'

This approach to social policy has received further support from the Government's developing strategy for boosting community involvement, performance management and performance monitoring. The performance indicators developed by the Audit Commission and the adoption of the Commission for Racial Equality's (CRE) Race Equality Standard have figured prominently in this new culture.

In a similar vein, there have been the developing demands imposed by 'Best Value'. In particular, there has been the need to consult with our diverse local communities, and to monitor the adequacy, effectiveness and relevance of our services.

There has also been the promotion of innovation and crosscutting approaches to tackle many of the longest standing aspects of social disadvantage. Here again, Camden has led by example by adopting a new and challenging approach to employment in September 2000. Called 'Valuing Diversity in Employment', this initiative is seeking to translate the same innovative and proactive approach of Valuing Diversity to employment issues in particular.

We have also seen the extension of the CRE's powers and the introduction of a new enforceable duty for all public bodies to promote racial equality. This has served to support the general widening of anti-discrimination legislation that has occurred. In addition, Camden has signed up to the CRE's 'Leadership Challenge'. This means that the organisation as a whole has an explicit commitment to creating 'a fair and open society'. Accepting the 'Challenge' also means that Camden's senior management agrees that:

> 'affording equality of opportunity in employment, and providing appropriate products and services to all sections of the population enhances the reputation of their organisation, makes it easier to recruit and retain staff, and is good for business.'

Camden is, however, very much aware that social priorities and policies are prone to change. Partly for this reason, the London Borough of Camden looks for overall guidance from a set of Valuing Diversity principles, which find their ethical basis in existing legislation. These principles are a central feature of Camden's declaration around Valuing Diversity and may be seen to inform the Council's *Policy Statement*.

Equalities in action
Appendix A – The statutory framework

Sex Discrimination Act 1975

In accordance with the statutory duty under the SDA 1975 and the European Commission's 'Code of Conduct (1992)', Camden Council – in the exercise of its functions – must not discriminate on the basis of sex either in whom it houses or employs. The *Equal Pay Act 1975/1986* specifically outlaws gender-based discrimination in payment for work.

Race Relations Act 1976/Race Relations Amendment Act 2000

In accordance with the statutory duty under the *RRA 1976*, Camden Council – in the exercise of its functions – must not discriminate on the basis of 'race' either in whom it houses or employs. It should provide different types of accommodation to meet the needs of all types of household and ensure that access is available only on the basis of need. It also has a duty under *section 71* of the *RRA 1976* to eliminate any unlawful racial discrimination and to promote equality of opportunity and social harmony between different racial groups.

The *Amendment Act*, adopted in 2000, strengthens this duty. In practice, its aim is to ensure that local authorities, as well as other public bodies, strive towards equality of opportunity in employment, in service delivery and in partnership arrangements. This past year has also seen the adoption at the level of the European Union of a new race directive, which widens the definition of indirect discrimination. This will be incorporated into UK law by 2003.

Disability Discrimination Act 1995

This legislation has certain similarities with the Acts from the 1970s against gender and race-based discrimination. The Act provides a definition of disability, based on the so-called 'medical model', and bars 'less favourable treatment' of people with disabilities in both employment and the provision of services. It also stipulates a duty to make 'reasonable adjustment'. In some ways, its implications for both employment and service provision may prove more far-reaching, but much will depend on the interpretation of the law by tribunals and the courts.

The Protection from Harassment Act 1997

This legislation will offer vulnerable residents – particularly women – added protection from various forms of harassment.

The Crime and Disorder Act 1998

This legislation provides new instruments (including Anti-Social Behaviour Orders), to tackle crimes such as racial harassment.

Human Rights Act 1998

This legislation took effect from 2 October 2000 and introduces into UK law the 18 Articles of the European Convention on Human Rights. In particular, Article 14 of the Convention states that the Act's 'rights and freedoms ... shall be secured without discrimination on any ground such as sex, race, colour, language, religion' etc.

Article 13 of the Amsterdam Treaty 1997 promises to make this factor even more significant for equalities by enabling the European Court of Justice to preside over national cases that involve complaints of discrimination.

A definition

Valuing Diversity embodies an evolving, systematic approach to equalities that seeks to go beyond just fighting discrimination and towards the positive promotion of diversity. It sees Camden's multicultural population as a source of great strength, while recognising the importance of past struggles for civil rights and greater equality. The policy aims to enhance both the quality and effectiveness of Camden's services in meeting the needs of everyone within the Borough.

Valuing Diversity, as developed in Camden since 1995, is essentially about:

- moving beyond an anti-discrimination approach that emphasises processes to a proactive approach that focuses on actual outcomes;

- recognising that there are great gains – both social and economic – to be made from positively embracing the diversity of a community;

- providing a common policy framework for addressing the needs of socially excluded groups (whether as employees, residents or users of public services);

- developing co-ordinated equality plans and monitoring systems for both employment practices and service delivery;

- ensuring equality becomes a mainstream responsibility for all managers and service providers rather than just for specialists; and

- actively driving the policy from the top levels of the organisation in order to ensure substantial progress.

The policy statement

The London Borough of Camden recognises the following.

- In society generally and in all organisations' activities, there are many different forms of discrimination (whether intentional, unintentional, institutional or otherwise), which affect vulnerable sections of the community – in particular women, black and ethnic minority people, older people, lesbians and gay men, and people with disabilities.

- All members of Camden's diverse communities have a right to enjoy the highest possible quality of life.

- A healthy community requires that all of its members feel that they are included and that their contributions are genuinely valued.

- To be efficient, public bodies need to address the psychological and financial costs that arise from the existence of inequality and discrimination.

- The Council must embed the concept of Valuing Diversity in all its policies and practices in order to ensure that Camden is and remains a suitable place to live and work.

- Camden Council's accountability and leadership role within the democratic process give it additional responsibilities for championing Valuing Diversity both locally and beyond.

The London Borough of Camden will therefore strive to do the following.

- Ensure that it does not tolerate any forms of prejudicial discrimination, whether intentional, unintentional, institutional (or otherwise).

- Work in partnership with all sections of its diverse communities and ensure their maximum involvement in the democratic process.

- Ensure that representative structures – including Council committees and school governors' bodies – equitably reflect our diverse communities.

- Ensure that, through consultation and growing user involvement, its services are designed to suit the needs of its diverse communities, and are delivered fairly (in terms of quality, quantity and timing): a standard to be tested through Best Value Reviews.

- Ensure that the diversity of its workforce and its employment policies and practices (concerning recruitment, retention, promotion, training and discipline) are designed to equitably reflect and protect the communities that Camden serves.

- Ensure that the Valuing Diversity theme is reflected in all of its publications.

- Ensure that the distribution of its grants and finances generally reflect the needs of its diverse communities.

- Promote Valuing Diversity through its work with all of its potential partners from the voluntary, community and private sectors.

- Play a leading role locally, London-wide and nationally in promoting Valuing Diversity.

- Ensure that all of its officers are made fully aware both of the meaning of the Valuing Diversity agenda and of their individual responsibility to make it happen.

- Set up effective systems of quality and equality monitoring to ensure that action on Valuing Diversity is being continuously evaluated and improved.

- Be prepared to innovate in providing solutions to Valuing Diversity issues and maintain Camden's leading-edge work in the field of equalities.

- Make sure that the community as a whole recognises the contributions made by Camden's diverse communities to the Borough's economic, social and cultural wellbeing.

JPMorgan Chase's Diversity Vision and Harassment Policy

Diversity Vision

At JPMorgan Chase, we win by creating a culture that sparks creativity, leadership and exceptional performance. Our success depends on enabling and challenging each other to contribute our best in an environment that is inclusive, open, flexible, fair and courageous.

Our commitment to an inclusive workplace:

- We respect and harness individual strengths and differences to surface the best ideas and insights.
- We hold every colleague accountable for living our vision and for promoting our diversity efforts with colleagues, clients, suppliers and communities.
- We excel by building diverse teams.
- We measure progress rigorously and often.
- We engage everyone in making this vision a reality.

Harassment Policy

Policy statement

JPMorgan's policy on harassment reaffirms our commitment to the personal dignity and worth of every employee and reflects the value we place on fostering a non-discriminatory work environment.

JPMorgan does not tolerate any form of harassment by or against any of its employees. The Firm operates and maintains an inclusive and productive working environment in which all workers are treated with respect and dignity.

This policy applies equally to everyone at JPMorgan. Employees have a responsibility to comply with the policy and treat all colleagues with dignity and respect. Managers have a responsibility for treating seriously and ensuring full investigation of any complaint of harassment against a member of their staff, and ensuring their staff comply with the policy. The policy also applies to agency workers, contractors and third parties directly connected to JPMorgan (eg outside vendors, consultants and clients).

Harassment is wholly unacceptable both in the workplace and in any work-related setting outside the workplace such as business trips and business-related social events.

Definition

Harassment in the context of this policy means misconduct of a physical, verbal or non-verbal nature which is unwanted and personally offensive to the recipient (it includes inappropriate behaviour towards employees based on their race, ethnic or national origin, gender, sexual orientation, age, religion or disability), and which causes them to feel humiliated, threatened, patronised, bullied, denigrated, distressed or harassed. Action may also be considered as harassment if it disrupts or interferes with another employee's work performance, employment opportunities, job security or any other employment decision such as salary increases or promotions.

It is important to note that harassment is often defined *by the way it feels to the recipient*, rather than by the intent of the person causing offence. It cannot, therefore be excused or justified by claiming that it was unintentional or humorous. The implications of harassment are serious and the Firm will take appropriate disciplinary action against the harasser.

Examples of harassment

Some examples of unacceptable behaviour that are covered by the policy include (but are not limited to) the following.

- Physical conduct.

  Unwanted physical conduct including unnecessary touching, patting or pinching, physical threats and insulting or abusive behaviour or gestures.

- Verbal conduct.

  Unwelcome advances, propositions or pressure for sexual activity or offensive flirtations; innuendo; lewd comments or abusive language which denigrates or ridicules; insults which are gender, age, race or nationality related or which relate to disability or sexual orientation and offensive comments about dress, appearance or physique.

- Non-verbal conduct.

  Exclusion from workplace conversation or social events, unfair allocation of work and responsibilities, the display of pornographic or sexually suggestive pictures (including emails and pin-ups); offensive objects or written materials; the making of abusive or offensive gestures including leering and whistling; the display, creation or transmission of sexually or racially offensive written or verbal material, including PC pornography; graffiti; open or covert hostilities to employees on the grounds of their race, gender, nationality or sexual orientation or any other unacceptable behaviour which denigrates another person for whatever reason.

Procedure

Harassment on any grounds is a disciplinary offence. All allegations of harassment will be promptly investigated and any employee found by JPMorgan to have violated the policy, or who fails to properly address harassment issues, will be subject to appropriate disciplinary action – up to and including immediate dismissal – depending on the circumstances.

Under the law, employees may be personally liable for their actions and can be personally liable to pay compensation. In more serious cases harassment may constitute a criminal offence.

No person who makes a claim of harassment or who takes part in an investigation will be retaliated against.

The Firm would expect such a complaint to be made as soon as possible and certainly within three months of the alleged incident (or the last of them).

Informal procedure

Do not wait until working levels reach an intolerable level or your personal wellbeing is being affected. Wherever possible an employee who believes that he/she has been the subject or harassment should tell the person responsible that he/she finds the behaviour offensive and asks them to stop – they may not be aware that their behaviour is inappropriate or objectionable and any misunderstandings may be resolved speedily.

Formal procedure

If the employee is unable to confront the person carrying out the harassment or the harassment continues, then the employee should report the incident(s) either to their manager or to their Human Resources Generalist in line with the Firm's Grievance Policy.

The Firm understands that this is a sensitive area and that many instances may be embarrassing to discuss. You are therefore assured that your case will be treated with the utmost sensitivity and that your claim will not affect your future employment with JPMorgan in any way.

Once you have discussed the issue with your Human Resources representative, you will be asked to co-operate in an investigation. The investigation will take place as soon as is reasonably practicable (usually within seven working days) and will decide whether or not disciplinary action should be taken in accordance with the Firm's disciplinary

procedure. Any investigation will be conducted confidentially in an independent and objective manner by a Human Resources representative.

During the investigation, where appropriate, the alleged harasser may be transferred to another department or suspended on full pay. Such action does not imply any guilt. Where the outcome of the investigation is found to uphold the allegation efforts may be made to permanently move one of the parties involved, if appropriate.

The employee who has made the complaint will be notified of the outcome of any disciplinary procedure.

If a complaint is found to be malicious or without foundation, the complainant may himself or herself become subject to appropriate action by the Firm that may result in disciplinary action.

Role of managers

All managers are responsible for supporting this policy and taking preventative action in situations that might be considered harassment. Managers who become aware of an incident or behaviours which may be considered harassment should immediately report the information to their Human Resources representative, or Employee Relations.

Managers are responsible for identifying problem situations and referring them to Human Resources, whether or not anyone complains. Failure to act promptly in this regard may put the Firm at risk. Managers, however, should never attempt to conduct an investigation themselves – all situations should be referred to Human Resources.

Informal procedure

Do not wait until working levels reach an intolerable level or your personal wellbeing is being affected. Wherever possible an employee who believes that he/she has been the subject or harassment should tell the person responsible that he/she finds the behaviour offensive and asks them to stop – they may not be aware that their behaviour is inappropriate or objectionable and any misunderstandings may be resolved speedily.

For further guidance please see 'Guidance for Handling Harassment Informally'.

Equal opportunities

The success of JPMorgan as an organisation depends upon the full and effective use of the abilities of each of our employees. With this principle in mind, the Firm is committed to providing equal opportunities by striving to create a working environment that encourages diversity. JPMorgan undertakes to ensure that it is free of discrimination on grounds of race, colour, ethnic origin, religion, gender, gender identity, marital status, disability, age and sexual orientation. The policy of equal opportunities applies to all recruitment practices, including, but not limited to, interviewing, advertising, promotion, terms and conditions of employment, performance appraisals, social and recreational programs, training, employee development, compensation, redeployment and termination.

The responsibility for upholding this commitment is shared by, and is intended to benefit, every employee.

Wherever it is practical, JPMorgan will make any reasonable changes to the work environment which prove necessary to ensure that employees with special needs, including disabled employees, are given the same opportunities as able-bodied employees in fulfilling their roles effectively.

Addressing concerns

If you have any concern, personal or otherwise, about discrimination, you should contact Human Resources or your manager for confidential advice. Allegations of discrimination will be handled promptly, seriously and in confidence. A thorough investigation will be carried out with due concern for the rights of all employees involved. Should this reveal that there has been discrimination, JPMorgan will address the problem and take steps to ensure that it does not happen again. Any employee who is found to have discriminated against another will be liable to disciplinary action, which may result in dismissal.

Nationwide Building Society's Equal Opportunities Policy

At Nationwide we want our employees to take pride in working for an organisation that lives by values. These apply equally to our customers and our employees. In order to achieve this we strive to ensure that all employees are treated equally and fairly regardless of age. We have policies to enable this and monitor the effectiveness regularly – one example being via our annual employee survey, 'Viewpoint'. Apart from any other consideration, this is commercially the right thing to do.

Keith Astill
Head of Corporate Personnel, Nationwide Building Society

Equal Opportunities Policy

1. Statement of intent

The Nationwide Building Society declares itself to be an Equal Opportunities Employer and is unreservedly opposed to any form of discrimination being practised against its employees or potential employees on the grounds of their race, creed, sex, marital status, age, physical or mental disability, political opinion, religious or sexual persuasion. The Society will ensure that, whenever practicable, physical disability is in itself no bar to recruitment or promotion.

The Society expects and places an obligation upon all its managers and employees to respect and act in accordance with both the letter and the spirit of the policy.

2. General operation

Provided it does not conflict with any statutory enactment, this policy will apply in respect of conditions of work including pay, hours of work, holiday entitlement, overtime and shift work, work allocation, sick pay, recruitment, training, promotion and redundancy. This policy will be communicated to employees using various media, eg advertisements, application forms, induction material, handbooks, notices, posters and appropriate training courses.

In particular, management and supervisory employees will be made aware of both the general contents of this policy and their specific responsibilities under relevant legislation.

Individual positive action targets will be agreed with each Divisional Director within the Society.

Overall responsibility for the enactment of this policy will rest with the Head of Personnel.

3. Recruitment and promotion

External applicants will be informed of the policy by a statement included in all advertisements and application forms, where appropriate, that Nationwide Building Society is an Equal Opportunities Employer.

Advertising media will be chosen in line with job requirements and job advertisements placed in a manner consistent with this policy in order to reach the widest possible range of potential applicants. All vacancies notified to the Job Centres will indicate that the Society is an Equal Opportunities Employer.

The same declaration will also be included in the advertisement of all internal vacancies. Wording in advertisements and job specifications will ensure that the Society is conforming with the policy and does in no way conflict with the law.

The operation of recruitment, selection and appointment procedures will be non-discriminatory in accordance with this policy and guidelines for management and employees involved in recruitment and selection will be issued.

4. Training

Through the use of Performance Management and the appraisal of performance, managers will be required to pay special attention to the needs of employees for training to improve their job performance, development or career potential.

Opportunities for training and retraining will continue to be brought to the attention of employees. Such training opportunities will include positive action for groups of employees who are under represented in certain parts of the Society.

Employees, especially those involved in management, selection and dealing with the public, will be given information, awareness training and guidance on the law relating to Equal Opportunities, their own personal liability under the law and the nature of discrimination.

Awareness training will be provided for employees by inclusion, where appropriate, in existing and future management courses or by means of special programmes as necessary. Equal Opportunities in training will be included in all training literature.

5. Employees with disabilities

Full consideration will be given to all disabled applicants and employees and every effort will be made to accommodate physical disability. The use of the Employment Service's nationally recognised disability symbol reinforces the Society's commitment to the employment of people with disabilities. Information on grants and facilities for disabled employees will be issued to managers within the Society.

6. Monitoring

Appropriate information systems in respect of applicants, new recruits and existing employees will be established for the purposes of monitoring the effectiveness of this policy. This will require relevant data to be provided by employees and applicants for employment. The Society will compare the information gathered with comparative practice amongst other Building Societies and financial institutions.

In accordance with the provisions set out by the Commission for Racial Equality, Equal Opportunities Commission and Disability Rights Commission, monitoring will be carried out across the Society. Should such monitoring reveal any areas of concern, these will be investigated and necessary action taken in line with the policy.

7. Grievances

Where employees consider that they have been subject to discrimination in employment which is in direct conflict with this policy, they should normally register a complaint for investigation and resolution through the agreed grievance procedure. In cases of particular sensitivity where an employee feels unable to raise such a grievance directly with his or her manager/supervisor, the employee may seek guidance from his or her local Personnel Manager and Staff Union Representative. The appropriate stage at which the grievance should be considered within the procedure will then be determined.

8. Discipline

Appropriate disciplinary procedures will apply where employees have acted in a deliberately discriminatory manner.

Yorkshire Electricity: Equal Opportunities Policy

1.1 Equal opportunities in Yorkshire Electricity

This document sets out the company's equal opportunities policy. It describes the measures the company and employees should take to ensure that no employee, contractor, temporary recruit, worker or job applicant receives less favourable treatment than another person on the grounds of their sex, race or disability.

This policy relies on the understanding and support of everyone involved to make this policy a success.

1.2 Our policy

Yorkshire Electricity is an equal opportunities employer and is committed to the policy in its employment and recruitment practices. Our policy will ensure that no potential or existing employee or worker receives less favourable treatment than another on the grounds of sex, race, disability or on the grounds that they are a member or non-member of a trade union or have taken or propose to take parental leave or maternity leave.

Individuals will be selected, promoted and treated on the basis of their abilities and merits and according to the requirements of the job. They will be given equal opportunity to show their ability and to progress within the organisation.

It is unlawful to discriminate against any employee, worker or job applicant on the grounds of sex, race or disability either directly (ie treating them less favourably on the basis of the person's sex, race, etc.) or indirectly (by setting a requirement or condition which less of a certain group can comply with, unless that requirement is justified*).

* Note that the legal definition of indirect discrimination has now changed, and applies to a 'provision, criterion or practice'.

Unlawful discrimination against employees, workers or job applicants on the grounds set out above can have serious results, including:

- unlimited financial penalties for the company;

- personal liability for the manager or fellow employee or worker responsible for the discrimination, including unlimited financial penalties; and

- adverse publicity for the company and employees involved.

It is therefore very important that all staff comply with the equal opportunities policy at all times when managing staff or dealing with each other. This is particularly important when:

(a) recruiting staff;

(b) making decisions on promotion, pay rises and allocations of training;

(c) dealing with requests for part-time working;

(d) managing pregnant workers and working parents;

(e) making selections for redundancy; and

(f) dealing with colleagues on a daily basis particularly in email correspondence.

1.3 Sex and race discrimination

Sex and race discrimination occurs when someone treats a fellow employee or worker less favourably on the grounds of their race or sex or due to a characteristic or assumption about their sex or race. For example, if someone assumes that a female employee with children cannot work as well as male members of the team and therefore gives her less quality work than the others, this would constitute direct discrimination.

1.3.1 Harassment

Sex and race discrimination can also take the form of harassment. Harassment is a type of direct discrimination and is defined as being conduct of a sexual or racial nature which the recipient finds unwelcome or offensive. This is a subjective test which means that it is not what you consider to be offensive, but what the person you say or do something to considers offensive.

Although this document refers specifically to sexual and racial harassment, which are unlawful, it also applies to conduct relating to an individual's personal characteristics. You as an employee have a right not to be harassed and have a responsibility not to harass other people.

Conduct which can constitute harassment can include the following types of behaviour:

- unwanted physical contact;

- unwanted oral or written abuse including offensive language, suggestive remarks, suggestive whistling or emails containing material of a sexual or racial nature (whether you consider this material to be amusing is not relevant);

- visual display of offensive posters, graffiti, suggestive gestures or use of pornographic or inappropriate internet sites; and

- conduct such as sexual or racial ridicule, offensive flirting, leering, intimidation or abuse.

We all have a right to work without harassment. If you think that you are being harassed, you should make a complaint in accordance with the company's grievance procedure for harassment or bullying complaints.

Employees should also note that harassment can take place on work-related events and so you should behave responsibly towards colleagues at all times.

1.4 Disability discrimination

Discrimination against people with disabilities can take two forms, namely less favourable treatment on the grounds of their disability or a failure to make reasonable adjustments to accommodate someone with a disability.

It is important that we all realise that not only people with visible disabilities fall within the definition of people who are disabled. The definition actually extends to anyone who has a serious physical or mental impairment which has lasted for a long time and which has a substantial effect on their normal daily activities. People who have conditions such as diabetes and epilepsy will probably be covered and so it is essential that you do not treat these people any differently if you are aware of their condition.

Also if you are a supervisor or manager and realise that someone is having difficulties due to a disability, you have an obligation to discuss this with them to see if any assistance can be offered to them by the company.

1.5 Victimisation

It is a discriminatory act to treat anyone less favourably if they have made a complaint about discrimination either during present or previous employment, they intend to make a complaint or they have assisted someone else's complaint by giving evidence or corroborating a story. If for example someone informs you that they have previously brought a claim for discrimination in the tribunal, you should not use this information to treat that person less favourably than others, eg by assuming that they are a trouble maker.

1.6 Bullying

Whilst there is no specific law against bullying at present unless the bullying is actually discrimination or harassment, Yorkshire Electricity considers bullying to be a serious matter and will not tolerate bullying within the workplace. Bullying is any persistent behaviour, directed against an individual or a group of employees, which is intimidating, cruel, offensive, humiliating or malicious and which undermines the confidence and self-esteem of the recipient(s).

These persistently negative attacks on personal and professional performance are typically unpredictable, irrational and often unseen. Bullying is therefore capable of identification not merely by what has actually been done but also by the effect it has on the recipients of the behaviour. Bullying is often, though not exclusively, linked to an abuse of power.

Legitimate, constructive and fair criticism of an employee's performance or behaviour at work is not bullying. An occasional raised voice or argument is not bullying.

If you believe that you are being bullied, you have the right to bring a grievance complaint within the bullying and harassment grievance procedure.

1.7 Breaches of the equal opportunities policy

As we all have a responsibility not to be offensive to colleagues or to condone harassment or discrimination by others, harassment, discrimination or victimisation of any kind is treated as serious or gross misconduct by the company. Formal disciplinary proceedings will be taken against anyone suspected of discrimination and this may lead to summary dismissal from the company.

Employees may also be personally liable to an employment tribunal claim being brought against them for either an act of discrimination or for allowing discrimination to occur or to continue without taking appropriate action. This could lead to an award of damages being made against an individual.

Bradford & Bingley: Equal Opportunities Policy

Overview

Bradford & Bingley is committed to provide equal opportunities to all employees, ensuring that the talents, abilities and competencies of its employees are used to the full. In addition, the Group aims to eliminate discrimination wherever it exists.

All employees and job applicants will be treated fairly and equally and will not be discriminated against in respect of race, gender, sexual orientation, gender identity, disability, marital status, religion, nationality, employment status, age, trade union membership or non-membership, infection or alleged infection, serious illness including mental illness. This is not an exhaustive list and other forms of discrimination can be included.

Scope

The policy covers all employees of any Bradford & Bingley Group company, which includes Bradford & Bingley Plc, Charcol Ltd, Mortgage Express and Bradford & Bingley International Ltd.

Policy

In consideration of this, Bradford & Bingley will take every reasonably practicable step to:

- recognise its legal obligations under the appropriate Employment Acts;

- recruit, train and promote individuals on the basis of ability, competence, the requirements of the job and similar objective and relevant criteria;

- ensure that the policy is consistently applied by carefully monitoring its operation for both job applicants and employees;

- provide facilities for any employee who believes that the Group has applied inequitable treatment within the scope of this Policy to raise the matter through the appropriate grievance procedure;

- encourage and assist any disadvantaged groups to achieve a position from which equality of opportunity can operate;

- review periodically its selection and recruitment procedures to ensure that in accordance with this commitment the Group is satisfied that the Policy is being effectively implemented;

- promote awareness of this policy within the Group by distributing and publicising the policy statement throughout the organisation and elsewhere as appropriate, and by training employees in respect of best practice.

It is a requirement of all employees to accept their personal responsibility for the practical application of this policy. However, the Group acknowledges that specific responsibility falls upon management, team leaders and individuals who are professionally involved in recruitment, human resources and training. Any act of discrimination by employees or failure to comply with the terms of the policy will result in disciplinary action.

General

The policy is not contractual and does not form part of your terms and conditions of your contract and may vary from time to time, after consultation with UBAC [the recognised trade union].

Harrogate Borough Council: Policy and Guidance Relating to the Prevention and Management of Harassment and Bullying at Work

1. POLICY STATEMENT

1.1 'Harrogate Borough Council believes that all of its employees have the right to be treated with dignity and respect and that harassment and bullying is totally unacceptable. It will deal effectively with any form of harassment or bullying and take any steps it sees fit to either stop or prevent it'.

2. INTRODUCTION

2.1 This policy should be read in conjunction with other Council policies and procedures such as; the Equal Opportunities Policy, Whistleblowing Policy, Code of Conduct, Disciplinary Rules and Procedures and Grievance Procedure. This new policy relating to harassment and bullying incorporates and replaces the policy on Harassment at Work introduced in October 1993.

2.2 Employees are the Council's most valuable and important resource and it has a legal, moral and ethical duty to ensure that the environment in which they work enables them to contribute to their fullest potential and that they feel confident and happy about that working environment.

2.3 As well as considering the welfare of its employees, there is a strong business case for ensuring the elimination and prevention of harassment and bullying such as; the financial impact (eg cost of reduced performance), health and safety (eg physical and emotional affects on staff) and public and employee relations (eg people will not want to come and work here if the Council has a bad reputation and employee turnover).

3. SCOPE OF THE POLICY

3.1 This policy covers harassment and bullying by Officers and Members of Harrogate Borough Council. It does not cover harassment and bullying from the public or contractors and in these cases employees should report any such behaviour to their manager who will take appropriate action. Complaints from the public (eg that their child has been bullied by staff) are not covered by this policy and instead will be managed through the complaints procedure and disciplinary procedure. This policy should however link in with operational policies.

4. AIMS OF THE POLICY

4.1 The information given below shows how harassment and bullying can affect both individuals and the Council and demonstrates the need for such a policy. The aims of having a harassment and bullying policy are as follows:

- To ensure that all of the Council's employees are treated with dignity and respect.

- To ensure that harassment and bullying is prevented.

- To ensure that action is taken to stop harassment and bullying if it does occur.

- To ensure that the working environment is such that each employee feels confident and happy about the way they will be treated whilst at work.

- To ensure that all of the Council's employees know what harassment and bullying is and what the Council's policy is.

- To explain the responsibilities of Members, Chief Officers, management and employees.

- To explain the procedures for dealing with harassment and bullying.

5. WHAT IS HARASSMENT AND BULLYING?

5.1 Definitions

5.1.1 Harassment and bullying are closely linked and a general definition could be 'conduct which is unwanted and offensive and affects the dignity of an individual or group of individuals'. The key words here being 'unwanted' and 'dignity of the individual'.

5.2 Sexual harassment

5.2.1 A definition of sexual harassment is 'conduct of a sexual nature or other conduct based on sex affecting the dignity of men and women at work'. This definition would also cover the harassment of lesbians and gay men.

5.2.2 The following are examples of inappropriate behaviour:

- *Physical* – unwanted physical contact including unnecessary touching, patting, pinching or deliberately brushing against another employee's body, assault and coercing sexual intercourse.

- *Verbal* – unwelcome sexual advances, propositions or pressure/blackmail for sexual activity, continued suggestions for social activity outside the workplace after it has been made clear that such suggestions are unwelcome, offensive flirtations, suggestive remarks, innuendoes or lewd comments.

- *Non verbal* – the display of pornographic or sexually suggestive pictures, objects or written materials, leering, whistling, or making sexually suggestive gestures.

- *Gender based conduct* – which denigrates or ridicules or is intimidatory or physically abusive of an employee because of his/her sex, such as derogatory or degrading abuse or insults which are gender related and offensive comments about appearance or dress.

5.3 Racial harassment

5.3.1 A definition of racial harassment is 'racially motivated actions and behaviour which are directed at people because of their race, colour, ethnic origin, cultural differences, creed and/or nationality and which cause offence and distress'. The Stephen Lawrence Report defines a 'racist incident as any incident which is perceived to be racist by the victim or any other person'.

5.3.2 As with sexual harassment described above, racial harassment can be expressed in a range of behaviours such as; physical or verbal conduct (eg assault, derogatory name calling, malicious comments, jokes, hostile attitudes), non-verbal conduct (eg graffiti, display of racial insignia or material), damage to personal property, denial of opportunities and exclusion from social activities.

5.4 Harassment of disabled people

5.4.1 As with sexual and racial harassment described above, there are a range of behaviours which are unacceptable such as; staring and/or uninvited touching, exclusion from social events, speaking to others rather than to the disabled person directly, asking intimate questions about a person's impairment, making assumptions about disabled people (eg that they do not have a social, sexual or private life), physical abuse or intimidation, unreasonably questioning a disabled person's work capacity and/or ability by making inappropriate demands or requirements, making assumptions about a person's impairment and sickness record, jokes and mimicking the particular disability.

5.5 Bullying

5.5.1 It should be noted that bullying does not just occur in manager/subordinate relationships (ie where the manager bullies the subordinate or vice versa), it can occur when there is unacceptable peer pressure or pressure by others in a position of 'authority', eg Members. Bullying can be defined as 'offensive, intimidating, malicious, insulting or humiliating behaviour, abuse of power orauthority which attempts to undermine an individual or group of employees and which may cause them to suffer stress'.

5.5.2 Examples of bullying are shown in 5.5.3. below but these must be put into context. One instance of someone being aggressive does not make them a bully and therefore the behaviours shown below would have to be deliberate and persistent and would, in effect, follow a pattern of continuous behaviour. Anyone who thinks they are being bullied should consider this point very carefully.

5.5.3 Bullying behaviour can include:

- all forms of harassment;
- aggressive, insulting and unco-operative attitude;
- destructive innuendo and sarcasm;
- constant unjustified criticism, unilaterally removing responsibilities and replacing them with trivial tasks to do instead;
- shouting at staff to get things done;
- persistently picking on people in front of others, or in private;
- insisting that their way of doing things is always right without discussion;
- unreasonable use of disciplinary/competence procedures;
- unreasonable refusal of requests (eg leave or training);
- deliberately ignoring or excluding individuals from activities;
- unreasonably overloading anyone with work and reducing deadlines;
- constantly attacking a member of staff in terms of their professional or personal standing;
- persistently undervaluing an employees efforts;
- setting out to make a person appear incompetent, or to make their lives miserable, in the hope of getting them dismissed or simply of making them resign;
- making someone the butt of jokes;
- 'flame-mail' (ie aggressive e-mail) can also be a source of bullying.

6. THE LEGAL FRAMEWORK

6.1 Supporting the harassment and bullying policy is a legal framework. Harassment and bullying are illegal on a number of grounds and the key legislation is as follows:-

6.1.1 Sex Discrimination Act 1975 and Race Relations Act 1976

Where there is a sexual or racial element to harassment or bullying, employees may be able to take their case to an Employment Tribunal under these acts. This would certainly be the case where someone was being victimised after making a complaint.

6.1.2 Health and Safety at Work Act 1974

Under this act employers are responsible for providing a healthy and safe working environment. Harassment and bullying undermines that and is included in the Health and Safety Executive's definition of violence. Therefore failure to take action to prevent or deal with any known occurrences could be in breach of the act.

6.1.3 Employment Rights Act 1996

An employee could take a case to an Employment Tribunal and complain of 'constructive dismissal' where they felt that they had to resign because they were being harassed or bullied and their employer was taking no action either to stop or prevent it.

6.1.4 Criminal Justice and Public Order Act 1994

Any intentional harassment is a criminal offence and a person commits an offence when they intentionally cause a person harassment, alarm or distress, where they use threatening, abusive or insulting language or behaviour, disorderly behaviour or displays, or any writing, sign or other visible representation which is threatening, abusive or insulting causing that other person harassment, alarm or distress. If found guilty, it could lead to a fine and/or imprisonment.

6.1.5 Disability Discrimination Act 1995

It is unlawful to victimise disabled people who make use of, or try to make use of, their rights under the Act. People who help disabled people complain about discrimination are also protected.

Note: The Equal Treatment Directive is being amended to make sexual harassment unlawful. The Directive on Racial and Ethnic Discrimination is also relevant.

7. PROVIDING A SUPPORTIVE CULTURE

7.1 The Council will strive to ensure that there is a positive and supportive culture which is free from harassment and bullying. This will encourage high morale and productivity, low absenteeism and turnover and provide an environment where people will feel comfortable about attending work. In order to achieve this the following responsibilities have been identified.

8. RESPONSIBILITIES UNDER THE POLICY

8.1 *Chief Officers* – will have the following responsibilities:

- To implement this policy in their department.

- To promote a positive and supportive culture in their department.

- To promote, maintain and enforce good standards of conduct and behaviour in their department.

8.2 *Managers* – will have the following responsibilities:

- Compliance with the policy.

- Creating/ensuring that there is a supportive working environment.

- Treating their colleagues with dignity and respect.

- Having an awareness of their own standards of behaviour and setting a good example to others.

- Making it clear that they find harassment and bullying unacceptable.

- Making sure that their staff know the details of this policy and ensuring compliance with it.

- Making sure that their staff know what standards of behaviour are expected of them.

- Taking complaints of harassment and/or bullying seriously and dealing with them as quickly and effectively as possible.

- Intervening to stop harassment and/or bullying.

- Ensuring that recipients of harassment and/or bullying receive any support they need including counselling (note: consideration should be given as to whether the harasser/bully should be given access to counselling).

- Dealing with complaints under the informal or formal procedure (see below).

- Ensuring that matters are dealt with confidentially and impartially.

- Ensuring that their staff attend any corporate training requirement.

- Liaising with Human Resources on how to deal with cases that arise.

8.3 *Human Resources Division* – will have the following responsibilities:

- Publicising the policy.

- Maintaining the policy in light of any legislative changes.

- Providing advice and support to Chief Officers, managers and employees (including recipients).

- Assisting Chief Officers and managers to maintain a positive and supportive culture in the Council.

- Arranging formal counselling.

- Managing and co-ordinating the 'Listener' system, including training 'Listeners' and providing them with support, advice and guidance.

- Providing any training that is necessary.

- Evaluate the effectiveness of the policy (eg through regular meetings with 'Listeners', discussions with the trade unions, generic feedback from counsellors, exit interviews and analysis of specific cases).

8.4 *Employees* – will have the following responsibilities:

- Complying with this policy.

- Treating their colleagues with dignity and respect.

- Being aware of their own standards of behaviour and setting a good example to others.

- Making it clear that they find harassment and bullying unacceptable.

- Reporting harassment and supporting management with the investigation of complaints.

- Intervening to stop harassment and/or bullying and give support to recipients.

- Understanding that it is a manager's role and responsibility to set targets and review performance as part of the normal managerial process. Bullying will only occur when a manager abuses their authority (eg deliberately sets too many or unachievable targets and discredits good performance).

8.5 *Members* – will have responsibilities for:

- Supporting and promoting the policy.

- Treating other Members and employees with dignity and respect in accordance with the aims and objectives of this policy.

9. THE PROCEDURE FOR DEALING WITH HARASSMENT AND/OR BULLYING

9.1 Those who consider that they are being harassed or bullied have the right to seek redress through either the informal or formal procedure. Only if the matter is brought to the attention of the harasser/bully or manager can action be taken to stop the behaviour.

9.2 The decision as to how any case of harassment and bullying should be pursued should, in the first instance, rest solely with the person being harassed or bullied. He/she must not feel pressurised to deal with the matter informally just because it would be easier for management. However, if the harassment or bullying is serious (eg assault or rape) then clearly the matter should be dealt with formally and will be reported to the Police since a criminal act has taken place.

9.3 'Listeners' and their role

9.3.1 Whilst all types of harassment or bullying are serious there are varying degrees of such behaviour. In order to help the recipient assess the seriousness of the problem and to help and guide them, there are a number of people within the Council who will act as 'Listeners'. Listeners are trained staff volunteers who are accessible in the first instance by telephone, but where necessary, can arrange face-to-face meetings. Listeners are supported by internal experts if they want advice themselves on how to deal with a particular case but whatever happens the matter will remain confidential. Details of who the 'Listeners' are is shown in the internal telephone directory, staff handbook and noticeboards. Alternatively, recipients may, if they prefer, contact their line manager, head of service, personnel officer, trade union representative or colleague for advice and guidance.

9.3.2 The 'Listeners' will not be required or expected to support a recipient through any formal disciplinary process, other than to confirm when the recipient first raised the problem with them.

9.4 Whatever the circumstances of the case, it is very important that a written record is kept by the recipient of any incidents of harassment or bullying in case of the need for subsequent action.

9.5 Informal action

9.5.1 Whenever possible and appropriate to do so, recipients should ask the person who is harassing or bullying them to stop such behaviour making it clear that it is offensive and unwelcome. This can be done face to face or in writing.

9.5.2 If the recipient feels that they cannot approach the harasser/bully themselves then this initial approach can be made by a friend, colleague, personnel officer, trade union representative or manager.

9.5.3 A written record should be kept by the recipient, or any of the individuals mentioned in 9.5.2 above, which notes what action has been taken or agreed.

9.5.4 It is possible that some people may not have realised that their behaviour was offensive and when this is pointed out to them they will stop causing offence. The sooner an issue is raised the better it may be.

9.5.5 Where the matter has been raised once by the recipient with the harasser/bully and they take no notice and continue to behave inappropriately, the recipient has the choice of asking an appropriate manager to deal with the matter which may result in disciplinary action.

Notes:

1. If an 'incident' is witnessed by a manager there is no need for a 'complainant' and the manager can deal with the matter as they see fit.

2. Anyone who feels that they have been harassed or bullied may, if they wish, obtain support from personnel officers within the Human Resources Section. Personnel officers are also available to provide advice and guidance to managers and the alleged harasser/bully.

9.6 Formal action

9.6.1 Where the informal procedure has failed or when a serious incident occurs, formal action can be taken. The recipient must raise a formal complaint against the harasser/bully in accordance with this policy and procedure. Any complaint must be made in writing and be given to their immediate manager. If the complaint is against the immediate manager it should be given to his/her manager. If the recipient prefers, the complaint may be given to the Head of

Human Resources who will discuss it with an appropriate manager within the department.

9.6.2 At this stage the matter will be investigated as part of and under the Council's Disciplinary Rules and Procedures. The Chief Officer will determine who will investigate the matter and this could include Human Resource Officers.

9.6.3 It should be noted that under the Disciplinary Rules and Procedures and depending on the severity of the alleged offence, the harasser/bully may be suspended on full pay pending the outcome of the investigation and, if appropriate, disciplinary hearing. Similarly, the Chief Officer has the right under this policy and procedure to require the alleged harasser/bully to be transferred to an office where they cannot come in contact with the recipient/complainant, whilst the investigation/disciplinary hearing is taking place. Each case will be judged on its own merits as to whether suspension or transfer is an appropriate course of action.

9.6.4 The usual representation will apply to the alleged harasser/bully and the recipient can be supported throughout the process by a person of their choosing.

9.6.5 If, at the conclusion of the investigation, there is a case to answer, the case will be put before the disciplining officer. The recipient should be given feedback after the conclusion of the hearing. If it is decided after the investigation or the hearing that there is no case to answer, an explanation must be given to the recipient. It should be noted that the recipient does not have a formal right of appeal or the right to raise a grievance against any decision affecting the harasser/bully following an investigation or disciplinary hearing.

9.6.6 If the disciplinary officer decides that the allegations are proven he/she has the right under this policy and procedure to require the harasser/bully to be permanently relocated to another office away from the recipient/complainant.

9.6.7 If, following the investigation of the complaint, it is determined that the recipient has made a malicious and unfounded complaint then this may constitute harassment in itself and be dealt with under the disciplinary procedure.

9.6.8 If the matter involves a complaint against a Member, the Chief Executive and the Monitoring Officer must be informed and, following investigation, a report should be submitted to the Standards Committee.

10. COUNSELLING

10.1 The Council will offer both parties (ie the recipient and harasser/bully) the opportunity to receive formal counselling and will arrange this for them if they so wish.

11. MONITORING AND REVIEW

11.1 This policy will be reviewed two years after implementation and thereafter in line with any legislative changes.

INDEX

A

Abadeh v British Telecommunications
plc   179
Age discrimination   2, 4, 7, 11, 13, 14, 18,
        28, 29, 37, 42, 43, 49, 60–62, 65, 78,
        79, 81, 109–112, 115, 119, 120, 130,
        145–147, 162, 189, 190, 192, 194,
        206, 207, 213, 214, 262, 263, 265,
        266, 269, 274, 275, 277, 278 283
Amsterdam Treaty 1997   272
Appraisal   11, 18, 19, 22, 53, 54, 89–92,
        99–101, 106, 107, 121–123, 144,
        145, 149, 161, 228, 246, 277, 279
Auditing   10–12, 14, 17, 18, 20

B

BAC Ltd v Austin   125
Baynton v Saurus General Engineers Ltd
                                       182
Bedfordshire Constabulary v Graham
                                       156
Bowers v Schroder Securities Ltd   139,
                                       172
Bullying   15, 16, 86, 89, 90, 99, 127–135,
                151, 190, 262, 282–292
Burden of Proof Directive   164
Burton and Rhule v De Vere Hotels   170

C

Career breaks   11, 15, 16, 18, 38
Chartered Institute of Personnel and
        Development (CIPD)   5, 18, 135
Chaudhary v BMA   173
Chief Constable of Avon and Somerset
        Constabulary v Chew   36, 37
Chief Constable of Bedfordshire Police v
        Liversidge   164, 170
Chief Constable of Cumbria v
        McGlennon   164, 170
Childcare   11, 15, 36, 37, 57–59, 137, 138,
                143, 144, 163
Code of Practice: Equal Opportunity
        Policies, Procedures and Practices in
        Employment   167

Code of Practice: Protecting the Dignity
        of Women and Men at Work   167
Code of Practice for Age Diversity   14,
                                       192
Code of Practice for the Elimination of
        Discrimination in the Field of
        Employment Against Disabled
        Persons or Persons who have a
        Disability   176, 180, 181
Code of Practice on Equal Pay   140, 141,
                                       142
Code of Practice on Rights of Access to
        Goods, Facilities, Services and
        Premises   26, 27, 125
Code of Practice on the Dignity of
        Women and Men at Work   128, 129
Commission for Racial Equality   12, 18,
        77, 78, 105, 108, 139, 140, 160, 171,
                172, 190, 234, 240, 255, 270, 280
Commission for Racial Equality v
        Dutton   157
Constructive dismissal   126, 127, 130,
                131, 167, 288
Coote v Granada Hospitality Ltd   171
Corporate Social Responsibility (CSR)
                30, 47, 48, 50, 60–62, 70, 71,
                97–99, 99–101
Cotterill and Westmoreland v (1)
        Millenium Air Products Ltd, (2)
        Majestic Enterprises UK Ltd, (3)
        Kevin Robinson, (4) Malcolm Billing,
        (5) Craig Russell, (6) Lindsey
        Broderick   27, 28
Crime and Disorder Act 1998   271
Criminal Justice and Public Order Act
        1994   288

D

Dawkins v Department of the
        Environment   158
Disability   2, 7, 11, 13, 15, 16, 18, 24–28,
        33, 34, 49, 63, 65, 70, 71, 73, 78–80,
        97–99, 104, 108–115, 117–125, 130,
        144–148, 158, 175–183, 189, 194–
        207, 217–231, 234, 257, 266, 268,
        269, 271, 274, 275, 277, 280, 282,
        283, 286, 288

NOTES

NOTES

NOTES

NOTES

NOTES

NOTES

NOTES

NOTES

NOTES

NOTES

NOTES

NOTES

IRS Managing Diversity in the Workplace

Executive Editor

Sue Johnstone
Editor of *Equal Opportunities Review* and www.EORdirect.com

Members of the LexisNexis Group worldwide

United Kingdom	LexisNexis IRS, member of the Eclipse Group Ltd, 18–20 Highbury Place, LONDON N5 1QP
Argentina	LexisNexis Argentina, BUENOS AIRES
Australia	LexisNexis Butterworths, CHATSWOOD, New South Wales
Austria	LexisNexis Verlag ARD Orac GmbH & Co KG, VIENNA
Canada	LexisNexis Butterworths, MARKHAM, Ontario
Chile	LexisNexis Chile Ltda, SANTIAGO DE CHILE
Czech Republic	Nakladatelství Orac sro, PRAGUE
France	Editions du Juris-Classeur SA, PARIS
Hong Kong	LexisNexis Butterworths, HONG KONG
Hungary	HVG-Orac, BUDAPEST
India	LexisNexis Butterworths, NEW DELHI
Ireland	Butterworths (Ireland) Ltd, DUBLIN
Italy	Giuffrè Editore, MILAN
Malaysia	Malayan Law Journal Sdn Bhd, KUALA LUMPUR
New Zealand	LexisNexis Butterworths, WELLINGTON
Poland	Wydawnictwo Prawnicze LexisNexis, WARSAW
Singapore	LexisNexis Butterworths, SINGAPORE
South Africa	Butterworths SA, DURBAN
Switzerland	Stämpfli Verlag AG, BERNE
USA	LexisNexis, DAYTON, Ohio

A CIP Catalogue record for this book is available from the British Library.

ISBN 0 754 519 554

Typeset by Kerrypress Ltd, Luton, Beds

Printed and bound by Bookcraft, Midsomer Norton, Bath

Visit LexisNexis IRS at www.irsonline.co.uk